Home Inspector License Exam Prep

All-in-One Review and Testing to Pass
the Home Inspector License Examination® (NHIE®)

First Edition

Bruce Barker
Stephen Mettling
Ryan Mettling

Performance Programs Company
6810 190th Street East
Bradenton, Florida 34211
www.performanceprogramscompany.com

© 2025 by Performance Programs Company
6810 190th Street East, Bradenton, FL 34211
info@performanceprogramscompany.com
www.performanceprogramscompany.com

ISBN 978-1965482100

Contents

Introduction

Welcome licensee candidates and future Home Inspectors!

We know you have worked hard just to get here – you have completed or nearly completed your pre-license curricula, and now all you have to do is pass the license exam. But, admittedly, easier said than done. That is where we at Performance Programs Company come in. We know the exam can be tough, and very nerve-wracking to prepare for. That's why we created our *Home Inspector License Exam Prep (HILEP)* the way we did. Since we have been developing and publishing real estate curriculum programs and products for forty years, we know how all this works – or fails to work. And let us assure you – you have made the right decision acquiring this publication to prepare for your National Home Inspector Examination® exam. Our content and organization streamline and reinforce the learning process.

As you will see, HILEP is comprehensive in that it contains both key content review and testing practice. HILEP specifically follows the National Home Inspector Examination® outline as promulgated by Examination Board of Professional Home Inspectors (EBPHI) testing officials. This outline sets the standard for content coverage, test section weighting, and, essentially, what is on the NHIE® test.

A word about HILEP's organization. Consistent with the promulgated NHIE license examination outline, the main sections of the exam prep cover:

> Property and Building Inspection
> Analysis of Findings and Reporting
> Professional Responsibilities

Following the review section are practice tests to test your mastery of the subject material. This is further reinforced by explanations in the Answer Key to each test. Exam candidates should also note that all content to our exam prep is tersely presented in bullet point lists. We make every effort to present only the essential material that you need to learn the test outline subjects.

Finally, our HILEP challenges candidates to take and pass one 100-item practice test covering the entire test outline. Again, the practice test comes with an answer key and explanation.

Taken as a whole, if you learn the content in our exam prep resource, we know you will pass the NHIE® license examination. Testing officials went into great detail outlining what would be presented in the NHIE® license exam. And we went to great lengths to explain all this content in our publication.

So, at this point, it's all up to you. There's a lot of material to be learned in our text's 175+ some-odd pages. And it will take some real concentration and hard work to prepare for this examination. There are no guarantees of passing, and don't be fooled by those who would say otherwise. But we are also very confident that, with focused studying and preparation, you will be successful! So good luck!

About the Authors

Bruce A. Barker.   Bruce A. Barker is the author or editor of books including: The NHIE Home Inspection Manual, Everybody's Building Code, Commentary on the ASHI Standard of Practice for Home Inspections, A Practical Guide to Evaluating Decks, and books in the Black & Decker series including Codes for Homeowners, Deck Codes and Standards, and The Complete Guides to Wiring, Advanced Wiring, Plumbing, and Decks. He also wrote The Word column in The ASHI Reporter. Bruce is an American Society of Home Inspectors (ASHI) Certified Inspector who served as the 2021 ASHI President.

Bruce has been building and inspecting homes for over 35 years. He is an ICC certified Residential Combination Inspector, a licensed contractor, and a licensed home inspector in multiple states. Bruce has a BSBA in Accounting, and an MBA in Information Systems.

Stephen Mettling.   For over fifty years, Stephen Mettling has been actively engaged in real estate education. Beginning with Dearborn Publishing in 1972, then called Real Estate Education Company, Mr. Mettling managed the company's textbook division and author acquisitions. Subsequently he built up the company's real estate school division which eventually became the country's largest real estate, insurance and securities school network in the country. In 1978, Mr. Mettling founded Performance Programs Company, a custom training program publishing and development company specializing in commercial, industrial, and corporate real estate. Over time, Performance Programs Company narrowed its focus to real estate textbook and exam prep publishing. Currently the Company's texts and prelicense resources are used in hundreds of schools in over 48 states. Mr. Mettling has authored over 100 textbooks, real estate prelicense programs and exam prep manuals.

Ryan Mettling.   As President and publisher of Performance Programs Company, Ryan Mettling is an accomplished online curriculum designer, author and textbook developer specializing in real estate, license training, and exam prep manuals. To date, Ryan has managed the development and all revision work for our 70-title product line involving author recruitment, product design, executive management, production, printing and marketing. Mr. Mettling graduated Valedictorian from the University of Central Florida's College of Business Administration in 2012.

Home Inspector License Examination® (Exam): Overview

About the National Home Inspector Examination® (NHIE)

➢ **NHIE Exam developed and maintained by The Examination Board of Professional Home Inspectors, Inc. (EBPHI)**

  - independent, volunteer-governed, not-for-profit organization
  - not affiliated with a government, professional association, or other group

➢ **Exam used in approximately 35 states, some Canadian Provinces, and some professional associations (e.g., the American Society of Home Inspectors) for home inspector regulation and for membership qualification**

  - refer to EBPHI, state/province home inspector license authority, and professional association for information about requirements for licensing and membership

➢ **Exam is psychometrically valid**

  - a psychometrically valid exam outline and exam questions provide fair assessment of candidate's knowledge
  - the NHIE is the only known psychometrically valid home inspector exam as of the publication date of this material

➢ **Exam consists of 200 multiple choice questions, 175 of which are scored**

  - twenty-five questions are test questions that help maintain the exam's psychometric validity
  - you will not know which questions are scored
  - time to complete the exam: four hours

➢ **Questions and correct answers come from specific references**

  - refer to EBPHI website for current references

➢ **Exams administered beginning 21 January 2024 will be based on a new exam outline**

  - this book uses the new exam outline

➢ **Focusing study efforts on the exam outline makes preparation more efficient**

  - exam outline provides percentages of exam questions based on knowledge areas

➢ **Rules regarding exam registration and administration are specific and may be inflexible**

  - refer to EBPHI website for current rules

Exam Outline (2024)

- ➤ **Section 1: Inspecting the Property and Building (70%)**

  - Unit 1:   Site Conditions
  - Unit 2:   Exterior Components
  - Unit 3:   Roof Components
  - Unit 4:   Structural Components
  - Unit 5:   Electrical Systems
  - Unit 6:   Cooling Systems
  - Unit 7:   Heating Systems
  - Unit 8:   Insulation, Moisture Management, Ventilation
  - Unit 9:   Exhaust Systems
  - Unit 10: Plumbing Systems
  - Unit 11: Interior Components
  - Unit 12: Fireplace and Chimney Systems
  - Unit 13: Life Safety Equipment and Systems

- ➤ **Section 2: Analyzing and Reporting Inspection Findings (20%)**

  - Unit 1:   Inform Client What Was Inspected
  - Unit 2:   Inform Client What Was Not Inspected
  - Unit 3:   Inform Client About Systems That Are Deficient
  - Unit 4:   Inform Client About Systems Than Need Evaluation or Action

- ➤ **Section 3: Performing Professionally and Responsibly (10%)**

  - Unit 1:   Understanding Pre-Inspection Agreements
  - Unit 2:   Maintaining the Quality and Integrity of the Inspection Process

Section I: Property and Building Inspection

Unit 1: Site Conditions

Unit 2: Exterior Components

Unit 3: Roof Components

Unit 4: Structural Components

Unit 5: Electrical Systems

Unit 6: Cooling Systems

Unit 7: Heating Systems

Unit 8: Insulation, Moisture Management, Ventilation

Unit 9: Mechanical Exhaust Systems

Unit 10: Plumbing and Fuel Distribution Systems

Unit 11: Interior Components

Unit 12: Fireplaces, Fuel-burning Appliances, Chimneys, Vents

Unit 13: Life Safety Equipment and Systems

Unit 1: Site Conditions

Topics covered in this Unit include:
- **Knowledge Areas**
- **Retaining Walls**
- **Grade and Drainage**
- **Vegetation**
- **Driveways, Walkways, and Patios**
- **Swimming Pool and Spa Access Barriers**

Knowledge Areas

➤ **Knowledge areas in-scope of a home inspection and in-scope of the exam**

- retaining walls and vegetation likely to adversely affect the building
- grade and drainage
- driveways, walkways, and patios

➤ **Knowledge areas out-of-scope of a home inspection but in-scope of the exam**

- swimming pool and spa access barriers

Retaining Walls

➤ **Description**

- **retaining wall**: a system that keeps soil or other material on one side of the wall from moving beyond the wall
- retaining walls control erosion and create level areas on sloped lots
- retaining walls may be any height
  - ○ retaining walls more than four feet tall (measured from the top of the footing) may need to be designed by an engineer, and may require a **building permit**

➤ **Common materials**

- wood (preservative-treated landscape timbers, creosote-treated railroad ties)
- precast concrete (concrete blocks, landscape/garden blocks)
- masonry (bricks)
- natural stone and rubble

➤ **Construction**

- build retaining walls on stable and level footing
- build wood and precast concrete retaining walls on compacted sand or gravel
- build masonry, concrete, and stone/rubble retaining walls on poured concrete footing or a similar solid footing
- taller retaining walls (especially wood retaining walls) should have components, such as **tiebacks / deadmen** or **buttresses**, to reduce wall failure

➢ **Drainage**

- retaining walls should have means to allow water to drain through the wall
- gaps between wood retaining wall members normally allow for drainage
- openings in masonry, concrete, and stone retaining walls (weep holes) enable drainage

➢ **Typical defects**

- **water pressure behind retaining walls** may lead to retaining wall damage and failure
- deterioration and insect damage (wood walls)
- rotation (wall leans outward from vertical)
- bowing (wall protrudes outward from horizontal)
- cracking
- inadequate reinforcement of taller retaining walls (no deadmen or buttresses)
- wall too tall for material used
- spalling (material flaked off of concrete and masonry wall surfaces)
- efflorescence (white powder on concrete and masonry wall surfaces)
- erosion under footings
- lack of means to drain water from behind wall

Grade and Drainage

➢ **Definitions**

- **grade**: level and slope of soil and hard surfaces outside of building
- **grading**: act of establishing grade
- **swale**: shallow channel (depression) in soil that directs water toward collection points or off property

➢ **General**

- **improper grade, drainage, gutters, and downspouts are common reasons for moisture inside buildings;** for foundation damage; and for deterioration of building components
- drainage occurs when water flows away from building either toward collection points, such as retention ponds, or off property
- drainage established by grading, and by establishing other storm water management systems, such as gutters and downspouts
- grade should slope away from the foundation *minimum 6 inches within the first 10 feet horizontally* from foundation
- hard surfaces, such as driveways and patios, should slope away from foundation *minimum ¼ inch per foot*
- uncontrolled water can cause erosion that can damage foundations and retaining walls, and can damage landscaping
- moisture near foundations attracts wood-destroying organisms, such as termites
- moisture near foundations applies (hydrostatic) pressure against foundations that can cause foundation deterioration and failure
- moisture near foundations can cause some types of soil, such as expansive clay, to expand or contract, and cause significant foundation damage
- moisture near foundations can freeze and cause soil to expand and damage foundation (**frost heave**)

- ➢ **Common drainage systems**
  - underground drains (French Drains) collect water and use pipes to direct water toward collection points or off property
    - ○ surface water may be collected in a catch basin
    - ○ **channel drain**: a long catch basin installed when grade slopes toward foundation, such as at garage vehicle door
    - ○ **downspouts** may deposit water directly into underground pipes
  - splash blocks and downspout extensions direct roof water away from the foundation, and usually should be installed at all downspouts

- ➢ **Typical defects**

  - **grade slopes toward foundation;** grade does not adequately slope away from foundation
  - grade established above the level of building's wood framing and wall coverings
    - ○ includes planters installed above wood framing and wall coverings
  - water collects on property (water may remain in swales up to 48 hours)
  - gutter and downspout defects, such as improper gutter slope, deterioration and damage, and inadequate discharge of water away from foundation
  - swales blocked, such as by debris and plant roots, and by homeowner and contractor alterations
  - underground drains and catch basins blocked
  - underground drain terminations blocked or not visible
  - soil settled in utility trenches
  - soil erosion

Vegetation

- ➢ **General**
  - vegetation includes trees, shrubs, turf grasses, and ground covers
  - **vegetation condition is out-of-scope of a home inspection**, unless the condition is likely to adversely affect the building
    - ○ example: dead tree which is likely to fall on building may be a reportable condition
  - appropriateness of the vegetation for the location is out-of-scope
    - ○ example: foundation plants that may grow to touch building, but do not touch building at the time of inspection, are out-of-scope

- ➢ **Typical defects**
  - **plants touch wall coverings or roof coverings**, including vines growing on wall coverings
  - plants likely to touch wall coverings or roof coverings when the wind blows
  - tree limbs hang over roof
  - trees lean toward building
  - trees obviously dead, diseased, or distressed that are likely to fall on building
  - tree limbs hang over electrical service drop, cable, or telephone wires
  - plants closer than about one foot away from air conditioning condensers

Driveways, Walkways, and Patios

➢ **Definitions**

- **driveway**: a private road intended for use by vehicles, and located on private property
- **walkway**: a private path intended for use by people, and located on private property
- **patio**: an outdoor recreation area located near building, located on the ground

➢ **Common materials**

- concrete, asphalt, gravel, soil, flagstone, pavers
- concrete may be covered by finish materials, such as tile or outdoor carpet
- walkways and steps occasionally constructed using preservative-treated wood and railroad ties
  - o these materials can deteriorate rapidly, especially in environments that are constantly damp

➢ **General construction practices**

- **driveways, walkways, and patios rely on soil or material underneath for support** to resist settlement, cracking, and other defects
- soil and other materials should be compacted, and should be free from vegetation and other materials that can deteriorate, such as wood construction debris,
  - o especially important for materials such as flagstone and pavers
- these systems should slope away from building ***minimum ¼ inch per foot*** where they abut the building
- an isolation joint should be at building to resist cracking and other defects caused by different movement rates and directions between system and building
- if soil is between these systems and the building, these systems should be installed so **water is not trapped** between system and building
  - o a walkway that is higher than the soil between the walkway and the building is a common defect

➢ **Concrete driveways, walkways, and patios construction**

- minimum thickness about 3½ inches
- locate control joints about every 10 feet
  - o joint depth about one quarter of concrete thickness

➢ **Asphalt driveways, walkways, and patio construction**

- minimum thickness between 2 and 4 inches

➢ **Typical defects**

- **inadequate slope away from building**
- system higher than soil between system and building, and does not allow water to drain
- concrete cracks (larger than about ¼ inch wide or ¼ inch vertical displacement)
  - o no generally accepted standard regarding reportable concrete crack size

- many possible causes, including soil settlement, uplift caused by tree roots, and improper finishing during installation
- **concrete crazing** (numerous surface cracks that look like a spider web)
  - often caused by improper finishing, or by rapid drying during installation
- **concrete delamination/spalling** (separation of finished surface that exposes aggregate)
  - often caused by improper finishing during installation, and by deicing salt
- **concrete pop-outs** (localized separation of finished surface that exposes aggregate, often deeper than delamination)
  - same causes as delamination
- **concrete dusting** (white powder continues to appear on surface)
  - often caused by improper finishing during installation
- ruts, erosion, and thin coverage in gravel
- loose or unstable flagstones and pavers
- staining and other evidence of water accumulation (ponding)
  - water more than ⅜ inch deep for more than 24 hours may be reportable
  - slip hazard, especially where water freezes

Swimming Pool and Spa Access Barriers

➢ **General**

- **objective: keep children away from swimming pools and spas** to reduce death and injury by drowning
- **child should not be able to get through, climb over, or crawl under barrier**
- typical barriers: fences, walls (including building walls), and pool and spa covers
- standards and regulations vary significantly between jurisdictions, including different jurisdictions in the same state and county

➢ **Common materials**

- metal, including chain link, aluminum, iron, and steel
- preservative-treated wood
- concrete blocks

➢ **General standards – fences and gates**

- fences and gates **minimum 45 inches tall**
- openings between vertical fence components maximum 4 inches if horizontal components less than 45 inches apart
- openings between vertical fence components maximum 1¾ inches if horizontal components less than 45 inches apart
- horizontal components on pool side of fence or gate if components are less than 45 inches apart
- space under fences and gates maximum 2 inches if loose material, such as soil or gravel, under fence or gate
- space under fences and gates should maximum 4 inches if solid material, such as concrete, under fence or gate

- single gates should be self-closing and self-latching, and **should swing away from pool** or spa
- a gate latch should be minimum 54 inches above adjacent walking surface

➢ **General standards – access doors**

- doors allowing access to pool or spa should be **self-closing** and self-latching, and should swing into building
- latches on doors allowing access to pool or spa should be minimum 54 inches above walking surface
- **pet doors** and similar components **not allowed if they allow access to pool** or spa
- approved alarm may substitute for door closers and latches

➢ **Typical defects**

- **fence, gate, or wall can be climbed, crawled under, or entered**
- damage or deterioration
- no barrier, or inadequate barrier
- gate swings toward pool or spa
- gate or door not self-closing and self-latching
- door alarm not functioning
- pet door allows access to pool/spa area

Unit 2: Exterior Components

Topics covered in this Unit include:
- **Knowledge Areas**
- **Exterior Wall Coverings and Trim: General & Types**
- **Wall Flashing**
- **Eaves, Soffits, and Fascia**
- **Exterior Doors**
- **Windows**
- **Decks**
- **Balconies, Stoops, and Porches**
- **Garage Vehicle Doors and Operators**

Knowledge Areas

➢ **Knowledge areas in-scope of a home inspection and in-scope of the exam**

- wall coverings and trim, wall flashing, eaves, soffits, and fascia
- doors and windows (including egress requirements)
- decks, balconies, stoops, and porches
- stairs, guards, and handrails (including egress requirements)
- garage vehicle doors and door operators

➢ **Knowledge areas out-of-scope of a home inspection but in-scope of the exam**

- safety glazing

Exterior Wall Coverings and Trim – General

➢ **General**

- **wall coverings impose loads on building and foundation**; most not structural elements
  - some wall coverings, such as wood panels, may provide lateral (racking) resistance
    - fastener type and spacing are important in this case
- **water-resistive barrier (WRB) and flashing prevent water intrusion into building**
  - WRB materials include house wraps and building paper (felt)
  - flashing materials include galvanized steel, aluminum, rigid plastics, and newer peal-and-stick materials
  - most wall coverings shed water and protect the WRB
- **absent or improperly installed WRBs, flashings, and sealants (caulk), are common defects**, and common causes of **water intrusion**
  - common wall flashing locations
    - around windows, doors, and transitions between wall covering types
    - kick out flashing at roof/wall intersections

- compliance with manufacturer's installation and maintenance instructions, and with building code requirements, is essential to avoid water intrusion and other problems, such as deterioration
  - typical instructions and requirements include a **drainage plane** consisting of WRB and flashing, and a means to drain water, such as **weep holes** and **weep screeds**
  - most wall coverings have instructions and requirements about fastener type, installation, and spacing, and about distance between the wall covering and soil, roofs, and hard surfaces such as patios, walkways, and driveways
  - failure to comply with manufacturer's instructions and code requirements are common causes of typical defects

➤ **Wall covering types**
- **attached veneers**: wall coverings supported by building and fastened to building
  - sidings (all types) and exterior insulation and finish system (EIFS)
- **anchored veneers**: wall coverings supported by foundation, or by framing supported on foundation, and fastened to building to prevent rotation away from building
  - masonry (bricks) and natural stone
- **adhered veneers**: wall coverings supported by building and "glued" to building
  - adhered masonry veneer (artificial stone) and stucco

Exterior Wall Coverings and Trim – Types

➤ **Adhered masonry veneer (AMV) - description**
- **most common 1980s to present**
- manufactured material looks like natural stone or brick
- sometimes called "lumpy stucco" because it is installed like stucco
- **weep screed** often required at locations, such as foundation and above windows and doors, to allow water drainage
- **known problematic wall covering because it is often improperly installed**
  - water intrusion common, often not visible during an inspection

➤ **Adhered masonry veneer – typical defects**
- **absent or improperly installed flashing**
- **insufficient distance above grade**, hard surfaces, and roof coverings
  - distance depends on manufacturer
    - typical 4-6 inches above soil when applied over wood framing
    - typical 1-2 inches above hard surfaces and roof coverings
- **weep screed absent**, improperly installed, or openings blocked
- cracks, usually between stones
- **deformation** (bulging)

➤ **Aluminum siding and steel siding – description**
- most common 1950s and 60s; less common recently in most markets
- interlocking horizontal strips about 6 inches to 8 inches wide
- WRB and flashing required behind siding

- electrically grounding this siding is ineffective, and not required by electrical codes; may be required by local authorities

➢ **Aluminum siding and steel siding – typical defects**
- absent or improperly installed flashing
- damaged or deteriorated siding and trim
- faded or pealed finish

➢ **Asbestos cement siding – description**
- most common 1920s to 1950s
- shingles about 18 by 24 inches
- **asbestos banned in building materials in 1973**
- **working with asbestos-containing materials, including removal, requires mitigation protocols that can be very expensive**
- presence or absence of asbestos can only be confirmed by a laboratory
  - report all materials that may contain asbestos as: "possible asbestos-containing material" and recommend laboratory analysis

➢ **Asbestos cement siding – typical defects**
- same as aluminum and steel siding
- cracks and damage can allow friable asbestos, which is dangerous

➢ **Brick and stone veneer – description**
- used since ancient times; commonly used today
- bricks are **hygroscopic**, they absorb water
  - water stains and algae near soil means bricks absorbing water from soil by capillary action
- a WRB and flashing required behind veneer
  - minimum 1 inch space required between veneer and wood-framed walls to allow water to drain out the weep holes
- weep holes required at locations, such as windows, doors, and at foundation to allow water to drain
  - locate weep holes **minimum 33 inches on center; minimum $^3/_{16}$ inch opening**
- base flashing and counterflashing required at roof/wall intersections and around chimneys
- mortar binds bricks and stones to each other
  - mortar joints should be about ⅜ inch thick, may vary between ¼ and ½ inch
  - joints tooled so water does not collect on the brick and deteriorate mortar
- steel lintels support veneer above openings, such as doors and windows, and where veneer is supported by wood framing, such as sidewall above garage roof
  - lintels should be painted on all sides
  - rusted lintels can expand and cause cracks in veneer
- wall ties should be embedded in mortar and fastened to wall to prevent veneer from rotating (bowing) away from building
  - wall ties rarely visible during an inspection; bowing wall covering may be visible

➤ **Brick and stone veneer – typical defects**
- absent, deteriorated, damaged, or improperly installed flashing
- cracks in mortar
- **cracks in bricks or stone** (usually more serious than cracks in mortar)
- deteriorated (spalling) bricks
- damaged bricks or stone
- **absent or deteriorated mortar**
- rusted lintels
- deformed lintels
- deformed (bowing) walls
- absent weep holes (common in older buildings)
- efflorescence (white powder on veneer often indicating water management problems)
- water stains near soil, often gutter problem or lack of gutters

➤ **Fiber cement siding – description**
- common beginning in the mid-1980s
- sometimes called Hardie® board; a brand name, not a wall covering type
- lapped strips 6 inches to 8 inches wide; also 4 feet wide panels
- WRB and flashing required behind siding

➤ **Fiber cement siding – typical defects**
- absent or improperly installed flashing
- damaged or deteriorated siding and trim
- faded or pealed finish
- absent or improperly installed blocks around wall penetrations, such as exhaust duct terminations and hose bibbs (a newer manufacturer's requirement)
- insufficient distance above grade, hard surfaces, and roof coverings
  - distance depends on manufacturer
    - **typical 4 - 6 inches above soil when installed over wood framing**
    - **typical 1 - 2 inches above hard surfaces and roof coverings**
- absent movement joint at vertical surfaces, such as corner boards, windows, and doors

➤ **Hardboard (composite wood) siding – description**
- common 1930s to the present
- plywood, oriented strand board (OSB) and wood are not hardboard siding
- lapped strips about 6 inches to 8 inches wide; also 4 feet wide panels
- WRB and flashing required behind siding
- **some types of this siding installed before about 1990 are problematic because they were often improperly installed and improperly maintained**
  - class action litigation settlements have been exhausted

➤ **Hardboard (composite wood) siding – typical defects**
- absent or improperly installed flashing
- inadequate distance above soil, hard surfaces, and roof coverings
  - distance depends on manufacturer
    - typical 6 inches above soil
    - typical 1 - 2 inches above hard surfaces and roof coverings

- damaged or deteriorated siding and trim, especially at the bottom edge
- faded or pealed finish
- absent finish on bottom edge, especially low on wall
- absent movement joint at vertical surfaces, such as corner boards, windows, and doors

➤ **Stucco (cement/exterior plaster) – description**
- three-coat stucco (two coats over masonry) used since ancient times; uncommon in many markets today; scratch, brown, finish coats
- one-coat and two-coat stucco are proprietary systems; common in some markets, uncommon in others
  - should be installed according to manufacturer's instructions
  - finish coat is paint for one-coat systems
- WRB, flashing, and lath required behind stucco (WRB not required over masonry)
  - these components usually installed over foam insulation board with one-coat and two-coat systems
- proper curing of stucco (keeping it moist for several days) necessary to avoid cracking and similar defects, especially in hot/dry weather
  - rarely done, so stucco cracks are a common defect

➤ **Stucco (cement/exterior plaster) – typical defects**
- same as adhered masonry veneer
- cracks, especially at windows and doors
- damage, especially one-coat and two-coat systems
- faded or pealed finish
- loose trim
- trim slopes toward wall

➤ **Stucco (Exterior Insulation and Finish System (EIFS)) – description**
- proprietary system that looks like stucco, **but is not stucco**
  - **do not describe EIFS as stucco, if unsure, recommend evaluation, especially for systems installed before the early 2000s**
    - water intrusion a common problem, and often not visible during inspection
- **sometimes called Dryvit®;** a brand name, not a wall covering type
- popular from the late 1970s to early 90s; uncommon in recent residential construction
- two types: barrier system and drained system
- barrier system relied on sealants around penetrations to keep out water
  - **barrier systems are problematic because they were often improperly installed**
  - class action litigation settlements have been exhausted
  - **barrier systems no longer allowed**
- drained system relies on WRB, flashing, and weep screeds; similar to stucco

➤ **Stucco (Exterior Insulation and Finish System (EIFS)) – typical defects**
- same as stucco

➤ **Vinyl siding – description**
- common 1960s to present

- interlocking lapped strips about 6 inches to 8 inches wide; also panels and strips that mimic wood shingles and shakes
- WRB and flashing required behind siding

➢ **Vinyl siding – typical defects**
- absent or improperly installed flashing and channel trim
- damaged or deteriorated siding and trim
  - melting caused by heat exposure and by reflection of sunlight off of low emissivity windows
- faded finish
- absent movement joint at vertical surfaces, such as corner boards, windows, and doors
- inadequate lap at seams between pieces (should be about 1 inch)
- excessive waviness (sometimes caused by fastening siding too tightly)

➢ **Wood structural panel siding – description**
- common 1930s; most popular between the 1940s and 90s, less common today
- 4 feet wide by 8 feet or 9 feet tall panels
- made using plywood; hardboard panels are different materials
- sometimes called T1-11, referring to the profile of lower (1 inch) and raised (11 inch)
  - many different profiles and textures; not all are T1-11
- WRB and flashing required behind the siding

➢ **Wood structural panel siding – typical defects**
- same as hardboard panel siding

➢ **Wood siding – description**
- used since ancient time; less common today
- vertical planks (board and batten), horizontal planks (lapped, rabbet joints, tongue-and-groove joints), shingles, and shakes

➢ **Wood siding – typical defects**
- same as hardboard panel siding

➢ **Wall covering trim – description**
- located at corners of buildings, around windows and doors, and at transitions between different wall covering materials
- may be wood, engineered wood, or wall covering manufacturer-supplied materials, such as vinyl J channels and F channels
- serves an aesthetic function, and gives installer convenient and uniform surface against which to terminate wall covering
- not required unless by wall covering manufacturer

➢ **Wall covering trim – typical defects**
- same as hardboard panel siding
- trim slopes toward building

Wall Flashing

➢ **General**

- **integrate wall flashing with water-resistive barrier (WRB) to keep water out of building**
- flashing installed at
  - wall penetrations, such as windows, doors, exhaust duct terminations, and pipes
  - intersections between different materials, such as roof/wall intersections
- flashing installed at joints between wall covering materials
  - Z-flashing between horizontal joints of panel siding
  - flashing strips behind joints of fiber cement siding strips (newer manufacture's recommendation)
  - flashing not required if joints between wall covering materials effectively shed water, such as lapped joints, rabbet joints, tongue-and-groove joints)
- wall flashing may be under wall coverings, such as window flashing, or outside of the wall covering, such as brick base and counterflashing
- flashing materials include galvanized steel, aluminum, rigid plastics, and newer peal-and-stick materials
- water that penetrates behind wall coverings should have a place to drain
  - weep screeds for stucco and adhered masonry veneer
  - weep holes for brick and natural stone
- incompatible flashing materials should not touch or be located above each other
  - steel (including galvanized), copper, and aluminum are incompatible with each other
- **sealants (caulk) do not replace flashing**

➢ **Typical defects**

- flashing absent
- flashing too small
- flashing or sealants loose, deteriorated, or damaged
- use of sealants as a substitute for flashing (excessive sealants may be attempt to address leaks)
- absent drainage openings (weep holes and weep screed)
- incompatible flashing materials, especially when touching

Eaves, Soffits, and Fascia

➢ **General**

- eaves created by rafters that extend beyond exterior walls
  - visible rafters called open eaves
  - enclosed rafters called boxed or closed eaves, or (boxed) cornice
- eaves not required, but beneficial
  - eaves protect wall below from sun and rain
- cornice: fascia (vertical) and soffit (horizontal); may include decorative materials, such as moldings and a frieze
- common materials: wood, plywood, composite materials, vinyl, and aluminum

➤ **Typical defects**

- deterioration or damage (materials and paint)
- absent, damaged, or blocked ventilation screens
- openings that allow vermin entry
- penetration by wall covering that could allow water infiltration

Exterior Doors

➤ **Hinged doors**

- door swings on hinges; usually swings into building, may swing out
  - pick-proof hinges recommended for security if door swings out
- types: single door (slab); double door, one or both slabs operable; bulkhead door (a slanted door opens into basement from exterior)
- dimensions: usually 80 inches high; widths 36 – 72 inches
- typical materials: solid wood; engineered wood with hollow core; steel, fiberglass, or aluminum with foam core
- door parts: hinge and lock jambs (vertical), rails (horizontal), mullion (center)
- installation: set plumb and square in rough opening; shim as needed to achieve even ⅛ inch space between door and frame; fasten; seal wood on all sides to reduce shrinking and swelling caused by moisture
- locks: entry (lockable); single cylinder deadbolt (key exterior, knob interior); double cylinder deadbolt (key both sides), not allowed on egress door

➤ **Sliding doors**

- door slides horizontally on top and bottom tracks; one or more operable leaves
- dimensions: usually 80 inches high; widths 60 – 72+ inches
- typical materials: fiberglass, aluminum
- door parts: tracks, rollers; often equipped with a screen door
- installation: set plumb and square in rough opening; shim as needed; fasten
- locks: entry (lockable)

➤ **Requirements**

- at least one egress door required (usually the front door)
  - minimum 32 inches **clear opening between door face and stop** (usually a 36 inch wide by 78 inch tall door)
  - lock must be operable from interior without key or special knowledge (no double-cylinder deadbolt locks or combination locks)
  - height between exterior landing and top of threshold maximum 7¾ inches if door does not swing over the landing; otherwise maximum 1½ inches
  - other doors not required to meet egress door requirements
- **landing required on interior and exterior sides of all doors to exterior**
  - minimum as wide as the door and minimum 36 inches deep in direction of travel
  - maximum two risers on exterior side of door; door may not swing over landing if risers present
- weatherstripping around door perimeter, and a threshold and sweep at bottom of door (or something similar), required to seal against air and water intrusion

➢ **Safety glazing requirements**
  - safety glazing: material that does not break into large pieces that can cause injury
    ○ examples: tempered glass and plastic
  - safety glazing required **in doors**
    ○ exception: decorative glass, such as cut glass and stained glass
  - safety glazing required for windows within 24 inches horizontally and 60 inches vertically of operable door
    ○ numerous exceptions
  - permanent label required on each pane of safety glazing (usually etched on glazing)
    ○ exception: divided-light glazing, label required on one pane
  - safety glazing requirements apply to exterior and interior doors

➢ **Flashing**
  - see wall flashing for more about door flashing

➢ **Typical defects**
  - improper lock operation
  - improper door operation, such as sticking or rubbing on frame
  - uneven gap between door and frame
  - damage, deterioration, of door or door finish; warping of door
    ○ sliding door tracks and rollers especially prone to deterioration with age and poor maintenance (cleaning/lubrication)
  - water stains or other leak evidence around and under door
    ○ bulkhead doors especially prone to leaking
  - door closes by itself (sometimes called **ghosting**)
  - loose, damaged, deteriorated hinges
  - slide bolt not functioning on double-hung door fixed slab
  - door from garage to building not fire-rated, or not self-closing and self-latching
  - wood door not sealed on all sides
  - threshold or lower track (sliding doors) not supported
  - lack of safety glazing where required
  - absent or damaged weatherstripping, sweep, or threshold
  - double-cylinder deadbolt lock on egress door

Windows

➢ **General**
  - types
    ○ operable (one or more sashes operable)
    ○ fixed (sash not operable)
  - common styles (several others)
    ○ **single hung** (bottom sash operable, top sash fixed)
    ○ **double hung** (both sashes operable, top often stuck shut)
    ○ **transom** (window above a door, usually fixed)
    ○ **sidelight** (window beside a door, usually fixed)
    ○ **casement** (window opens out horizontally, operated by crank)

- o **sliding** (window slides horizontally in frame)
  - common materials
    - o wood, aluminum, vinyl, vinyl-clad aluminum

➢ **Parts**
- glazing: area through which one can see
  - o usually glass, but may be other material such as plastic
- sash: material that surrounds the glazing
  - o most hung windows have two sashes
- frame: material that holds the sashes in place
- muntin: material that divides panes in a divided-light sash
  - o glazing putty and glazing points secure glazing to muntin in single pane windows
- mullion: vertical material that covers joint between window frames, such as when two or more windows are joined to make one window unit
- sash cords (older windows) or springs hold operable sashes in place when window open
  - o worn or broken cords and springs are reportable defect, and can allow injury if sash falls
- sash locks prevent opening sash
  - o improperly operating sash locks are reportable defect, and can indicate window installation or operational problems

➢ **Safety glazing requirements**
- all glazing less than 60 inches above walking surfaces in bathtub and shower walls, and near swimming pools and spas
- glazing more than 9 square feet in one piece if glazing less than 18 inches vertically above walking surface and within 36 inches horizontally of walking surface
- glazing less than 36 inches above stair risers and intermediate landings, or glazing less than 36 inches above bottom landing within 60 inches of the bottom stair tread

➢ **Escape and rescue opening requirements**
- at least one opening required in every sleeping room and habitable attic, and in many basements (newer requirement)
  - o opening may be a window or a side-hinged or sliding door
- clear opening dimensions minimum 20 inches horizontal, 24 inches vertical; area minimum 5.7 square feet (5 square feet at grade)
- opening minimum 44 inches above interior walking surface
- no keys or combination locks allowed
  - o bars or similar security devices may be installed if can be opened from inside
  - o fall protection opening controls maximum 70 inches above walking surface
- window (area) well required if any part of window below grade
  - o well floor area minimum 9 square feet; depth minimum 36 inches
  - o ladder required if well floor more than 44 inches below grade
    - ▪ step width minimum 12 inches; height minimum 18 inches
  - o well should have means to drain water, such as a catch basin and pipe

➢ **Operable windows near floor (fall protection, newer requirement)**
- window opening maximum 4 inches if bottom of window opening less than 24 inches above interior floor and more than 6 feet above exterior grade

➢ **Energy efficiency**
- single pane glazing installed in older buildings (very inefficient)
- two or more pane glazing installed in newer buildings
  - o partial vacuum between panes in most double pane windows to increase energy efficiency
  - o more expensive windows have inert gas between the panes to increase energy efficiency
  - o windows with condensation between panes are deficient and should be reported (replacement can be expensive)
- newer windows may have a low emissivity (low-e) coating that reflects infrared light (heat) to make window more energy efficient

➢ **Flashing**
- see wall flashing for more about window flashing

➢ **Inspection**
- inspect minimum one window in every room (many inspectors inspect all windows)
- look carefully for water infiltration above, around, and under windows

➢ **Typical defects**
- operable sash difficult to operate, painted shut
- sash cords or springs broken, damaged, or deteriorated
- damaged or deteriorated glazing, frame, muntin, or putty
- hardware, such as sash locks and casement window operating hardware, broken, damaged, or deteriorated
- water intrusion, or evidence of water intrusion
- fogging between panes
- egress openings absent, wrong size, too high above floor
- fall protection absent where required
- absent or damaged weatherstripping
- lack of safety glazing where required

Decks

➢ **General**
- deck: outdoor recreation area usually attached or adjacent to building
- decks usually built using preservative (pressure)-treated wood, or naturally durable wood such as redwood and cedar
  - o flooring and rails may be built using composites (such as Trex®), metal, wire cables, and plastic
- type of preservative treatment used on deck wood is indeterminable and best estimated by reading the label attached to the wood

- most deck wood should be ground contact rated (UC4A or better)
- deck hardware and fasteners should be galvanized steel (G180 or better) or stainless steel
- connections between deck components may not use nails subject to withdrawal
  - connections may be subject to withdrawal unless components are restrained against lateral (horizontal) movement

- ➤ **Flashing**
  - **essential for reducing water intrusion that can damage building components**
    - damage can contribute to deck collapse
  - integrate flashing with water-resistive barrier at and above deck ledger, and at doors opening on to deck, to create a drainage plane
  - aluminum flashing not allowed

- ➤ **Ledger attachment**
  - **deck ledger**: lumber that connects the deck to the building
    - **deck ledger connection failure is common cause of deck collapse**
  - minimum deck ledger lumber: #2 grade, 2 inch thick, preservative-treated or naturally durable wood
  - minimum material (band joist/rim board) to which the deck ledger may be connected: 2 inch-thick dimensional lumber or 1 inch-thick engineered wood
    - deck ledger connection to other materials, such as floor trusses and concrete foundations, allowed in some cases
    - deck ledgers may not be connected to cantilevered framing, such as a bay window or a framed chimney
    - deck ledgers should not be installed on through wall coverings, such as siding, brick, and stucco (some exceptions)
  - deck ledger connection to building should resist vertical (downward) load, and resist minimum 3,000-pound lateral (horizontal) load
  - minimum fasteners to resist the vertical load ½ inch diameter machine bolts or lag screws with washers
  - minimum connectors to resist lateral load two connectors rated minimum 1,500-pounds or four connectors rated minimum 750-pounds
  - may use other approved fasteners or connectors when installed per manufacturer's instructions, or when designed by engineer

- ➤ **Stairs and landings**
  - **applies to exterior stairs and interior stairs**
  - stair components: **stringers** (stair support structure), **risers** (vertical), **treads** (horizontal)
  - flight of stairs runs between two landings
    - stairway could have one, two, or more flights of stairs
  - stringers should be attached to the deck using stringer connector; uncommon
    - stringer attachment using screws or nails can work if properly installed, and if stringers restrained against lateral (horizontal) movement
  - **stair riser height maximum 7¾ inches**
  - **tread depth minimum 10 inches**

- winder tread depth minimum 6 inches at any point on tread; minimum depth 10 inches at walk line
- provide **tread nosing** if solid risers, in addition to 10 inch tread depth
  - tread nosing minimum ¾ inch; tread nosing maximum 1¼ inch
- difference between riser heights and tread depths in a flight of stairs maximum ⅜ inch
- open area between treads should not allow a 4 inch diameter sphere to pass
- stairway width minimum 36 inches above handrail
- stairway headroom height minimum 80 inches from line connecting adjacent treads
- **spiral stairways**
  - tread depth minimum 7½ inches at 12 inches from narrow side
  - riser height maximum 9½ inches
  - stairway width minimum 26 inches at and below handrail
- landing should be present at top and bottom of every flight of stairs
  - landing should be at least as wide as the stairs, and at least 36 inches deep in direction of travel

➤ **Guards**

- guard prevents falls from a higher level to a lower level
- guard required if walking surface more than 30 inches above a surface within 36 inches horizontally from the walking surface
- guard height minimum 36 inches tall
- guard resists minimum 200 pound per square foot load applied at top of guard
- guard fill-in, such as balusters, resists minimum 50 pound per square foot load
- horizontal guard fill-in should not allow 4 inch diameter sphere to pass
- stair guard fill-in should not allow 4⅜ inch diameter sphere to pass
- triangle between stair guard bottom rail, stair riser, and tread, should not allow 6 inch diameter sphere to pass

➤ **Handrails**

- **handrail required when stairway has four or more risers**
- top of handrail should be between 34 and 38 inches above a sloped line connecting leading edge of treads
- handrails should begin and end with a return or a post (newel)
- handrails must be graspable
  - only certain shapes and dimensions allowed
  - dimensional lumber handrails, such as a 2 x 4, not graspable, but common; 2" x 2" handrail is generally considered graspable

➤ **Typical defects**

- flashing at deck ledger absent, damaged, or deteriorated (especially aluminum flashing)
- sealant damaged, deteriorated, or excessively applied (usually attempt to repair leak)
- evidence of water intrusion at or below deck ledger
- deck ledger attached only with nails
- deck ledger screws or bolts improper size, improper spacing, too close to deck ledger or band joist edges, deteriorated (rusted)
- deck ledger lateral load connectors absent (common)
- deck ledger attached through wall coverings

- deck ledger attached to cantilevered framing
- stairs inadequately attached to deck
- stairs pulling away from deck
- stairs riser opening more than 4 inches
- stair landings absent, too small
- stair stringers or treads deteriorated, damaged, loose
- guard or handrail absent, loose, deteriorated, damaged, not continuous above all stair treads
- handrail not graspable such as 2 x 4 handrail
- guard or handrail height too low
- notched deck guard posts
- guard baluster opening more than 4 inches (4⅜ inches for stair guards)

Balconies, Stoops, and Porches

➢ **General**
- balcony: outdoor recreation area located at or above second story
  - o usually self-supported (cantilevered), or supported by columns (posts)
  - o evaluate as a deck if supported by columns and ledgers and attached to house
  - o may serve as a roof for area below
    - ▪ roof covering should be designed for use as walking surface
    - ▪ water intrusion through the roof covering/balcony walking surface and at penetrations, such as for guard posts, is common defect
- stoops: small landings on exterior side of exterior doors
- porches: outdoor recreation areas on or near ground
- all may be covered by roof and enclosed with insect screens
- **stoops and porches should slope away from building** minimum ¼ inch per foot
- wood-framed cantilevered balconies should have **minimum 2 feet of floor joist span inside the building (backspan) for every 1 foot of cantilever**
  - o maximum cantilever distance determined by floor joist depth, spacing, and snow load

➢ **Common materials**
- concrete, bricks, concrete blocks, pavers, stone, wood

➢ **Typical defects**
- Same as decks if wood-framed, and driveways, walkways, and patios if other materials
- evidence of water intrusion, especially cantilevered balconies and balconies serving as a roof

Garage Vehicle Doors and Operators

➢ **Garage vehicle doors – general**
- garage vehicle door: operable door large enough to allow a vehicle to enter/exit
  - o common widths 8 and 16 feet; common height 7 feet
  - o may be narrower (for golf carts), or wider (such as 18 feet)

- o may be taller for trucks and recreational vehicles
- most vehicle doors are sectional doors consisting of panels about 18 inches tall
- some (mostly older) vehicle doors are one one-piece (tilt-up)
- **vehicle doors can be dangerous if they close on people or property**
  - o wood doors can weigh 400 pounds or more
  - o metal and fiberglass doors can weigh 200 pounds or more
- vehicle doors require a **torsion (coiled) spring** (common) or extension springs to help them open
  - o worn or improperly adjusted springs are common defect
- reinforcement required for doors in high wind zones

➢ **Garage vehicle doors – installation**

- attach door tracks and springs directly to framing
  - o attachment to or through wall coverings, such as drywall, not allowed
- wood, called bucks, usually nailed at door jambs (sides of the door) and above center of door
  - o buck attachment through wall covering is common defect
- remove rope attached to door for opening/closing if operator installed
- adjust sectional door springs so door remains stationary when half-way open
- install containment cables on extension springs so that springs do not cause injury or damage if they break
- install weatherstripping around the entire door to reduce water and air intrusion
  - o door not expected to be water and air tight

➢ **Garage vehicle doors – typical defects**

- damaged or deteriorated door panels, glazing, or weatherstripping
- damaged, deteriorated, or improperly adjusted springs
  - o door moves when half way up may indicate spring defects
- absent, damaged, deteriorated, or loose door hardware
- door makes unusual noise or binds when operated
- absent containment cable on extension springs
- lock not operating properly (should be disabled if operator installed)
- buck pulling away from framing (especially where springs attached)

➢ **Garage vehicle door operators – general**

- commonly called garage door openers
- usually an electric motor that drives a chain, belt, or screw in a trolly, and attached by operator arm to vehicle door
  - o jackshaft openers installed above or at side of door, uncommon
- common safety features
  - o pressure reverse sensor: operator should reverse direction when closes on a 1 inch high object; frequently improperly adjusted
  - o optical reverse sensor: operator should reverse when the beam is interrupted
    - ▪ **sensors should be located not more than 6 inches above floor**
  - o manual release rope at door arm: maximum 72 inches above floor
  - o wall switch: minimum 60 inches above floor

- extension cords to power operator and splicing of operator power cord not allowed
- operator should be on a GFCI-protected circuit (newer requirement)

- ➢ **Garage vehicle door operators – typical defects**
  - attachment of operator arm to vehicle door not reinforced
    - o door may be damaged by the pressure reverse system
  - operator does not operate when wall switch used
  - operator operates only when the wall switch continuously depressed
  - optical reverse sensors bypassed or otherwise not functioning properly
  - door does not reverse direction when striking object (common defect)
    - o considerable controversy whether and how to test this feature during inspection
  - safety features improperly installed
    - o sensors too high, wall switch or release rope too low
  - operator unusually noisy
  - drive mechanism (chain, belt) loose, drooping
  - extension cord or spliced operator power cord
  - operator does not disengage from door (vehicle door cannot be used if power out)
  - operator light does not function

Unit 3: Roof Components

Topics covered in this Unit include:
- **Knowledge Areas**
- **Roof Coverings: General**
- **Roof Coverings: Steep Slope**
- **Roof Coverings: Low Slope**
- **Roof Drainage Systems**
- **Roof Flashing**
- **Skylights**

Knowledge Areas

➢ **Knowledge areas in-scope of a home inspection and in-scope of the exam**

- roof coverings
- roof drainage systems
- roof flashing
- skylights and other roof penetrations

Roof Coverings – General

➢ **General**

- **roof coverings**: materials on roof framing to prevent water intrusion into building
  - ○ "the roof" consists of **rafters** and **roof sheathing**; roof coverings cover the roof
- **underlayment** required under most steep slope roof coverings
  - ○ may be building paper (felt, traditional type), synthetic material (newer), or roll roofing
- **valleys are lower slope than rest of roof**
  - ○ valley slope may be too low for roof covering if roof framing is near minimum allowed slope for roof covering
- roof penetrations, such as plumbing vents, should not be located within 12 inches of valley center line due to increased risk of water intrusion around penetration
- roof covering manufacturer's instructions may supersede general (code) requirements
- **water stains on interior finish materials may not be roof covering leaks**
  - ○ condensation can occur under some roof coverings, especially metal
  - ○ condensation can occur in attics due to poor attic ventilation, air leaks between the building and the attic, and HVAC duct leaks
  - ○ condensation can occur when interior finish materials are attached to rafters, usually because of poor ventilation and air leaks around penetrations such as recessed lights

➢ **Roof covering types**

- roof pitch and slope describe the same concept; terms often used interchangeably

- o roof pitch describes the roof slope as a ratio of vertical rise to 12 inches of horizontal run
  - **steep slope roof coverings:** for roof slopes **2 inches or more rise for every 12 inches** run (2/12)
    - o examples: asphalt shingles, metal shingles, slate, tile, wood
    - o **steep slope roof coverings are water-shedding, not waterproof**
      - ▪ **underlayment is the water-resistive barrier**
  - **low slope roof coverings:** for roof slopes less than 2 inches rise for every 12 inches run (2/12)
    - o examples: built-up membranes (BUR), modified bitumen membranes, single-ply membranes, such as EDPM, and some metal panels, such as standing seam
    - o low slope roof coverings are waterproof
    - o low slope roofs should **slope minimum ¼ inch vertical for every 12 inches** horizontal toward a water drainage point
      - ▪ "flat" roofs (a common description of low slope roofs) are deficient and should be reported because they retain water

Roof Coverings – Steep Slope

➢ **Asbestos cement shingles - description**
  - most common 1910s to 1950s
    - o uncommon in many markets because these shingles are beyond their 50 – 75 year service life
  - usually between ¼ to ½ inch thick
  - asbestos banned in building materials in 1973
    - o shingles no longer made; finding replacements may be difficult and expensive
  - **working with asbestos-containing materials, including removal, requires mitigation protocols that can be very expensive**
  - the presence or absence of asbestos can only be confirmed by a laboratory
    - o report all materials that may contain asbestos as: "possible asbestos-containing material" and recommend laboratory analysis

➢ **Asbestos cement shingles – typical defects**
  - absent, damaged, deteriorated, loose shingles and flashing
    - o cracks and damage can allow friable asbestos, which is dangerous
  - improperly installed flashing

➢ **Asphalt (fiberglass, composition) shingles - description**
  - most common roof covering in United States
  - made from asphalt-impregnated base (usually fiberglass) covered with stone granules
  - seal strip near center of shingle adheres shingles to each other
    - o seal strip at first course necessary to reduce shingle uplift by wind
  - types
    - o 3-tab strip (flat profile, least expensive)
    - o 3-tab dimensional (raised profile, moderately expensive)

- o laminated (raised profile, two layers of shingles adhered into one strip, expensive, heavy, uncommon)
  - service life 18-20 years for strip shingles to 25-35 years for laminated shingles
    - o faster deterioration usually on south and west-facing roofs due to sunlight
    - o algae and moss common on north facing roofs

➤ **Asphalt (fiberglass, composition) shingles – installation**
- install on solid sheathing
- roof slope minimum 4/12
  - o may be allowed as low as 2/12 with double underlayment
- underlayment required
  - o minimum #15 building paper, synthetic materials common on recent installations
  - o lap horizontal seams minimum 2 inches, and vertical seams minimum 4 inches
  - o double underlayment required in high wind zones
- ice barrier required at eaves in cold climates
  - o install minimum 2 feet horizontally inside exterior walls
- drip edge flashing required at eaves and rakes
  - o install underlayment above drip edge at eaves, and under drip edge at rakes
- common valleys: closed cut and woven; open valleys allowed, uncommon
  - o flashing, such as 36 inch wide roll roofing, required in valleys
  - o trim cut side of closed cut valley minimum 2 inches from valley center line, and seal cut side with roofing cement
- minimum 4 nails per strip most areas; 6 nails per strip high wind zones
  - o staples may be allowed by some manufacturers, but not recommended
  - o nail locations per manufacturer's instructions, usually not above seal strip
- flat profile cap shingles at hips and ridges, not dimensional or laminated shingles

➤ **Asphalt (fiberglass, composition) shingles – typical repairs**
- replace shingles with similar material and integrate into existing shingles
- patch using roofing cement; roofing cement deteriorates rapidly; not permanent repair
- algae considered cosmetic; not a defect
- moss can damage shingles by loosening granules; a defect if widespread

➤ **Asphalt (fiberglass, composition) shingles – typical defects**
- absent, damaged, deteriorated, loose, aged shingles and flashing
  - o evidence of deterioration or age: granule loss, curling at edges, visible fibers at edges, stiffness, cracking
  - o damage often caused by tree limbs, hail, foot traffic
- improperly installed shingles and flashing
  - o common: no seal strip at first shingle course; too few nails; nails above seal strip; cut side of closed cut valley not cut back from center line and sealed; exposed fasteners
  - o shingle slots not offset per manufacturer's instructions
- more than two layers of shingles
  - o two layers allowed, not recommended

- determine by counting layers at rakes, or by looking for flashing that does not appear to have been replaced
- widespread moss
- use of dimensional or laminated shingles as cap shingles at ridges and hips

➢ **Concrete and clay tiles - description**
- common in some markets, such as desert Southwest, uncommon in most other markets
- types
    - concrete: hard, more durable than clay
    - clay: soft, easily broken
    - common profiles: Spanish (S shape), Mission (C shape, clay), curved, flat
- very heavy; roof framing must be designed to bear the load
- service life 100+ years
    - tiles usually have much longer service life than common #30 felt underlayment; all tiles may need to be removed to replace underlayment

➢ **Concrete and clay tiles – installation**
- install on solid sheathing or spaced sheathing
- roof slope minimum 2½/12
    - 4/12 industry recommendation
- underlayment required
    - minimum #30 building paper
    - **lap horizontal seams minimum 2 inches, and vertical seams minimum 4 inches**
    - lap underlayment over rake minimum 1 inch
    - double underlayment required on roof slopes between 2½/12 and 4/12
- ice barrier required at eaves in cold climates
    - install minimum 2 feet horizontally inside exterior walls
- common valleys: closed and open (more common)
    - flashing, such as 36 inch wide #30 building paper and 22 inch wide galvanized steel with a 1 inch splash diverter ridge, required in valleys
- securing tiles depends on securing method used and on the wind zone
    - tiles may rest on and be secured to wood battens
    - secure all tiles within 36 inches of eaves, rakes, and ridges
    - mud balls (mortar) used to secure tiles at ridges and hips
- typical head lap minimum 3 inches
    - head lap: distance upper tile extends over lower tile

➢ **Concrete and clay tiles – typical repairs**
- reposition and secure loose tiles
- replace cracked tiles; adhesive not permanent repair
- replace cracked mud balls if necessary to secure tiles at ridges and hips
- replace damaged and deteriorated underlayment

➤ **Concrete and clay tiles – typical defects**
- absent, loose, and damaged, tiles, mud balls, and flashing
- improperly installed tiles and flashing
  ○ tiles not secured at perimeter
  ○ inadequate head lap
- damaged or deteriorated underlayment, common at eaves and rakes
- overcut tiles exposing underlayment

➤ **Metal shingles - description**
- uncommon in many markets
- metal shingles defined as maximum 3 square feet exposed area
  ○ metal panels defined as 3 square feet or more exposed area
- shingle materials: steel (common), aluminum, copper, stainless steel (all uncommon)
- shingle coatings: zinc (galvanized steel), liquid coatings, granules
- some metal shingles designed to look like slate, wood shakes, and tile
- service life 50+ years; dependent on local environment and maintenance of coating

➤ **Metal shingles – installation**
- install on solid sheathing or closely spaced sheathing
- roof slope minimum 4/12
- underlayment not required by code, but may be required by manufacturer
  ○ condensation possible under metal if no underlayment
- ice barrier may be required by local authorities at eaves in cold climates
- valley flashing of same material as shingles; minimum 16 inches wide over 36 inch wide underlayment

➤ **Metal shingles – typical repairs**
- repair rust by removing rust and replacing coating
- patch small holes by soldering patch made from same metal as shingle to shingle

➤ **Metal shingles – typical defects**
- absent, damaged, deteriorated, loose shingles and flashing
- improperly installed shingles and flashing

➤ **Metal panels - description**
- common in many markets
  ○ may be used as accent covering above bay windows, or as covering for most or all of roof
- metal panels defined as 3 square feet or more exposed area
  ○ metal singles defined as less than 3 square feet exposed area
- types
  ○ lapped seam, unsealed seam: steep slope roof covering, minimum roof slope 3/12
  ○ lapped seam, sealed seam: low slope roof covering, minimum roof slope ½/12
  ○ standing seam: low slope roof covering, minimum roof slope ¼/12
- panel materials: steel (common), copper (common on small roofs), aluminum, stainless steel (both uncommon)

- panels coatings: zinc (galvanized steel), liquid coatings
- service life 50+ years, heavily dependent on local environment and maintenance (of coating)

➤ **Metal panels – installation**
- install on solid sheathing or spaced sheathing
- underlayment not required by code, but may be required by manufacturer
  - condensation under metal possible if no underlayment
- ice barrier may be required by local authorities at eaves in cold climates
- valley flashing of same material as panels; minimum 16 inches wide with splash diverter rib over 36 inch wide underlayment

➤ **Metal panels – typical repairs**
- same as metal shingles

➤ **Metal panels – typical defects**
- absent, damaged, deteriorated panels and flashing
  - rust
  - faded, deteriorated coating
- improperly installed panels and flashing
  - overdriven fasteners (washer splayed), lapped seam panels
  - absent, loose, or underdriven fasteners, lapped seam panels
  - improper seam lap, lapped seam panels
  - improper or inadequately secured roof penetration flashing
- excessive ripples in panels (oil canning)

➤ **Slate shingles - description**
- made from stone quarried mostly in Northeast United States and Eastern Canada
- used mostly in Northeast; uncommon in most other markets
- very heavy; roof framing must be designed to bear load
- service life 100+ years; fasteners likely to deteriorate before slate

➤ **Slate shingles – installation**
- install on solid sheathing; may see spaced sheathing at older buildings
- roof slope minimum 4/12
- underlayment not required by code, but may be required by manufacturer, or by local authorities
- ice barrier may be required by local authorities at eaves in cold climates
- head lap depends on roof slope
  - head lap minimum 4 inches
  - head lap distance upper tile extends over lower tile
- common valleys: open and closed
  - flashing required, such as 36 inch wide #30 building paper and 15 inch wide galvanized steel
  - closed valleys limited to 8/12 or more roof slopes

- ➢ **Slate shingles – typical repairs**
  - reposition and secure loose shingles
  - replace cracked and delaminated shingles; adhesive not permanent repair
  - chips usually do not need repair if small and not widespread

- ➢ **Slate shingles – typical defects**
  - absent, damaged, deteriorated (delaminated), and loose shingles, flashing, and fasteners
    - o lower quality slate can present chipping and delamination; a defect if widespread
  - improperly installed shingles and flashing, such as inadequate head lap

- ➢ **Wood shakes and shingles - description**
  - made from naturally durable wood (cedar, redwood) or preservative-treated wood
  - shakes
    - o made by splitting wood, rough surface texture
    - o ⅝ - ¾ inch thick at butt end
    - o standard lengths of 16 and 24 inches
  - shingles
    - o made by sawing wood, uniform surface texture
    - o ½ inch thick at butt end
    - o standard lengths of 16, 18, and 24 inches
  - service life 30 years, heavily dependent on local environment, drying potential of wood, and maintenance

- ➢ **Wood shakes and shingles – installation**
  - install on solid sheathing or spaced sheathing
    - o spaced sheathing better, allows wood to dry from below and above
  - roof slope minimum 3/12; 4/12 industry recommendation
  - underlayment not required by code, but may be required by manufacturer
  - interlayment required between shake courses; #15 building paper or better
  - ice barrier may be required by local authorities at eaves in cold climates
  - 2 fasteners per shingle or shake
    - o fastener location shingles: maximum ¾ inch from sides, and maximum 1 inch above butt end of shingle above
    - o fastener location shakes: maximum 1 inch from sides, and maximum 2 inches above butt end of shingle above
  - **keyway** (slot, space) required between each shingle and shake; allows for wood expansion and contraction because of moisture
    - o shingles: between ¼ and ⅜ inch
    - o shakes: between ⅜ and ⅝ inch
    - o offset keyways minimum 1½ inches between each adjacent course
  - exposed area of shingles depends on depends on shingle length, grade, roof slope
    - o between 5 and 7½ inches
  - exposed area of shakes depends on shake length
    - o 7½ inches for 18 inch long shakes
    - o 10 inches for 24 inch long shakes

- common valleys: open; swept (uncommon); closed valleys allowed, uncommon
  - flashing: minimum 20 inch corrosion-resistant metal required in valleys

➢ **Wood shakes and shingles – typical repairs**
- reposition and secure loose shingles and shakes
- replace deteriorated and damaged shingles and shakes with similar material and integrate into existing materials
- roofing cement deteriorates rapidly; not permanent repair
- algae considered cosmetic, not a defect
  - may indicate wood not drying which could reduce service life
- moss can damage wood; a defect if wide spread

➢ **Wood shakes and shingles – typical defects**
- absent, damaged, deteriorated, aged, loose, shingles, shakes, **interlayment**, and flashing
  - splitting and curling edges and cupping typical for deteriorated and aged wood
- improperly installed shingles, shakes, and flashing
  - improper exposure length
  - improper keyway size or offset distance
- exposed fasteners
- widespread moss

➢ **Ice dams**
- occur when heat from building melts snow on roof; melted water freezes at eaves forms ice dam; melted snow (water) stopped at ice dam, flows into building
- visible evidence
  - ice and icicles at eaves and gutters
  - water stains and damage at eaves and at walls and ceilings near exterior walls
- preventing ice dams
  - **reduce heat entering attic by air sealing ceiling penetrations, sealing HVAC supply ducts in attic, adding insulation, and ensuring adequate ventilation in ventilated attics**
- heat strips at eaves sometimes used to reduce ice dams, but not as effective as addressing ice dam causes

Roof Coverings – Low Slope

➢ **Built-up membranes (BUR) - description**
- two or more layers of building paper (felt) or other membranes, bitumen (asphalt/coal tar) installed between each layer, then covered with gravel
  - also known as tar and gravel roof coverings
  - gravel protects the paper from sunlight, rain, and wind
- common leak locations
  - transitions between roof covering types, such as steep slope to low slope
  - roof penetrations, such as plumbing vents, exhaust openings, skylights, and curbs for equipment

- o **parapet walls** (walls that extend above roof covering)
- service life 10 to 40 years, heavily dependent on number of membrane layers, local environment, and maintenance

➢ **Built-up membranes (BUR) – installation**
- install on solid sheathing, including rigid insulation
- roof slope minimum ¼/12
- raised platform (curb), flashed as necessary, to support equipment such as HVAC
- install cant strip at vertical walls, such as parapet walls, so membrane does not bend at sharp (90°) angle
- install gravel stop drip edge flashing where water drains over roof edge

➢ **Built-up membranes (BUR) – typical repairs**
- repair depends on problem and BUR materials
  - o usually a patch using same BUR material adhered to existing material

➢ **Built-up membranes (BUR) – typical defects**
- damaged membrane, such as holes and rips
- deteriorated membrane, such as deep and extensive **alligatoring**, and cracks that penetrate the membrane
  - o **alligatoring**: cracks in membrane that do not penetrate membrane and look like alligator skin
- deformed membrane, such as blisters and wrinkles
- openings at seams between membranes (**fishmouths**)
- evidence of water accumulation, such as standing water, dirt, and stains
  - o water may remain up to 48 hours after rain
- vegetation and debris on roof
- loose and deteriorated flashing around penetrations and parapet walls
- displaced gravel exposing membrane
- fasteners withdrawing and penetrating membrane
- improper or inadequately flashed equipment support
- upslope seams lapped above lower seams
- absent cant strip at vertical walls

➢ **Mineral-surfaced roll roofing - description**
- asphalt-impregnated base, which is usually covered with granules
- 36 inches wide
- roof covering for temporary structures, underlayment for roof coverings, such as tile, and valley flashing
- not recommended as roof covering for permanent structures because of ten year or less service life
- easy to confuse with modified bitumen roof covering
  - o modified bitumen is thicker and usually 39 inches wide

➢ **Mineral-surfaced roll roofing – installation**
- install on solid sheathing
- roof slope minimum 1/12, manufacturer may specify 2/12

- underlayment required minimum #15 building paper
  - lap horizontal seams minimum 2 inches; vertical seams minimum 4 inches
- secure at upper edge of material using nails long enough to penetrate sheathing minimum ¾ inch
- lap horizontal seam minimum 1 - 2 inches over lower course; seal with roofing cement
- lap vertical seam minimum 6 inches over adjacent material; seal with roofing cement

➤ **Mineral-surfaced roll roofing – typical repairs**

- patch using the same material adhered to existing material

➤ **Mineral-surfaced roll roofing – typical defects**

- same as built-up membranes (BUR), except granule loss instead of displaced gravel

➤ **Modified bitumen roofing - description**

- polymer-modified bitumen-impregnated base; may be covered with granules
  - two-membrane systems may be used on commercial buildings, single membrane systems more likely on residential buildings
- usually 39 inches wide, compared to 36 inches wide for roll roofing
- common leak locations same as built-up roofing (BUR)
- service life 10 to 20 years, heavily dependent on local environment and maintenance

➤ **Modified bitumen roofing – installation**

- install on solid sheathing
- roof slope minimum ¼/12
- nails at the upper edge of material that penetrate sheathing minimum ¾ inch
  - fasteners should not be exposed
- lap horizontal seam minimum 3 inches over lower course, seal per manufacturer
- lap vertical seam minimum 6 inches over adjacent material, seal per manufacturer
- install **cant strip** at vertical walls, such as parapet walls, so membrane does not bend at sharp (90°) angle
- do not use adhesive to secure modified bitumen roof covering to roof sheathing; sheathing may move a different rate than roof covering and damage roof covering

➤ **Modified bitumen roofing – typical repairs**

- patch using the same material adhered to existing material

➤ **Modified bitumen roofing – typical defects**

- same as built-up membranes (BUR), except granule loss instead of displaced gravel

➤ **Polyurethane foam roofing - description**

- spray-applied closed cell foam that dries hard
  - cover with ultra-violet-resistant coating maximum three days after foam installed
  - reapply coating, coating service life depends on local conditions

- provides insulation value
- service life 30 years, heavily dependent on local environment and coating maintenance

➢ **Polyurethane foam roofing – installation**
- install on solid sheathing
- roof slope minimum ¼/12
- thickness minimum 1-1½ inches; maximum 4 inches
- foam provides flashing; no additional flashing required
- raised platform to support equipment, such as HVAC

➢ **Polyurethane foam roofing – typical repairs**
- as specified by the manufacturer

➢ **Polyurethane foam roofing – typical defects**
- damage by hail, foot traffic, scraping
- blisters
- "tree bark" texture
- evidence of water accumulation, such as standing water, dirt, and stains
  - water may remain up to 48 hours after rain
- vegetation and debris on roof
- deteriorated coating
- thin application
- improper or inadequately flashed equipment support

➢ **Single-ply membrane roofing - description**
- types
  - thermoplastics, such as Polyvinyl Chloride (PVC) and Thermoplastic Olefins (TPO); uncommon on residential buildings
  - thermoset membranes, such as Ethylene Propylene Diene Terpolymer (EDPM)
- common leak locations same as built-up roofing (BUR)
- service life 30 years, heavily dependent on membrane thickness, local environment, and maintenance

➢ **Single-ply membrane roofing – installation**
- install on solid sheathing
- roof slope minimum ¼/12
- lap horizontal seams minimum 3 inches over lower course; seal per manufacturer
- lap vertical seam minimum 6 inches over adjacent material; seal per manufacturer
- raised platform to support equipment, such as HVAC
- asphalt-based materials are incompatible with these roof covering materials

➢ **Single-ply membrane roofing – typical repairs**
- patch using same material adhered to existing material

➢ **Single-ply membrane roofing – typical defects**
- damaged membrane, such as holes and rips

- deteriorated membrane
- deformed membrane, such as blisters and wrinkles
- openings at seams between membranes (fishmouths)
- evidence of water accumulation, such as standing water, dirt, and stains
  - water may remain up to 48 hours after rain
- vegetation and debris on roof
- loose and deteriorated flashing around penetrations and at parapet walls
- fasteners withdrawing and penetrating membranes
- improper or inadequately flashed equipment support
- upslope seams lapped above lower seams
- absent cant strip at vertical walls

Roof Drainage Systems

➤ **Gutters and downspouts – description**
- gutters and downspouts provide steep slope roof drainage
  - downspout may be installed under scupper to conduct water to ground
- **gutter** (trough, eaves trough): horizontal trough conducts water from roof to downspout
- **downspout** (conductor, downpipe, leader): vertical pipe discharges water away from building
- splash block or downspout extension: conducts water minimum 5 feet from foundation
- gutters not required in most markets
  - gutters required where collapsable or expansive soil present
  - lack of gutters in markets where gutters are common is a reportable issue
- determining appropriate gutter and downspout size out of scope of home inspection

➤ **Gutters and downspouts – types and materials**
- half round gutters
- L-shaped gutters, called K gutter
- gutters integrated into eaves, called Yankee gutters, uncommon
- common materials: aluminum, galvanized steel, vinyl
- less common material: copper, very expensive

➤ **Gutters and downspouts – installation**
- gutter securing methods
  - spike (nail) and ferrule (tube): typical for galvanized steel gutters
  - hidden hangers: typical for aluminum and vinyl gutters
- **ideal gutters slope toward downspout about $\frac{1}{16}$ inch per foot**
- gutters and downspouts should not discharge on roof coverings; amount and force of water can damage roof coverings
  - better to discharge into another gutter, or extend a downspout
  - discharge on roof coverings common; reporting as defect a judgment call
- gutters and downspouts should not discharge into foundation drains

➢ **Gutters and downspouts – typical defects**
  • gutter holding water; not sloped toward downspout
  • leaks, especially at joints and end caps
  • water stains on and damage to fascia
    ○ may indicate poor gutter installation, gutter overflow (poor maintenance), or poor roof covering installation
  • damage, deterioration
  • debris in gutters and downspouts, debris blocking gutter guards
  • depression in ground under gutter indicating possible gutter overflow
  • loose and poorly attached gutters and downspouts
  • downspout directed toward wall or foundation
  • absent splash block or downspout extension

➢ **Low slope roof drainage – types**
  • water discharged over roof edge; drip edge/gravel stop protects discharge area
  • scupper (opening in parapet wall)
  • internal drain pipes

➢ **Low slope roof drainage – installation**
  • single scupper or internal drain may not be only roof drain
    ○ secondary drain required located minimum 2 inches above primary drain

➢ **Low slope roof drainage – typical defects**
  • evidence of water accumulation, such as standing water, dirt, and stains
    ○ water may remain on roof up to 48 hours
  • vegetation and debris blocking scuppers and drain openings
  • leak evidence, especially around scuppers and drain openings
  • damage, deterioration, absent components, such as debris screens
  • lack of secondary drain where required

Roof Flashing

➢ **Roof flashing – description**
  • **sealants (caulk) do not replace flashing**
  • flashing of pipes that penetrate the roof are called boots, roof jacks, stack flashing, thimbles
    ○ terminology is regional; may differ depending on penetration type
    ○ pipe flashing should match roof slope to achieve reliable seal between pipe and flashing
    ○ flashing flanges should be integrated into roof covering to reduce leaks around flashing
    ○ roof penetrations should not be located in roof valleys
  • common roof flashing locations
    ○ roof penetrations, such as vents, chimneys, and skylights
      ▪ see wall flashing, for more about masonry chimney flashing
    ○ intersection of roof with sidewalls, headwalls, and parapet walls

o where roof changes direction or slope, including valleys
▪ see individual roof covering types for more about valley flashing
- incompatible flashing materials should not touch or be located above each other
o steel (including galvanized), copper, and aluminum are incompatible with each other

➤ **Plumbing vent flashing**
- called **boots** or stack flashing
- less expensive, shorter service life: neoprene and thermoplastic
- more expensive, longer service life: lead

➤ **Appliance vent and metal chimney flashing**
- called **thimbles**
- installed around gas and oil appliance vents, and around metal chimneys
- galvanized steel for gas vents and for chimneys; stainless steel for oil vents
- storm collar should be installed above the flashing to reduce storm water intrusion

➤ **Exhaust duct and attic ventilation opening flashing**
- called roof jacks
- installed at exhaust duct roof terminations, such as bathroom, kitchen, clothes dryer
- installed at roof-mounted attic ventilation openings, such as turtle-backs

➤ **Sidewall and headwall flashing**
- sidewall: where roof runs along and is parallel with sidewall
- headwall: where roof runs up to and is perpendicular to headwall
- typical flashing materials: galvanized steel and aluminum; copper has longer service life, but uncommon due to high cost
  o approved plastics and composites may be used
- flashing should consist of base flashing and counterflashing
  o counterflashing covers base flashing to prevent leaking
- long lengths of base flashing and counterflashing may be used to flash headwalls
  o called apron flashing
- small lengths of base flashing and counterflashing should be used to flash sidewalls
  o called step flashing
  o step flashing minimum 4 inches vertically and horizontally
  o step flashing on high side should lap lower step flashing minimum 2 inches
- flashing usually covered by siding-type wall coverings, such as fiber cement and vinyl
- stepped base flashing and counterflashing should be installed on exterior of bricks
  o counterflashing installed in groove cut into mortar and sealed with sealant
    ▪ counterflashing secured with fasteners or sealant; can work, but not recommended, needs regular inspection and maintenance
- base flashing installed under stucco and adhered masonry veneer; wall covering provides counterflashing

➤ **Parapet wall flashing**

- flash intersection of roof covering and parapet wall based on roof covering type and parapet wall type
  - example: modified bitumen and EDPM roof covering often run up a brick parapet wall, mechanically fastened with metal strip flashing, and sealed with a sealart
    - cant strip at roof/wall intersection avoids turning membranes at 90° angle
  - cap parapet wall with metal or concrete cap that extends beyond the wall and is sloped to drain water

➤ **Kick out flashing required where wall extends beyond a vertical sidewall**

- turns water away from the sidewall
- minimum 4 inches tall and 4 inches wide
- often absent or too small, a reportable defect

➤ **Roof flashing – typical defects**

- absent, deteriorated, damaged, loose flashing and sealants
- absent counterflashing
- absent kick out flashing
- counterflashing secured mechanically or with sealant
- flashing too small, not run far enough up wall
- upper step flashing lapped under lower step flashing
- flashing restricts vent opening area
- absent cant strip where appropriate

Skylights

➤ **Skylights – description**

- glazed opening in roof
  - glazing sloped more than 15° from vertical defined as skylight
  - glazing should be safety glazing (or other approved glazing) or acrylic

➤ **Skylights – types**

- rectangular
  - modern skylights usually manufactured system including flashing
  - skylights may be operable
  - skylights may be field-assembled, including opening covered by glazing
- round: called tubular skylight or tubular daylighting device
  - manufactured system; reflective tube runs from device on roof to opening ir room

➤ **Skylights – installation**

- install and flash manufactured skylights per manufacturer's instructions
- minimum 4 inch tall curb recommended for rectangular skylights; required if roof slope less than 3/12
  - step flashing, head flashing, and apron flashing curb recommended for skylights
- frame and insulate chase between a rectangular skylight and opening in room

- **do not cut or remove rafters, ceiling joists, and truss members when installing skylight**
  - dimensional rafters and ceiling joists may be notched or drilled
  - trusses may not be altered unless alteration is designed by engineer

- ➤ **Skylights – typical defects**
  - water leaks or evidence of water leaks
  - water stains caused by condensation
    - especially in high humidity rooms like bathrooms and kitchens
  - damaged or deteriorated glazing, including compromised seal between multiple-pane glazing
  - framing altered, cut, or removed
  - absent, removed, fallen chase insulation
  - absent, damaged, deteriorated, loose flashing
  - excessive sealant, usually an attempt to stop a leak
  - absent curb, not required unless roof slope less than 3/12, but lack of curb makes leaks much more likely
  - skylight poorly secured to framing/curb

Unit 4: Structural Components

Topics covered in this Unit include:

- **Knowledge Areas**
- **Forces Affecting Buildings**
- **Footings, Piles, Piers, Columns, Pilasters**
- **Basement Foundations**
- **Crawlspace Foundations**
- **Slab Foundations**
- **Floor Systems – General**
- **Dimensional Lumber Floor Joists and Beams**
- **Wood I-Joist , Engineered Wood Floor Joists and Beams**
- **Wood Floor Trusses**
- **Wall Systems – General**
- **Wood-Framed Walls**
- **Concrete Masonry Unit and Structural Brick Walls**
- **Roof Systems – General**
- **Dimensional Lumber Ceiling Joists and Rafters**
- **Wood Roof Trusses**

Knowledge Areas

➢ **Knowledge areas in-scope of a home inspection and in-scope of the exam**

- foundation
- floor structure
- wall and vertical support structure
- roof and ceiling structure

➢ **Knowledge areas out-of-scope of a home inspection but in-scope of the exam**

- engineering-related issues, such as how forces affect buildings, and soil types and characteristics

➢ **Structural components are often not visible during a home inspection**

- knowledge of structural components helps inspector evaluate visual clues that might indicate structural defects

Forces Affecting Buildings

➢ **Buildings move in any direction depending on the type and direction of force and on how much force is applied**

- buildings should resist forces from any direction whether applied individually or simultaneously
- buildings should resist forces known to exist in the area
  - ○ buildings near the Atlantic and Gulf coasts should resist wind force

- o buildings on the West coast, and near Memphis, TN and Charleston, SC should resist earthquake force
- o buildings in the far north, on mountains, and where lake-effect snow exists should resist snow loads
- modern buildings are built with more fasteners and connectors to resist applied forces compared to older buildings

➢ **Forces affecting the building**
- these forces are sometimes called **environmental loads** because they are generated by the environment
- gravity pulls building down
  - o gravity is resisted by foundation components, such as footings and piles
  - o foundation components **distribute gravity load to soil**
    - ▪ foundation subsidence (settlement) often due to poorly compacted soil, soil with poor load-bearing capacity, unstable soil, and erosion
- water causes building movement in any direction, sometimes changing direction rapidly (wave action)
  - o water can push walls horizontally (**hydrostatic pressure**)
  - o frozen water expands and can push foundations horizontally and upwards (**frost heave**)
    - ▪ bottom of foundation (footings) must be below local frost depth
  - o water acting on unstable (expanding/contracting) soil can move foundations up, down, and horizontally
  - o flood water can cause building to move horizontally in different directions, and can lift building off of its foundation
- wind pushes and pulls building walls horizontally
  - o push on windward side, pull on leeward side
  - o wind can push walls and roofs up, especially when windows and doors blown out
- earthquakes (seismic loads) can move foundations and walls in any direction
  - o earthquake forces change direction rapidly causing building to move up, down, and horizontally; this can cause buildings to slide off foundations, and can tear buildings apart
- snow can place significant downward load on structural components, especially roofs and decks

➢ **Types of loads on building components**
- **dead load**: load imposed by building materials and permanently installed components
- **live load**: load imposed by occupants and belongings, and by environmental loads, such as snow
- dead and live loads expressed in pounds per square foot (psf), and assumed to be uniformly distributed

➢ **Different soils have different load-bearing capacity, ability to drain water, and stability when moisture is applied or withdrawn**
- **Unified Soil Classification System** divides soil into categories based on characteristics
  - o bedrock has highest load-bearing capacity and stability, but poor drainage

- o gravel, sand, and mixtures have good load-bearing capacity, stability and drainage
- o organic clays, silt, and mixtures have poor load-bearing capacity and drainage, and are unstable
  - ▪ unstable soils may expand when water is applied and contract when water is withdrawn, causing significant foundation damage

Footings, Piles, Piers, Columns, Pilasters

➢ **Definitions**
- **footings and piles**: foundation components that transfer building loads to soil
  - o concealed in ground; rarely fully visible for inspection
- **piers and columns**: vertical structural components that transfer point loads to foundation
  - o **point load**: concentrated load, such as from a beam
- **pilasters**: vertical structural components that transfer building loads to soil, or that provide lateral support for foundation walls
  - o may be installed to stabilize rotated or bowed foundation walls

➢ **Footings**
- modern (last 100+ years): concrete spread footings
  - o 6 - 19 inches thick and 12 - 49 inches wide; may be steel-reinforced
- older: rubble stone, bricks, timbers, or no footings
- pad footing: footing that supports a pier or column
- bottom of footing should be minimum 12 inches below grade and below frost line

➢ **Piles**
- used where soil load bearing capacity is poor, such as beaches, swamps, and rivers
- wood driven into ground until load-bearing soil encountered, or deep enough that friction with soil provides load bearing support
  - o preservative-treated wood 8-14 inches diameter round, 6x6 or 12x12 inches square
- engineer designs pile foundations

➢ **Piers**
- piers: above ground supports for beams, sometimes below grade
- often concrete blocks and bricks
  - o mortar required between blocks and bricks; no dry stacking
  - o cores placed vertical, not horizontal
  - o solid cap block or solid-filled core at top of block piers
- often found in crawlspaces and under porches

➢ **Columns**
- columns: above ground support for beams
- wood (preservative-treated if outdoors or in crawlspaces), or rust-resistant coated steel
  - o wood minimum 4x4 inch; steel minimum 3 inch diameter, Schedule 40 thickness

- o telescoping columns not allowed as permanent columns
  - o **screw jack columns** allowed as permanent columns
    - ▪ screw may be at top or at bottom of column
- may be anywhere in a building
- secure columns at bottom, may also secure at top
- sometimes called a **post**

➢ **Footings, piles, piers, columns, pilasters – typical defects**
- footings inadequate size or thickness
  - o examples: open patio converted to enclosed space, decks
- footings cracked, uplifted, settled
  - o no standard about when a footing crack is a defect; ¼ inch wide, or ¼ inch vertical displacement sometimes used
- masonry piers: dry stacked, mortar absent or deteriorated, too tall, absent solid cap, rotated, cores installed horizontally, load not bearing in center ⅓ of pier
- columns: damaged, deteriorated, not secured at bottom, size too small, not plumb (rotated), bowed
  - o no standard about when a column bow or rotation is a defect; ¾ inch bow or rotation in 8 feet is sometimes used

Basement Foundations

➢ **General**
- **basement**: area mostly or entirely below grade
- usually 7 feet or more ceiling height and a concrete floor
  - o distinguish from a crawlspace
- called a cellar, especially if entirely below grade and impractical to convert into habitable space
- called a walk-out or daylight basement if a full-height door installed

➢ **Materials**
- modern walls
  - o cast-in-place concrete
  - o precast concrete panels
  - o concrete masonry units/blocks (CMUs)
  - o steel reinforcing rods
- older walls: brick, stone, clay tile
  - o older walls susceptible to water intrusion
- uncommon walls
  - o insulating concrete forms
    - ▪ styrofoam blocks, look like Legos
    - ▪ reinforcing bars placed, then concrete poured in forms
  - o permanent wood
- floors
  - o concrete (modern)
    - ▪ usually 4 inch thick slab, except thicker under load bearing components

51

- non-structural, except under load bearing areas
    - soil (older)

> **Moisture management**
- wall moisture management types
    - dampproofing
        - reduces water vapor intrusion
        - required if basement can be usable space
        - service life: 10-20+ years, depending on soil dampness
        - modern: bituminous coating, often spray applied
        - older: ⅜ inch mortar **parging**, often on CMU walls
    - waterproofing
        - reduces liquid water intrusion
        - recommended if basement can be usable space
        - service life: life of building
        - modern: proprietary systems
        - older and some modern: bituminous coating and 6 mil polyethylene
- floor moisture management
    - gravel and vapor retarder installed under slab for moisture and radon control
- foundation drains
    - required if basement can be usable space
    - modern: proprietary system, or 4 inch slotted plastic pipe covered with fabric sock, then pipe covered with gravel
    - older: clay tiles
    - slope drain to daylight or sump pump

> **Major defects**
- classification as major depends on type and extent of condition, whether and how to report is judgment call
- wall not plumb, rotation from vertical
- wall bulging
- wall cracks: crack in same plane as wall, non-uniform width
- wall cracks: crack not in same plane as wall, wall shearing
- wall cracks: crack diagonal or stair-step, especially when wide or runs through blocks and bricks
- wall moving on footing
- non-uniform foundation settlement or uplift, part of foundation subsiding or rising, with or without wall rotation and cracks
- evidence of prior repairs
- active water intrusion

> **Minor defects**
- classification as minor depends on type and extent of condition, whether and how to report is judgment call
- cracks: small uniform width, no bulging or rotation
    - small concrete cracks often caused when concrete shrinks while curing

- void in concrete wall finish, exposed aggregate (**honeycombing**), no evidence of water intrusion
- **spalling**, **delamination** of surface, if not widespread
- efflorescence, white powder on surface caused by water intrusion, if not widespread
- cold joint in concrete
  - lower part of wall began to cure before upper part of wall poured
- absent or deteriorated mortar, if not widespread
  - repair/replacement of old lime mortar with cement mortar can trap water behind wall and damage wall
- water stains, no evidence of active water intrusion

➢ **Typical repairs: water intrusion, non-structural cracks**

- hydraulic cement: good for smaller cracks
- polyurethane foam: good for larger cracks
- epoxy: good for many cracks
- liquid coatings: effectiveness varies, can make situation worse

➢ **Typical repairs: structural**

- buttress: vertical support for wall, usually concrete blocks
- steel beams: similar to buttress
- tieback anchors: rod through wall attached to helical anchor (a large screw) in soil
- plate anchors: similar to tieback anchors; plate in soil instead of helical anchor
- carbon fiber mats: adhered to wall with epoxy
- sister wall: new wall built next to defective wall
- push piers and helical piers: similar to tieback anchors; used to lift subsiding footings; also used to lift concrete slabs
- slab/foam/mud jacking: expanding materials injected under concrete slabs to raise slabs

Crawlspace Foundations

➢ **General**

- crawlspace: an area mostly or entirely below grade
- height 7 feet or less between floor joists and soil floor
  - height usually 18 - 36 inches

➢ **Materials**

- modern walls
  - concrete masonry units/blocks (CMUs)
  - poured concrete, uncommon
- older walls: brick, stone, clay tile; older walls susceptible to water intrusion

➢ **Moisture management**

- wall dampproofing and waterproofing not required
- foundation drains not required
  - if present, may indicate water management problem

- crawlspace ventilation: see Unit 8

➢ **Typical defects**
- same as basement

➢ **Typical repairs**
- same as basement

Slab Foundations

➢ **Slab-on-grade**
- monolithic, turned-down edge
  - footing dug to required width and depth around foundation perimeter; remainder of slab about 4 inches thick
  - used on level lots in any climate zone
- mat, floating
  - entire slab poured at footing thickness, unless a thicker slab required at some points to bear point load
  - used on level lots where frost depth is negligible, such as desert Southwest

➢ **Slab-on-stem wall**
- spread footing poured, stem walls (usually concrete blocks) built to required height, area inside stem wall filled, slab plumbing and electrical installed, slab poured
- used on sloped lots in any climate zone

➢ **Post-tensioned slab**
- steel cables installed before slab poured, contractor returns after slab cured to put cables under tension, cables hold slab together as unit
- used where unstable soil present to reduce slab displacement and cracking
- cables under significant tension; cut cable can rip through concrete causing injury
- post-tensioned slab must be permanently labeled

➢ **Reinforcement and crack control**
- reinforcement: reduces concrete shear under load
  - steel reinforcing bars, usually not required in slabs
  - crack control, not required
    - welded wire mesh (6x6 inch squares made with #10 wire), installed before concrete poured
    - fiberglass strands (mixed into concrete)

➢ **Major defects**
- classification as major depends on type and extent of condition, whether and how to report is judgment call
- cracks: wide crack in same plane as slab, especially if non-uniform width
- cracks: crack not in same plane, one side of crack higher than the other

- non-uniform slab settlement or uplift; part of slab subsiding or rising, with or without cracks
- evidence of prior repairs
- active water intrusion evidence, visible moisture

➢ **Minor defects**
- classification as minor depends on type and extent of condition, whether and how to report is judgment call
- cracks: small, deep, uniform width
  - small concrete cracks often caused when concrete shrinks while curing
- **crazing**: thin surface cracks that look like a spider web
- **spalling**: larger area of surface delamination; major if widespread
- **popout**: smaller area of surface delamination; major if widespread
- **efflorescence**: crusty white powder on surface caused by water intrusion; major if widespread
- **dusting**: fine white powder on surface
- water stains, no evidence of active water intrusion

Floor Systems – General

➢ **Common materials**
- concrete slab foundation
- dimensional lumber floor joists
  - sawn wood
  - some joists not straight; upward curve called crown
    - install crown side up
  - common species: Southern pine, Douglas fir, spruce, pine, fir (SPF)
  - common grades (quality): highest to lowest: #1, #2, #3
  - allowed joist span depends on species and grade, and on room use (living area and sleeping (bedroom) area)
  - nominal (rough) dimensions: 2 inches wide by 2 to 12 inches deep
    - examples: 2x4, 2x6, 2x8, 2x10, 2x12
  - actual (finished) dimensions: ½ inch smaller width by ½ to ¾ inch smaller depth
    - examples: 2x6 actual 1½ by 5½ inches; 2x10 actual 1½ by 9¼ inches
- I-joist floor joists
  - wood top and bottom flanges, ⅜ inch thick or larger oriented strand board (OSB) or plywood web set in a groove cut into the flanges
  - span longer distance than dimensional lumber
  - design and installation specified by engineer
  - I-joists also used as ceiling joists and rafters (uncommon)
- **trusses**
  - wood top and bottom chords and wood webs usually connected by metal plates
    - usually 2x4 lumber
  - trusses also used as ceiling joists and rafters
  - span longer distance than dimensional lumber
  - design and installation specified by engineer

- engineered wood (structural composite lumber)
  - wood or wood composites compressed together using adhesives, heat, and pressure
  - mostly used for beams and headers
  - span longer distance than dimensional lumber
  - design and installation specified by engineer
- floor sheathing (subfloor)
  - since 1950s: plywood panels
  - since 1960s: particleboard panels
  - since 1970s: oriented strand board (OSB) panels
  - nominal thickness of panels: ½ or ¾ inch
  - older, but may find anywhere: dimensional lumber, usually 1x4 or 1x6

> **Floor system characteristics**
  - **deflection**: structural member bends under load temporarily, springs back into original position when load removed
    - **modulus of elasticity** (E), measurement of resistance to deflection/deformation
    - too much deflection results in "spongy" floors; squeaks; cracking of stiff floor coverings, such as tile; and cracking of wall/ceiling coverings, such as drywall
  - **deformation**: when structural member bends under load permanently, and does not spring back into the original position when load removed
    - fiber stress in bending (F_b), design strength of joist
    - in extreme cases, the joist or truss will fail
  - when load applied from top of floor, member under compression on top, under tension on bottom

> **Floor system design loads**
  - **dead load**: usually 10 psf; uncommon 20 psf
  - **live load** living areas and decks: 40 psf
  - **live load** sleeping areas: 30 psf

> **Floor joist/truss bearing on support (minimum)**
  - 1½ inches on wood, such as sill plates, top plates, ledgers, and beams
  - 3 inches on masonry and concrete

> **Sill plates and sole plates (bottom plates)**
  - plates should be same width as wall framing
    - example: 2x4 inches plates for 2x4 inches wall framing
  - **sill plates**: wood installed on the foundation around building perimeter upon which joist/trusses bear; usually 2x4 or 2x6 inches
    - should be preservative-treated
    - should be secured to foundation using minimum ½ inch diameter bolts with nuts and washers, or approved straps
      - straps should be spaced minimum every 6 feet, and within 12 inches of corners and plate joints

- bolts should be spaced minimum every 6 feet, and within 12 inches of corners and plate joints, located in center ⅓ of plate, and maximum seven bolt diameters distance to plate joints
  - should be a **sill gasket** or sealant installed under plates between conditioned and unconditioned space (newer requirement, often not visible)
- sole (bottom) plates: wood installed under interior walls upon which wall studs bear

➢ **Wood clearance to soil in crawlspaces**
- minimum 18 inches between wood joists/trusses and soil
- minimum 12 inches between wood beams and soil
- clearance not required if wood is preservative-treated (uncommon)

➢ **Floor sheathing**
- panels
  - apply long dimension across minimum 3 floor joists
  - panel width at least 24 inches
- edges of panels and dimensional lumber sheathing supported by tongue-and-groove edges, or solid wood blocking

➢ **Joist hanger installation**
- install joist hangers per manufacturer's instructions; general rules
  - install fastener in round and oblong holes
  - use fasteners specified by manufacturer
  - position joist or beam in hanger not more than ⅛ inch from supporting member

Dimensional Lumber Floor Joists and Beams

➢ **Floor joist and beam span**
- floor joist and built-up beam span: maximum distance joist or beam may be installed without support
- see span tables in International Residential Code Chapter 5 for maximum joist spans and Chapter 6 for beam spans

➢ **Blocking (lateral restraint)**
- required at both ends of joists to reduce joist twisting
- provided by **band joists** at joist ends when joists bear on top of walls or beams
- provided by joist hangers or fasteners when joists attached to side of beams
- joists that meet above interior wall or a beam lapped minimum 3 inches and fastened

➢ **Bridging**
- required for joists larger than 2x12 to reduce joist twisting
  - frequently installed on smaller joists
- locate near center of joist span
- provided by lumber same depth as the joist, or by X bridging

➢ **Cantilever/backspan**

- cantilever used as less expensive way to increase square footage without the cost of additional foundation
- common locations: bay windows, framed fireplaces/chimneys, second stories, decks
- **cantilever**: the distance joist extends beyond supporting wall or beam
- **backspan**: the distance joist extends inside supporting wall or beam
- cantilever/backspan ratio for cantilevered joists supporting wall and roof: 1 foot cantilever/3 feet backspan
- cantilever/backspan ratio for cantilevered joists supporting balcony: 1 foot cantilever/2 feet backspan
- prescriptive span tables in International Residential Code Chapter 5
  - engineer may design other cantilever spans

➢ **Floor system openings**

- common locations: **stairways, chimneys**
- minimum two trimmer joists at each end of opening
- single header joists if opening not more than 4 feet wide
- double header joists if opening more than 4 feet wide

➢ **Partition (non-load-bearing) walls**

- partition walls may place additional, non-uniform, loads on joists
- install minimum two joists under partition walls running parallel with joists

➢ **Joist and beam notching and drilling**

- **notching**
  - notch depth: not more than $\frac{1}{6}$ of actual joist depth, except not more than $\frac{1}{4}$ of actual joist depth at joist ends
  - notch location: not in center $\frac{1}{3}$ of joist length
- drilling
  - hole size: not more than $\frac{1}{3}$ of actual joist depth
  - hole location: not closer than 2 inches to joist edges, and not closer than 2 inches to another hole or notch

➢ **Typical defects**

- floor not level, slopes
- improper size or location of notch or hole
- damaged or deteriorated wood (sills, joists, beams, subfloor)
- deformed (sagging, twisting, rotating) joist or beam
- absent joists and beams (may have been removed during remodeling)
- inadequate joist or beam bearing on wood, concrete, or masonry
- excessive deflection
- excessive floor squeaks
- joist, beam, subfloor span longer than allowed
- subfloor not supported at joints (blocking, tongue-and-groove)
- floor sheathing panels less than 2 feet wide

> **Typical modifications and repairs**

  - repair/modification/replacement of structural members requires a permit; may require engineer design
  - sister joist: additional joist adjacent to defective joist
  - blocking between adjacent functional joists: distributes some of load to functional joists
  - mending components: wood or steel to stiffen the defective member
  - columns, piers, and beams: provide support under the defective members

Wood I-Joist and Engineered Wood Floor Joists and Beams

> **General**

  - all aspects of I-joist and engineered wood floor joists and beams design, installation, modification, and repair specified by manufacturer and engineer
  - do not mix I-joists and dimensional lumber in same floor system
    - example: use manufacturer-supplied rim joists, not dimensional lumber band joists

> **Notching**

  - flanges may not be notched or altered

> **Drilling**

  - hole location and size specified by manufacturer
  - common specifications
    - no holes within 6 inches horizontally and vertically from supports
    - distance between holes minimum 2 times dimension of larger hole
    - leave minimum ⅛ inch of web between hole and flange
    - allowed hole size smaller closer to supports
    - holes in beams only in the center ⅓ of the beam horizontally and vertically

> **Backer blocks**

  - install backer block where an I-joist supports another I-joist

> **Filler blocks**

  - install filler block between two I-joists where they support another I-joist

> **Support under load-bearing walls**

  - option 1: web stiffeners on both sides of I-joists and blocking between I-joists
  - option 2: squash blocks on both sides of I-joists

> **Support under non-load-bearing walls**

  - web stiffeners on both sides of I-joists

> **Typical defects**
  - most dimensional lumber defects apply to I-joists and engineered wood
  - absent, improperly installed backer and filler blocks, web stiffeners, and squash blocks

Wood Floor Trusses

> **General**
  - all aspects of wood floor truss design, installation, modification, and repair specified by manufacturer and engineer
  - trusses usually bear on the bottom chord, occasionally on top chord

> **Modifications and repairs**
  - trusses may not be notched, drilled, altered, or repaired without written engineered design
  - repairs should be reported as possibly deficient unless engineer-designed written repair instructions available

> **Top chord-bearing trusses**
  - install top chord-bearing trusses maximum ⅛ inch from truss bearing point

> **Lateral bracing**
  - truss lateral bracing materials and location specified by manufacturer and engineer
  - truss bracing occasionally cut to install plumbing pipes and HVAC ducts

> **Metal gusset plates**
  - truss chords and webs usually connected by metal gusset plates
  - even slightly loose gusset plates weaken connection and weaken truss

> **Typical defects**
  - most dimensional lumber defects apply to trusses
  - damaged, deteriorated, modified trusses
  - absent, damaged, loose gusset plates
  - absent, damaged braces
  - improper top chord-bearing truss installation

Wall Systems – General

> **Framing systems – description**
  - platform: most common by far
    o first story floor joists/trusses and sheathing are platform on which first story walls built; first story walls support second story floor joists/trusses and sheathing on which second story walls built
  - balloon: very uncommon in modern construction

- walls bear on the foundation and extend full height to top plate at attic; floor joists secured to walls
  - post and beam and timber frame: uncommon
    - both systems use large lumber (posts) to support large beams; provides large open areas
    - post and beam uses mechanical fasteners to secure structural members
    - timber frame uses mortise-and-tenon joints to secure structural members

➢ **Common materials**

- dimensional lumber, most common by far
  - usually sawn wood
    - may be small pieces spliced together with finger-joints and adhesive (finger-jointed wood)
  - common grades (quality): highest to lowest: #1, #2, stud, #3
  - allowed wood height depends on grade and size
    - usually 2x4 inches
    - 2x6 inches walls where plumbing drain pipes installed; in exterior walls where extra strength or more insulation required; in newer basements
  - nominal (rough) and actual (finished) dimensions same as floor joists
- concrete masonry units/blocks (CMUs)
  - used in some markets, especially where wind load resistance required
  - blocks usually 8x8x16 inches
  - top block should be solid cap block, or top CMU cores fully filled with grout

➢ **Uncommon materials**

- structural bricks and stone; more common in older buildings
- structural insulated panels; wall panels factory-built and assembled on site
- insulating concrete forms; see floor system materials
- logs
- light-gage (cold-formed) steel; more likely in multi-family
- adobe brick, rammed earth, straw bale; more likely in dry climates

➢ **Characteristics**

- deflection and deformation same as floor systems
- most load applied vertically from above
- horizontal load possible, mostly from environmental loads
  - slamming a door can cause a wall to shake

➢ **Design parameters**

- maximum deflection for most walls: H/180 where H is wall height in inches
  - example: 96 inch tall wall/180 = maximum deflection ½ inch
- H/360 required for stucco wall coverings

61

➤ **Wall bearing on support**

- walls should fully bear on foundation, or on structural components that bear on foundation
- some wall overhang is acceptable
  - no standard for acceptable overhang amount

Wood-Framed Walls

➤ **Bottom and top plates**

- bottom plates, see floor systems-general
- top plates
  - resist vertical loads from above and horizontal (racking) loads
  - usually two top plates on load bearing walls
  - strap required across one plate if plates notched more than 50%
- offset top plate joints minimum 24 inches
- lap top plates to tie walls together where perpendicular walls meet

➤ **Headers at wall openings**

- headers: beams over openings in load bearing walls, such as windows and doors
- built using two or more pieces of #2 lumber, or engineered wood
- supported by king studs on sides of headers and jack studs under headers
  - number of jack studs depends on opening size

➤ **Wall bracing**

- wall bracing required to resist horizontal (racking) loads that can crack interior and exterior wall coverings, cause improper operation of doors and windows, and weaken connections between structural components
- bracing a complex subject; many requirements and methods of complying

➤ **Wall stud notching and drilling**

- **notching**
  - notch depth: maximum 25% of actual stud depth for load-bearing studs, maximum 40% of actual stud depth for non-load-bearing studs
- **drilling**
  - hole diameter: maximum 40% of actual stud depth for load-bearing studs, maximum 60% of actual stud depth for non-load-bearing studs
  - minimum ⅝ inch of wood at edge of hole

➤ **Support under point load**

- extra support required under multiple joists and trusses, and under beams and headers
- general rule: one extra jack stud for each extra joist or truss
- common problem location: interstitial space at floor and ceiling joists

- ➢ **Typical defects**
  - • water stains and damage
    - ○ rain water leaks, plumbing leaks, condensation
  - • wood-destroying organism evidence and damage
    - ○ termite tubes, holes in framing members and trim
  - • excessive stud notching and drilling
  - • excessive stud bowing/twisting
    - ○ bulge in wall
  - • wall not plumb
  - • inadequate support under point loads
    - ○ sagging ceilings and floors, sticking doors, cracks at doors and windows
  - • no strap at notched top plate
  - • inadequate top plate attachment to other walls
  - • improper wall bracing
    - ○ wall covering cracks

- ➢ **Typical modifications and repairs**
  - • repair/modification/replacement of structural members requires a permit; may require engineer design
  - • sister studs: additional studs adjacent to deficient studs
  - • blocking between adjacent functional studs; distributes some of load to functional studs
  - • stud shoe: manufactured product reinforces stud at excessive hole or notch

Concrete Masonry Unit and Structural Brick Walls

- ➢ **Concrete masonry unit (CMU) above ground walls – general**
  - • usually 8x8x16 inch blocks installed in a running bond pattern
    - ○ **running bond**: each block course offset by a half block
  - • top block should be solid cap block, or top block fully grouted
    - ○ **grout**: cement-based material used to fill cores in CMUs and bricks
  - • cores may be reinforced with steel and grouted, or may be left empty
  - • cinder blocks made using combustion waste products, such as burning coal
    - ○ cinder blocks can corrode metal
    - ○ uncommon in newer construction
  - • CMU's have good compressive load bearing, less lateral load-bearing unless cores reinforced and grout-filled
    - ○ lateral load-bearing provided by floor systems and ceiling joists

- ➢ **Typical defects**
  - • similar to brick veneer

- ➢ **Typical repairs**
  - • tuck pointing (repointing)
    - ○ avoid using cement mortar to replace lime mortar

- anchors (mostly used with structural brick)
  - wall mechanically secured to other structural components, or to stable structural brick walls

Roof Systems – General

➢ **Components**

- **roof system**: ceiling joists and rafter ties, rafters, collar ties, purlins, and roof sheathing
  - roof truss combines these components into one engineer-designed system
- ceiling joists secured to rafters or rafter ties to resist horizontal force on walls caused by rafters (**rafter thrust**)
  - **kicker** may be substituted for rafter ties
- **collar ties**: connect rafters that are across from each other to resist wind uplift of roof
- **purlins**: support rafters that would have a longer span than allowed without purlins
- **roof sheathing**: provides support for roof coverings and bracing for rafters
- tie-down connectors/straps: provide uplift resistance caused by wind
  - major issue in high wind design zones

➢ **Styles**

- common steep slope roof styles
  - **gable:** triangle-shaped roof; rafters are legs of triangle; ceiling joist is base; rafters run from ridge to supporting wall
  - **hip**: four three-sided or four-sided polygons connecting at ridge
  - **shed**: rectangle that slopes from another roof or sidewall
  - a roof system may have one or more styles
- less common steep slope roof styles: **mansard, gambrel** (barn)

➢ **Common materials**

- dimensional lumber
  - sawn wood
  - common species: Southern pine, Douglas fir, Hem fir, spruce, pine, fir (SPF)
  - common grades (quality): highest to lowest: #1, #2, #3
  - allowed ceiling joist span depends on species, grade, and attic storage potential
  - allowed rafter span depends on species, grade, roof covering load, and snow load
  - nominal (rough) and actual (finished) dimensions same as floor joists
- trusses
  - wood top and bottom **chords** and wood **webs**, usually connected by metal plates
    - usually 2x4 lumber; bottom chord may be 2x6 lumber when truss designed for attic storage
  - span longer distance than dimensional lumber
  - design and installation specified by engineer

- roof sheathing
  - same as floor sheathing
  - nominal thickness of panels: ½ inch

➢ **Characteristics**
  - deflection and deformation same as floor system

➢ **Design loads**
  - ceiling joist dead load: 5 psf no attic storage, 10 psf limited attic storage
  - ceiling joist live load: 10 psf no attic storage, 20 psf limited attic storage
  - rafter dead load: 10 psf most roof coverings, 20 psf heavy roof coverings
  - rafter live load: depends on snow load, and if interior finish attached to rafters

➢ **Bearing on support (minimum)**
  - 1½ inches on wood, such as top plates, walls, and beams
  - 3 inches on masonry and concrete

➢ **Sheathing**
  - panels
    - apply long dimension across minimum three rafters or joists
    - panel width should be minimum 24 inches
  - panel span limits printed on sheathing
    - example: 32/16 means 32 inch span when panel used on roof, and 16 inch span when used on floor
      - edge support assumed, usually provided by H clips on roofs

➢ **Fire damage**
  - evidence: blackened, chard wood; sometimes damage covered by paint
  - fire can weaken wood, refer to engineer for damage evaluation

➢ **Attic access**
  - required if attic area exceeds 30 square feet and more than 30 inches vertically between ceiling joist and rafters
  - minimum rough opening size 22x30 inches and at least 30 inches above opening
    - locate opening in hallway or similar accessible area
  - attic access requirements have changed over years; older buildings often do not comply

➢ **Attic ventilation**
  - most common ventilation ratio: 1 square foot free opening area for every 300 square feet of attic area
    - between 40% and 50% of free opening area within 3 feet of ridge, rest in bottom ⅓ of attic
  - conditioned (unventilated) attics allowed
    - rules are complex and depend on building location, and types of insulation and vapor retarders

Dimensional Lumber Ceiling Joists and Rafters

- ➢ **Rafter types**
    - **ridge**: highest point of roof; complex roof systems have multiple ridges
    - **common**: runs from ridge to supporting wall
    - **jack**: runs from ridge to a hip rafter or a valley rafter
    - **hip**: ascending rafter formed at intersection of adjacent hip sections
    - **valley**: descending rafter formed at intersection of adjacent roofs

- ➢ **Rafter cuts**
    - **plumb** cut: angle cut at ridge
    - **seat cut**: angle cut at a hip or valley rafter, or at a wall when rafter stops at a wall
    - **bird mouth**: triangle cut at wall when rafter extends beyond the wall to form eaves

- ➢ **Ceiling joist and rafter span**
    - ceiling joist, rafter, and built-up beam span is maximum distance that member may be installed without support
    - see span tables in International Residential Code Chapter 8 for maximum joist spans and Chapter 6 for beam spans

- ➢ **Blocking and bridging (lateral restraint)**
    - usually not required, but frequently installed

- ➢ **Roof system openings**
    - common locations: dormers, chimneys
    - same rules as floor system openings

- ➢ **Ceiling joist and rafter notching and drilling**
    - o same rules as floor joists

- ➢ **Ceiling joist installation**
    - usually bear on walls; may be attached higher on rafters, but ceiling joist span reduced
    - connect rafters on opposite sides of roof to resist rafter thrust
        - o may use rafter ties or kickers if not possible or practical to connect rafters to ceiling joists

- ➢ **Rafter installation**
    - install rafters across from each other at ridge
        - o may offset rafters maximum 1½ inches
    - full depth of rafter plumb cut and seat cut should bear on ridge and on support at wall or another rafter
    - hip and valley rafters occasionally spliced; should be supported at splice by brace bearing on load bearing wall

➢ **Purlin installation**
  • purlin should be at least as large as rafter it supports
    ○ example: 2x6 rafter should have 2x6 purlin
  • purlin brace
    ○ at least 2x4, double 2x4 if brace longer than 8 feet
    ○ installed at maximum 45° angle to horizontal
    ○ spaced maximum 4 feet on center
    ○ bear on load bearing wall

➢ **Typical defects**
  • deterioration and stains at roof penetrations: common cause: poor penetration flashing
  • deterioration and stains at valleys: common causes: poor valley flashing, debris in valley, roof penetrations in valley, fasteners penetrating flashing, ice dams
  • deterioration and stains at sidewalls: common causes: poor sidewall flashing, kick out flashing
  • deterioration and stains at eaves: common causes: ice dams, roof covering leaks, poor drip edge flashing
  • deterioration and stains at rafters and sheathing, rust on nails: common causes: roof covering leaks, condensation
  • improperly installed purlins or purlin braces: common defects: sagging rafters
  • deformed rafters and ceiling joists: common causes: excessive span, excessive load
  • improperly supported rafters and ceiling joists: common defects: sagging and slipping rafters
  • improper bearing of seat cut or plumb cut: common defects: slipping rafters
  • sheathing less than 24 inches wide: common defects: cracked deformed sheathing
  • inadequate attic access: common results: no way to inspect or repair, difficult access for firefighters
  • inadequate attic ventilation: common results: condensation, reduced roof covering service life; increased HVAC cooling costs

➢ **Typical modifications and repairs**
  • repair/modification/replacement of structural members requires a permit; may require engineer design
  • sister rafters and joists: additional rafter or joist adjacent to defective member
  • blocking between adjacent functional rafters or joists: distributes some of load to functional members
  • mending components: wood or steel to stiffen defective member
  • purlins: provides support under deficient members

Wood Roof Trusses

➢ **General**
  • all aspects of wood roof truss design, installation, modification, and repair specified by manufacturer and engineer
  • trusses usually bear on the bottom chord, occasionally on top chord

> **Modifications and repairs**
> - trusses may not be notched, drilled, altered, repaired, or have additional loads imposed without written engineered design
>   - additional loads include attaching roof for a room addition to trusses, or installing heavy roof covering on trusses designed for light roof covering
> - repairs should be reported as possibly deficient unless engineer-designed written repair instructions available

> **Installation**
> - install top chord-bearing trusses maximum ⅛ inch from bearing point
> - truss chords should be straight within 2 inches, or L/200 where L is length of truss chord in inches, whichever is smaller
> - trusses should be installed plumb within 2 inches, or D/200 where D is depth of truss in inches
> - piggyback (cap) trusses should be installed on 2x4 purlins spaced maximum 2 feet on center
>   - piggyback truss: truss installed on top of another truss because a single truss would be too large to transport

> **Lateral bracing**
> - truss lateral bracing materials and location specified by manufacturer and engineer
>   - bracing at gable ends usually required
> - additional bracing for long webs (strongbacks) may be required
> - truss bracing occasionally cut to install plumbing pipes and HVAC ducts

> **Metal gusset plates**
> - truss chords and webs usually connected by metal gusset plates
> - even slightly loose gusset plates weaken connection and weaken the truss

> **Typical defects**
> - most dimensional lumber defects apply to trusses
> - damaged, deteriorated, modified trusses
> - absent, damaged, loose gusset plates
> - absent, damaged truss braces
> - improper top chord-bearing truss installation
> - truss cord not straight, usually bottom chord
> - truss not plumb
> - owner belongings stored on or hung from trusses not designed for storage
>   - trusses designed for attic storage usually have a 2x6 or larger bottom chord

Unit 5: Electrical Systems

Topics covered in this Unit include:

- **Knowledge Areas**
- **Electrical System - General**
- **Grounding and Bonding**
- **Electrical Service Capacity**
- **Electrical Service and Service Entrance Wires**
- **Electrical Panels and Enclosures**
- **Overcurrent Protection Devices**
- **Ground Fault Circuit Interrupters (GFCI)**
- **Arc Fault Circuit Interrupters (AFCI)**
- **Electrical Panels with Known Problems**
- **Wiring Methods – General**
- **Wiring Methods – Types**
- **Receptacles, Switches, Lights**
- **Alternative Energy Systems and Generators**
- **Electrical Vehicle Equipment**

Knowledge Areas

➢ **Knowledge areas in-scope of a home inspection and in-scope of the exam**

- service components
- panels and subpanels
- wiring methods
- devices, equipment, and fixtures

➢ **Knowledge areas out-of-scope of a home inspection but in-scope of the exam**

  o alternative energy systems (wind, solar), generators, electric vehicle charging equipment

Electrical System – General

➢ **Electrical system types**
- **high voltage**: operate at 120/240 volts; provide power to appliances, equipment, lights
- **low voltage**: operate at less than 30 volts or 50 volts, depending on circuit
  o examples: doorbells, thermostats, and low voltage lights
- **signal**: usually operate at very low voltage
  o examples: cable television, computer, and telephone

➢ **Definitions**
- **American Wire Gauge** (AWG): electrical wire diameter; smaller number, larger wire
- **conductor**: a wire
- **energized**: electricity flowing

69

- **lug**: opening where a wire is inserted and secured with a screw, such as a circuit breaker or terminal bar
- **outlet**: where electricity is taken for use, such as a receptacle, light, or appliance
- **short circuit**: electricity flow between hot and grounded or grounding wires

➢ **Required dedicated branch circuits**

- two, 20 amp, 120 volt, serving only kitchen countertop receptacles and receptacles in breakfast and dining areas
- one branch circuit for each furnace or air handler
- one 20 amp, 120 volt serving only receptacles in laundry area
- one 20 amp, 120 volt serving only receptacles in bathrooms
- one 20 amp, 120 volt serving only receptacles in garage and on house exterior

➢ **Multiwire branch circuits**

- two hot wires share one neutral wire
- should be powered by adjacent slots on panel
- should have handle tie connecting circuit breakers
- examples: clothes dryer receptacle, split-wired receptacles (top and bottom half of receptacle served by different hot wire)

Grounding and Bonding

➢ **Grounded (grounding) definition**

- **intentionally connecting the electrical system to earth**
  - provides alternate return path for electricity to its source
    - primary return path is utility's neutral wire
  - protects system by directing electricity from outside system, such as lightning and voltage surges, to the earth
- in circuits: **grounded wire** insulated, usually colored **white**
  - **often called neutral wire**
- electric service wires: grounded wire usually uninsulated aluminum
- grounded wire carries electricity (current); **should be at zero volts**

➢ **Grounding electrode system at service equipment**

- service equipment: **circuit breakers, fuses**, or **switches** that shut off all electricity to a building
  - **six or fewer devices located in same area**; often located in main panel
  - label as service equipment
- system consists of one or more grounding electrodes and a grounding electrode wire
- common grounding electrodes types: rod and pipe, concrete-encased (Ufer electrodes), and metal water service pipes
- rod and pipe electrodes: minimum ¾ inch diameter corrosion-resistant steel pipe, or ⅝ inch diameter copper or copper-coated steel rod driven minimum 8 feet into ground
- metal water service pipe and rod and pipe electrode no longer allowed as only grounding electrode
  - two rod and pipe electrodes, or another grounding electrode required

- grounding electrode conductor (wire) size depends on service amperage and grounding electrode type
    - #6 AWG copper for 150 amps or more rod and pipe electrode
    - #8 AWG copper for 125 amp or more rod and pipe electrode
- splicing grounding electrode wire allowed if splice secured by welding, or by listed compression clamp

➢ **Grounding subpanels in main building**
- subpanel: electrical panel downstream from service equipment
- **grounding electrode wire connection point required to be at any accessible location at or upstream from service equipment**
    - downstream connections can create electrocution hazard
- do not connect neutral wires and equipment grounding wires together at subpanels

➢ **Grounding subpanels at detached buildings supplied by main building**
- detached buildings include garages, sheds, barns
- grounding electrode required at detached buildings with subpanels
- do not connect neutral wires and equipment grounding wires together in subpanel supplied by 4-wire feeder
- neutral wires and equipment grounding wires may be connected in subpanel supplied by 3-wire feeder

➢ **Bonding definition**
- connects non-current-carrying metal together
    - safety system; reduces electrical shocks
    - provides low resistance path that connects metal to service panel
    - during ground fault, electricity flows through path and trips circuit breaker

➢ **Common metal components required to be bonded**
- general rule: if it is **metal and could be energized, it should be bonded**
    - water and gas distribution pipes
        - bonding corrugated stainless steel gas tubing (CSST) required at first metal gas pipe or metal fitting after gas meter
        - **bonding jumper** required around interior water meters, water softeners, water filters, and similar devices
    - metal appliance and equipment cabinets
    - all metal parts of the electrical system, such as panel cabinets and conduit
        - cabinets and equipment grounding wires should be bonded
    - all accessible grounding electrodes
    - cable TV, telephone, satellite, and similar services

➢ **Bonding wire size**
- usually same size as grounding electrode wire

- ➤ **Equipment grounding wire**
  - not really a grounding wire; provides bonding connection at receptacles, lights, and appliances since 1960s
  - **wire usually uninsulated**, occasionally **green insulation with yellow stripe**
  - not allowed (dangerous) to connect neutral and equipment grounding wires together at devices, such as receptacles (bootleg ground)

- ➤ **Typical defects**
  - grounding electrode wire (GEC) loose, disconnected, damaged, corroded, or similar high-resistance connection at grounding electrode
  - GEC too small for service size
  - GEC improperly spliced
  - absent or improper bonding connection for cable TV, telephone, satellite, or similar
  - absent bonding jumper around metal water pipe connections at interior water meters, water softeners, water filters, and at repair of metal water pipe using plastic pipe
  - bonding jumper or bonding clamp loose, disconnected, corroded, damaged
  - bonding clamp connection corroded, painted, or similar high-resistance connection
  - disconnected, loose, damaged, corroded fittings at conduit and at conduit connections to enclosures
  - equipment grounding wires not bonded to cabinet; bonding jumper absent or not connected

Electrical Service Capacity

- ➤ **Minimum residential voltage**
  - no minimum voltage; 120/240 volts standard

- ➤ **Minimum residential current**
  - 100 amps minimum
  - 150 – 200 amps common for newer and upgraded systems

Electrical Service and Service Entrance Wires

- ➤ **Definitions**
  - **service drop**: overhead wires that bring electricity from utility transformer to building
  - **service lateral**: same as service drop wires, but run underground
  - **service entrance wires**: wires between service drop or lateral and service panel

- ➤ **Service drop components**
  - **service drop wires**: (two insulated hot wires, one uninsulated neutral wire)
    - o four wires: three-phase service, out of home inspection scope
  - **service entrance wires**: (two insulated hot wires, one uninsulated neutral wire)
  - **service point**: where service drop wires connect to service entrance wires
  - **drip loop**: down-sloping wires that reduce water flow down service entrance wires
  - **service head** (gooseneck): where service entrance wires enter service mast
  - **service mast**: pipe that supports and protects service entrance wires

- **flashing**: where service mast penetrates roof
- **meter base**: enclosure where electric meter installed
- components upstream from service point belong to utility, downstream belong to building owner

> **Service drop required clearances**
- **above roof**
  o 18 inches above eaves; 3 feet above roof slopes greater than 4/12; 8 feet above roof slopes less than 4/12; 10 feet above walkable roofs
- **above ground**
  o 10 feet above walking surfaces; 12 feet above residential driveways; 18 feet above streets
- to windows and doors (clearance to individual service drop wires, not to SE cable or conduit)
  o 3 feet to operable windows and to doors

> **Typical defects**
- service drop wires run through trees
- damaged, deteriorated, melted service drop wire insulation
- absent, damaged, deteriorated insulation where service drop wires connect to service entrance wires
- inadequate drip loops
- inadequate service drop wire clearances to roof, ground, openings
- loose connection of service drop wires at building
- loose, damaged, deteriorated meter base
- loose, damaged, deteriorated conduit at meter base or service panel
- electrical system current capacity increased without increasing service wires

Electrical Panels and Enclosures

> **Definitions**
- **electrical panel** (buss/panelboard): equipment on which circuit breakers or fuses are mounted; located inside an enclosure
- **enclosure**: cabinet that protects against accidental contact with energized parts inside
- **dead front cover**: cover inside an enclosure that protects against accidental contact with energized parts; must be removed to inspect enclosure interior
- **terminal bars**: metal bars inside enclosure where neutral and equipment grounding wires attached
- **tabs** (twistouts): removable opening covers on dead front cover; removed to install circuit breakers
- **knockouts:** removable opening covers on enclosures; removed to attach conduit

> **Electrical panel and enclosure types**
- **meter main enclosure**: electric meter, service equipment, and electrical panel in one enclosure
- **main breaker enclosure**: service equipment and electrical panel in one enclosure
- **main lug enclosure**: type of subpanel, electrical panel fed by another panel

- **single-bus panel**: circuit breakers/fuses mounted on one panel
- **split-bus panel**: two panels in one enclosure; upper panel feeds lower panel; older style
- some enclosures not rated for exterior installation

➤ **Enclosure location and working clearances**
- enclosure should be readily accessible
  - readily accessible: do not need to climb over or move obstructions, use ladder
- enclosure prohibited locations: bathrooms, clothes closets, storage areas, above stair steps
- enclosure working clearances
  - height of circuit breaker/fuse maximum 79 inches, handle in up position
  - clear area in front of enclosure: 36 inches deep, 30 inches wide, 78 inches tall; door must open at least 90°

➤ **Inspection safety**
- inspector required to inspect enclosure interiors by most Standards of Practice
  - except if inspector determines a risk to inspector, other people, property
- risks
  - electrocution: accidental contact with energized parts
  - **arc flash**: spark jumps from energized parts to grounded parts
- risk mitigation
  - exercise care when inserting anything into energized enclosures, and when removing and replacing dead front covers
  - wear rubber-sole shoes and eye protection when inspecting enclosure interior
  - use insulated tool if inserting tool into energized enclosure

➤ **Typical electrical panel and enclosure defects**
- multiple wires in one lug (double tap): not allowed, unless allowed by circuit breaker or equipment manufacturer
- multiple neutral wires in one terminal bar lug: wires may not be properly secured against movement
- absent tabs or knockouts: electrocution hazard; openings should be covered with something that protects like original tab or knockout
- rust inside enclosure: indication of water entering enclosure; increases electrical resistance and heat, fire hazard
- contaminants inside enclosure: such as paint or drywall joint compound; increases electrical resistance and heat, fire hazard
- damaged wires and insulation: nicked wires and multi-strand wires with absent strands can safely carry less electricity; increases electrical resistance and heat, fire hazard
- melted insulation or charred wires: indication of overheating
- absent or improper handle tie on 240 volt and multiwire branch circuit: one circuit breaker could trip, not the other, leaving half of circuit energized
- fasteners with pointed tips secure enclosure parts: pointed tips can penetrate wire insulation, contact wire, energize enclosure
- branch circuits not adequately labeled: circuits should be labeled to clearly indicate the protected circuit, safety requirement

- energized wire not color coded or marked as energized: wires **not used** as indicated by insulation color should be permanently marked to indicate actual use at every accessible location, such as enclosures and outlets
- circuit breaker manufacturer different from panel manufacturer: could create loose connections, increases electrical resistance and heat, fire hazard
- low voltage components inside high voltage enclosure or conduit: low voltage components could be energized with high voltage
- fused neutral wire: no apparent electricity flow if fuse blows, but circuit energized
- electrical cables or conduit not secured to enclosure: cables/conduit could come loose, be damaged
- enclosure physical damage or deterioration: could allow damage to or contact with components inside enclosure

Overcurrent Protection Devices

➤ **Overcurrent protection devices definition (OPD)**
- **overcurrent protection device**: device protects wires from overheating and starting fires by interrupting electricity (current) flow when too much electricity flowing

➤ **Circuit breaker**
- **circuit breaker**: device interrupts excess electricity (current) flow by sensing high temperature, high magnetic field, or both
- case types: full (1 inch) height 120 volt, half (½ inch) height 120 volt, double (2 inch) height 240 volts
  - 240 volt circuits and multiwire branch circuits protected by two full-height circuit breakers require approved **handle tie** so both circuit breakers trip at same time
- some panels limit number and location of half-height circuit breakers
  - information on panel label, usually located on enclosure door

➤ **Fuses**
- **fuse**: device interrupts excess electricity (current) flow using heat to melt a metal strip
  - fuse base screws into opening on panel
- fuse base types: Edison (Type T), Type S, cartridge
- Edison fuses have same base size regardless of current rating
  - easy to install larger fuse than allowed for circuit protected
  - old style, many have been replaced when panel updated
- Type S fuses have different base size for different current rating
- Fuse color coding: 30 amps green, 25 amps green or yellow, 20 amp red or orange, 15 amp blue or purple

➤ **OPD compatibility with protected wires**
- wires rated to carry limited electricity (current) to prevent overheating
  - rating depends on wire material, wire size (AWG), wire type and installation method, and circuit use
- **copper** wires contained in electrical cables, general limits
  - #14 AWG 15 amps; #12 AWG 20 amps; #10 AWG 30 amps; #8 AWG 40 amps

- **aluminum** wires contained in electrical cables, general limits
  - #12 AWG 15 amps; #10 AWG: 20 amps; # 8 AWG 30 amps; #6 AWG 40 amps
- **exception to general rule**: wires serving air conditioning condensers and certain motors
  - maximum OPD rating and minimum wire rating on condenser label
  - reason for exception: allows for temporary current surge without tripping OPD when condenser or motor starts; operating current is less than surge

Ground Fault Circuit Interrupters (GFCI)

➤ **Definitions**
- **ground fault**: metal that should not be energized, such as a water pipe or appliance, becomes energized; current flows through bonding system and trips OPD
- GFCI: protects people from electrical shock during ground fault
  - measures current flow difference between hot and neutral wires; OPD trips when difference exceeds about 6 milliamps
  - may be circuit breaker or receptacle
  - equipment grounding conductor not required for GFCI operation

➤ **Required locations for GFCI protected circuits**
- kitchen countertops, bathrooms, garages, laundry rooms, unfinished basements, unfinished detached buildings, crawlspace, outdoors, dishwashing machines, swimming pools
- date required depends on location: bathroom, outdoors earliest

➤ **Upgrading or extending circuits**
- upgrade to current standards not required of existing circuits
- upgrade to current standards required when upgrading or extending circuits

Arc Fault Circuit Interrupters (AFCI)

➤ **Definitions**
- **arc fault**: electricity flows (sparks/arcs) between wires (parallel fault) or along wires (series fault)
- AFCI: protects structures from fire during arcing fault
  - should be circuit breaker
  - may be receptacle in some replacement/remodel situations
- AFCI types
  - branch circuit: detects parallel arcing faults; not allowed since late 2000s
  - combination: detects series and parallel arcing faults

➤ **Required locations for AFCI protected circuits**
- currently required on most 15 and 20 amp branch circuits except outdoor, garage, basement, utility room, storage room
- date required depends on location: bedrooms earliest

➤ **Upgrading or extending circuits**
- upgrade to current standards not required of existing circuits
- upgrade to current standards required when upgrading or extending circuits

Electrical Panels with Known Problems

➤ **Definition**
- problem electrical panel: electrical panel with defects known in inspection profession; inspectors may be expected to report presence of these panels

➤ **Problem panels**
- **Federal Pacific Stab-loc**, also called Federal Electric and Challenger
- **Zinsco**, also called Zinsco-Sylvania
- Bulldog Pushmatic

➤ **Typical defects**
- circuit breakers may not trip during overcurrent condition
- circuit breakers may be energized when showing deenergized

Wiring Methods – General

➤ **Definition**
- **wiring method**: components conduct electricity between panels and from panels to outlets
  - o many types and installation requirements; only types commonly seen in houses presented in this book

➤ **Wiring method installation requirements – general**
- **support**: must be supported at specific intervals and close to outlets and enclosures
- wet or dry locations: some approved only for interior dry locations, others approved for exterior and wet locations
  - o wet locations include concrete block cores and conduit installed outdoors
- burial: some approved for burial, burial depth depends on wiring method type
- subject to physical damage: most not approved for installation where subject to damage; must be protected if exposed
  - o locations subject to physical damage not defined; subject to interpretation

➤ **Flexible cords, including extension cords**
- intended to connect appliance to outlet
- may not be altered, spliced, or extended
- may not be substituted for permanent wiring
- may not pass through walls, ceilings, floors

➤ **Wire insulation color coding**

- energized (hot): usually black or red, may be any color except white or green
- grounded (neutral): usually white, occasionally gray
- grounding (equipment): usually uninsulated in homes, may be green with yellow stripe
- permanently mark wire at all outlets and enclosures if use does not correspond to color code, such as using neutral as hot

➤ **Typical defects**

- splice or tap not in covered electrical box
- electrical box without approved cover
- electrical box loose, damaged, deteriorated, open knockouts
- electrical box concealed; boxes must be accessible
- not protected against physical damage
- installed in unapproved location, such as NM cable outdoors
- deteriorated or damaged insulation, sheathing, conduit, tubing
- loose or disconnected conduit or tubing at fittings or enclosures
- improper repair, such as by electrical tape
- not secured where required
- not secured by an approved securing method, such as a wire staple
- no anti-oxidant grease at aluminum wire connections
- extension cord used as permanent wiring
- extension cord passes through wall, ceiling, floor
- attachment plug used with permanent wiring, such as NM cable

Wiring Methods – Types

➤ **Armored cable (AC), also called BX**

- wires in flexible metal sheath
- support every 4½ feet
- install only in dry locations

➤ **Electrical metallic tubing (EMT), also called thin wall**

- rigid metallic tube available in 10 feet long pieces
- support every 10 feet
- approved for wet locations and burial if corrosion protected

➤ **Electrical nonmetallic tubing (ENT)**

- flexible corrugated nonmetallic tube
- support every 3 feet
- use in wet locations depends on manufacturer's instructions

➤ **Liquidtight flexible conduit**

- flexible nonmetallic tube
- support every 4½ feet
- approved for wet locations and burial

➢ **Nonmetallic sheathed cable (NM) and underground feeder cable (UF)**
  - NM often called Romex®, a brand name
  - NM most common wiring method in houses
  - wires enclosed in a nonmetallic sheath
    o plastic since 1960s; cloth 1940s – 1950s
    o cloth sheath may be damaged or deteriorated due to age and rodents
      ▪ homeowner insurance may be denied
  - support every 4½ feet and within 8 inches of most plastic boxes
  - NM approved only for dry locations; UF approved for wet locations and burial

➢ **Rigid polyvinyl chloride conduit (PVC), also called rigid nonmetallic conduit (RNC)**
  - rigid nonmetallic tube available in 10 feet long pieces
  - support every 3 feet for 1 inch and smaller, every 5 feet for larger
  - approved for wet locations and burial

➢ **Service entrance cable (SE)**
  - wires enclosed in a nonmetallic sheath
  - support every 2½ feet
  - approved for wet locations and burial

➢ **Knob and tube wiring**
  - individual cloth-covered wires supported by ceramic knobs and run through ceramic tubes in wood
  - installed 1900s – 1930s, 15 amp circuit, obsolete and past end of service life
  - splices to other knob and tube wiring soldered and covered with electrical tape
  - splices to other wiring methods in covered electrical box
  - do not cover with insulation or radiant barriers
  - homeowner insurance may be denied

➢ **<u>Solid conductor</u> aluminum wiring**
  - installed mid-1960s to mid-1970s
  - problems
    o galvanic corrosion when contact with copper, increased heat, fire hazard
    o became distorted and brittle when heated and cooled
      ▪ connections became loose, heat increased, fire hazard
  - repairs
    o devices labeled CO/ALR
    o COPALUM or AlumiConn connectors at all outlets and splices
  - does not apply to wire made after 1972, and to stranded aluminum wire
  - does not apply to copper-clad aluminum and tin-coated copper wire
  - homeowner insurance may be denied

Receptacles, Switches, Lights

➤ **Receptacles – general**

- **slots 120 volt receptacles**: three-slot grounded since 1960s; two-slot ungrounded, older
- **slots 240 volt receptacles**: four-slot grounded; three-slot ungrounded, older, common
- polarized: larger slot neutral, usually left, smaller slot hot, usually right, semi-circular slot equipment grounding slot, usually below
  - o reversed polarity is electrical shock hazard
- no gaps between cover plate and receptacle, and between cover plate and wall
- receptacle should not move when plug inserted

➤ **Replacing ungrounded two-slot receptacle with three-slot receptacle**

- install equipment grounding wire from three-slot receptacle to closest location where an equipment grounding wire present, or
- install GFCI receptacle and label receptacle "NO EQUIPMENT GROUND"

➤ **Receptacle location - habitable rooms**

- no point on wall more than 6 feet from receptacle, including on walls more than 2 feet long

➤ **Receptacle location - kitchen countertops, peninsulas, islands**

- no point on wall above countertop more than 2 feet from receptacle
- at least one receptacle serving peninsula or island more than 2 feet long
- additional requirements apply

➤ **Receptacle location - bathroom**

- one receptacle for every sink, maximum 3 feet from sink edge
- no receptacle above bathtub or in shower

➤ **Receptacle location - garage**

- one receptacle for each vehicle parking space

➤ **Receptacle location- outside**

- one receptacle at front and at back of house
- wet area receptacle cover (bubble) required if receptacle exposed to rain

➤ **Receptacle location - HVAC service**

- one receptacle within 25 feet from HVAC equipment, such as furnace and condenser

- ➤ **Switches – general**
  - types
    - ○ snap and rocker most common; push button and rotary, older, uncommon
    - ○ dimmer/control
      - ▪ rheostat, older; often do not work with fluorescent and LED lights
      - ▪ solid state
    - ○ 3-way and 4-way, control devices from multiple locations
      - ▪ 3-way, two locations; 4-way, three or more locations
      - ▪ sometimes improperly wired, one switch does not function when other switch in one position
  - height maximum 79 inches when switch in up position
  - no gaps between cover plate and switch and between cover plate and wall
  - switch should not move when operated
  - damp or wet area cover required if switch located outdoors

- ➤ **Appliance disconnects**
  - required for appliances that need maintenance, such as furnaces, condensers, dishwashers
    - ○ may be switch, fuse block, pull tab, circuit breaker, or plug
  - should be within sight of appliance, and less than 50 feet from appliance

- ➤ **Lights – required**
  - wall switch-controlled, wall or ceiling-mounted, light fixture required in bathroom, kitchen, hallway, stairway, attached garage; and in detached building if electricity present
    - ○ light may be switched outlet in other habitable rooms
  - stairway lights capable of illuminating all treads and landings
    - ○ switch at top and bottom landing if six or more risers
    - ○ switches should be accessible without walking on stairs
  - at least one light in basement, attic, crawlspace if used for storage or if contains equipment requiring service
    - ○ switch should be at entrance to space; light at equipment if present

- ➤ **Lights – prohibited locations**
  - no part of hanging lights, track lights, or ceiling fans within 8 feet vertically and 3 feet horizontally from highest point of bathtubs and showers
  - clothes closets contain shelves and rods intended for clothes storage
    - ○ no exposed incandescent bulb, or light fixture that could use exposed incandescent bulb, in clothes closet
    - ○ clearances to shelf and rod storage areas depend on light fixture and bulb type

- ➤ **Lights – recessed (can) fixtures**
  - 3 inches clearance required between insulation and recessed lights that are not insulation contact (IC) rated
    - ○ most newer recessed lights are IC rated

➢ **Typical defects**
- reversed polarity receptacle, hot and neutral reversed
- loose, damaged, deteriorated, painted switch or receptacle
- loose, damaged, deteriorated light
- loose, damaged, absent cover plate
- gap present between cover plate and switch, receptacle, or light, or between cover plate and wall
- no power at switch, receptacle, or light
- 3-way and 4-way switches do not operate light when switch in one position
- dimmer/control does not operate properly, or hums when operating
- switch, receptacle, or light installed where not allowed
- switch, receptacle, or light not installed where required
- damp or wet area cover not installed where required
- ceiling fan wobbles, noisy operation

Alternative Energy Systems and Generators

➢ **Generators**
- gasoline, natural gas, or propane-powered motor turns generator that produces electricity
- transfer switch: disconnects building electrical system from utility system and provides electricity to selected circuits, such as heating, refrigerator, well pump, lights
  - o required to protect utility workers from electric shock caused by generator electricity backflowing into utility system
  - o absence indicates generator may have been installed without a permit

➢ **Alternative energy systems – definition**
- no accepted definition: may include solar photovoltaic (PV), solar water heating, and wind turbines

➢ **Solar photovoltaic (PV)**
- types
  - o grid-tied: system uses utility power when needed and feeds solar power back to utility when building not using all solar power produced; most common
  - o stand-alone: system not connected to utility, common where utility power not available
  - o battery backup: provides electricity when PV system not producing enough electricity; common with stand-alone; becoming more common with grid-tied
- common components
  - o solar array: converts solar energy to direct current (DC) electricity
  - o two disconnect switches: one switch disconnects solar array from inverter, other switch disconnects inverter from building electrical panel
  - o inverter: coverts DC electricity to alternating current (AC) electricity
  - o circuit breaker in building electrical panel: connects inverter to building electrical system
    - ▪ circuit breaker must be secured against movement, and labeled as being fed by solar system
  - o conduit and wires; metal conduit should be bonded

- ➤ **Wind turbines**
  - components similar to solar photovoltaic, except wind turbine instead of solar array
  - surge protective device required between wind system and building electrical system to protect against lightning
  - wind turbine tower should be grounded for lightning protection

- ➤ **Solar water heating**
  - uses
    - solar assist: increases water temperature before water enters regular water heater
    - solar heating: provides domestic hot water directly to faucets; may provide water for space heating
    - swimming/spa pool heating: increases pool water temperature
  - types
    - direct: heats water in solar collector and distributes water through building pipes
    - indirect: heats transfer fluid in solar collector and transfers heat to water using heat exchanger
  - common components
    - solar collector
    - storage tank
    - temperature limiting device to prevent scalding in direct systems
    - backflow preventer to flow of water from building to solar collector

Electric Vehicle Equipment

- ➤ **Charger types (levels)**
  - level 1: 120 volt AC, 15 or 20 amp receptacle; very slow charging
  - level 2: 240 volt AC receptacle; slow charging
  - level 3: DC fast charger; requires charging station to convert AC to DC electricity

- ➤ **Attachment plug to vehicle**
  - type depends on vehicle

- ➤ **Receptacle requirements**
  - at least one receptacle for each vehicle parking bay in attached garage
    - voltage and current ratings not specified
  - dedicated branch circuit serving 240 volt, 20 amp or more charging outlet, if outlet installed

- ➤ **Safety**
  - avoid using a multi-outlet branch circuit for vehicle charging, continuous load could overheat wires and cause fire
  - see National Electrical Code 2023 Article 625 for additional information

Unit 6: Cooling Systems

Topics covered in this Unit include:

- **Knowledge Areas**
- **Cooling Systems – General**
- **Theory of Air Conditioning Operation**
- **Evaporative (Swamp) Coolers**
- **Whole-house Fans**
- **Condensate Management**
- **Thermostats**
- **Forced-air Distribution System**

Knowledge Areas

➢ **Knowledge areas in-scope of a home inspection and in-scope of the exam**

- cooling systems
- distribution systems

Cooling Systems – General

➢ **Cooling systems common types**

- split system: evaporator indoors, condenser outdoors
  - o includes systems attached to furnaces, air conditioning only systems, and mini-split (ductless) systems
- package system: evaporator and condenser in one unit
  - o includes central/whole house systems, window-mounted units, through-wall units
- evaporative (swamp) coolers: air pulled across water-soaked media is cooled and distributed through building; mostly used in dry climates
- heat pump: heats and cools by exchanging heat with a medium
  - o medium usually air (air source), sometimes ground (ground source, often incorrectly called geothermal), occasionally water (water source)
  - o may be split system or package system

➢ **Definitions**

- **British thermal unit** (Btu): heat required to increase one pound of water by 1° Fahrenheit (F)
- **compressor**: device inside condenser unit that compresses refrigerant and pumps it through air conditioning/heat pump system
- **condenser unit**: exterior part of air conditioning/heat pump system; expels heat from building in cooling mode, absorbs heat from medium in heating mode
- **evaporator unit**: interior part of air conditioning system/heat pump system; absorbs heat from building in cooling mode, expels heat from medium in heating mode
- **HSPF** (heat seasonal performance factor): energy efficiency rating of heat pump in heating mode

- latent load: water vapor that air conditioning/heat pump system removes (condenses) from air before removing heat from building; condensate (water) is produced
- liquid line: small tube in split air conditioning/heat pump system line set between condenser unit and evaporator unit
- SEER 2 (seasonal energy efficiency ratio 2): energy efficiency rating of cooling system effective 1 January 2023; slightly more stringent than previous SEER rating
- sensible load: heat removed from air after latent load removed
- short-cycling: air conditioner turns on and off rapidly (runs less than 10 – 20 minutes); does not sufficiently reduce latent load; may indicate system has too much capacity
- suction line: large, insulated, tube in the split air conditioning/heat pump system line set between condenser unit and evaporator
- ton of refrigeration: common term for capacity of air conditioning/heat pump system; 12,000 Btu equals one ton of refrigeration

➢ **Air conditioning and heating system inspection, central and through-wall systems**
- operate system using normal operating controls, such as thermostat
- open access panels provided for homeowner maintenance, and not sealed in place
- risks of operating air conditioner (or heat pump in cooling mode) below 60° F.
  - o inaccurate information about whether system is operating properly
  - o compressor damage
- report if air conditioning or heating system not inspected/operated, and report why
- air conditioning temperature drop measurement; not required but common practice
  - o measure as close as possible to evaporator
  - o measuring at supply and return registers can produce significant errors
  - o temperature drop can indicate acceptable operation when system malfunctioning

➢ **Service access, attic and crawlspace**
- access path minimum 24 inch wide, maximum 20 feet long
- service platform in front of unit minimum 30 inches wide and deep
- attic and crawlspace clear opening size large enough to remove all equipment
  - o attic clear opening minimum 20 x 30 inches
  - o crawlspace clear opening minimum 22 x 30 inches

Theory of Air Conditioning Operation

➢ **Theory of energy and moisture**
- heat energy flows from hot to cold
- hot air rises because it is less dense than cold air (stack effect)
- moisture flows from area with more moisture to area with less moisture
- hot air holds more moisture than cold air
- **much more energy is needed to change the state of matter**, such as from liquid to gas, than is needed to change the temperature of matter within a state

➢ **Air conditioner and heat pump operation cycle, cooling mode**
1. compressor receives cool gas from suction line and compresses gas to hot gas
2. hot gas enters condenser coils, releases heat, condenses into liquid
3. liquid flows in liquid line to metering device (expansion valve) at evaporator

4. liquid expands in evaporator, absorbs heat, boils, changes state to cool gas, returns to compressor
   - **temperature difference between liquid and suction lines is <u>estimate</u> of heat removed from building, and of temperature drop across evaporator**

➢ **Heat pump operation cycle, heating mode**
   - reversing valve in condenser reverses refrigerant flow direction
   - operation cycle same as air conditioner except condenser unit acts as evaporator and absorbs heat, evaporator acts as condenser and releases heat

➢ **Air conditioner and heating capacity**
   - one or more permanently installed heat sources capable of maintaining habitable rooms minimum 68° F is required
     - air conditioning not required
   - air conditioning and heating capacity determined by Air Conditioning Contractors of America (ACCA) Manuals J (load requirement) and S (size/capacity for required load)
     - hot water and steam heat capacity determined by manufacturer's instructions
   - air conditioner and heat pump usually should be within about ½ ton of Manual S value
   - out of inspection scope to determine or verify capacity
   - general rules for estimating capacity (such as ton per square foot) can be significantly incorrect
     - insulation, windows, climate, other criteria impact capacity

➢ **Typical defects – general**
   - system does not activate using normal operating controls
   - poor temperature distribution between rooms or stories
     - common causes: one unit, two stories; poor duct design and installation
   - inadequate, damaged, deteriorated unit supports
   - system uses R-22 refrigerant (Freon), obsolete, expensive to replace

➢ **Typical defects – evaporator unit**
   - evaporator or condenser damaged, deteriorated corroded
   - evaporator or condenser not level, condensate may not drain properly from evaporator, vibrations may damage compressor
   - evaporator or condenser icing: causes: poor air flow, other causes; significant defect
   - evaporator or condenser unusual noise or vibration when operating
   - air leakage at cabinet, especially where evaporator connects to furnace
   - evaporator coils blocked by debris and fungus
   - evaporator size (more than ½ ton) or manufacturer different from condenser unit
   - evaporator installed before furnace blower; condensate may damage furnace
   - absent caps on evaporator drain openings

➢ **Typical defects – condenser unit**
   - damaged or deteriorated unit support pad
   - unit at or below ground or mulch; should be at least 3 inches above
   - absent, damaged, deteriorated suction line insulation
   - absent, damaged, deteriorated, improperly wired electricity shutoff

- overcurrent device larger than maximum on label; common when unit replaced
- wires smaller than minimum on label
- fins/coils blocked by debris
- oil around or in unit; possible refrigerant leak
- clothes dryer exhaust or combustion appliance vent too close
  - recommended 3 – 6 feet separation to condenser
- too close to obstructions, distances per manufacturer's instructions
  - minimum 30 inches on service side, 6 – 12 inches on sides, 48 inches above

Evaporative (Swamp) Coolers

➤ **Evaporative coolers**
- components: fan (blower), water source, pads made from plastic or wood fibers
- water flows down pads, fan pulls outside air through water-soaked pads, air cooled by evaporation when pulled through pads, fan blows cooled air into ducts
- used in dry climates where evaporation is more effective
- older technology, used before widespread central air conditioning; many replaced by central air conditioning; replaced systems often abandoned in place

➤ **Typical defects**
- abandoned system
- deteriorated or damaged components, such as pads, drive belt, cabinet, supports
- water leaking from cabinet
- water leaking around or through unit or ducts into building
- absent backflow preventer on water supply (common)

Whole-house Fans

➤ **Whole-house fans**
- 24 – 36 inch diameter fan usually located at ceiling opening in central hallway; louvers open during operation and close when fan not operating
  - windows should be open when fan operating to provide air flow
- cools by evaporating moisture from skin, like any fan
- benefit: much less expensive than air conditioning
- problems: noisy, louvers allow significant air escape during winter (unless opening sealed and insulated), potential for backdrafting combustion byproducts, potential for asbestos exposure if asbestos materials in attic

➤ **Typical defects**
- fan does not activate using normal controls, abandoned
- some or all louvers do not open or close
- fan damaged, deteriorated, unusually noisy
- fan drive belt loose or deteriorated
- winter cover absent, loose fitting, deteriorated

Condensate Management

➢ **Condensate management – general**

- air conditioners produce significant water when removing water vapor from air (latent load)
- water may be disposed of outdoors, into a floor drain, or upstream from a plumbing drain trap
- most disposal systems drain by gravity; pump required if gravity disposal not possible
- condensate from high efficiency combustion appliances can be acidic; disposal into plumbing systems and sewers with metal pipes can damage pipes

➢ **Primary condensate disposal system**

- pipe size minimum ¾ inch, usually PVC
- slope toward drain point minimum ⅛ inch per foot
- trap on pipe usually required by manufacturer; trap depth per manufacturer
- pipe should have accessible and capped opening for cleaning

➢ **Auxiliary condensate disposal system**

- primary condensate systems occasionally blocked by debris and algae
- auxiliary system required if condensate overflow could damage the building

    o in practice, auxiliary disposal system installed at most condensate sources

- auxiliary system options
    o drained pan under evaporator with float switch in pan, or pan drained to outdoors
    o float switch installed at evaporator

➢ **Typical defects**

- pipe damaged, disconnected
- pipe not sloped toward discharge point
- pipe trap not installed, or sloped so trap drains and does not retain water seal
- running trap, insufficient depth for adequate water seal
- pipe not insulated where appropriate, such as humid climates when condensation on pipes could cause damage, or where pipe could freeze in winter when used for high efficiency furnace condensate
- pipe drains on roof, into plumbing vent, or other unapproved location
- absent auxiliary condensate disposal system
- drained pan not sloped to drain
- water, water stains, refrigerant or refrigerant stains in pan
- evidence of water flow at auxiliary drain termination

Thermostats

➢ **Thermostats – general**

- thermostat: a temperature-sensing switch
- old thermostats: bimetal spring, spring tilts mercury vial that completes or interrupts electrical circuit to turn system on and off
    o should be level for proper operation

- o mercury is hazardous material
- new thermostats: thermistor sensor
- thermostat should be located away from heat/cold sources that may affect accuracy, such as doors, windows, sunlight, kitchens, HVAC supply registers
  - o often located near HVAC return
- programmable thermostat required for new construction and replacements

➢ **Dampers/zoned systems**

- zoned systems use multiple thermostats that open and close mechanical dampers to control air flow in different areas (zones) of a building
  - o allows one HVAC system to provide better temperature control in multiple areas, such as first and second stories
- may be equipped with a pressure-relief damper between the supply and return plenums that equalizes pressure when a zone is open and others are closed, not required at all systems

➢ **Typical defects – thermostats**

- loose, damaged, deteriorated, absent parts
- bimetal spring thermostat not level
- poor location

➢ **Typical defects – zoned systems**

- dampers not operating or not fully opening or closing
- pressure-relief damper absent or not operating

Forced-air Distribution System

➢ **Common materials – low pressure ducts**

- applies to air conditioning and force-air heating
- sheet metal: galvanized steel or aluminum
  - o usually older buildings; should be insulated on inside or outside of duct
- duct board: rigid fiberglass board with integrated insulation
  - o current and older buildings
- flexible duct: usually plastic cover over insulated plastic core, occasionally flexible metal
  - o common in current buildings
- framing cavities, floor joist and stud cavities
  - o older buildings, not allowed in new construction because difficult to seal
- duct insulation required if duct outside conditioned space, such as attic and crawlspace
  - o at least R-8 insulation for ducts 3 inches diameter and larger

➢ **Duct support**

- sheet metal: minimum ½ inch wide compatible material every 10 feet
- duct board: minimum 1½ inch wide compatible material every 6 - 8 feet

- flexible duct: minimum 1½ inch wide compatible material every 4 feet horizontally, 6 feet vertically, and 1 foot from bends, fittings, and splices
- support plenums independently from ducts

➢ **Duct and plenum securing and sealing**
- secure ducts at collars and fittings using pop rivets, screws, or zip ties
- secure and seal ducts and collars so leakage less than requirement; confirm by pressure testing
- sealing materials include approved foil tape and mastic

➢ **Duct bends, sag, and compression**
- flexible duct bends maximum one duct diameter
- flexible duct sagging maximum ½ inch per foot between supports
- flexible ducts should not be compressed so that duct area is reduced

➢ **Return air prohibited locations**
- unconditioned attic and crawlspace, bathroom, closet, garage, kitchen, mechanical, boiler, or furnace room
- closer than 10 feet to combustion appliance with open flame or a draft hood, or to a fireplace

➢ **Filters**
- filters primarily intended to protect HVAC equipment
- dirty filters reduce air flow
  - reduced air flow reduces system efficiency and cooling effectiveness, and can damage system

➢ **Typical defects**
- duct support inadequate, especially if duct sagging or compressed
- duct bend or compression excessive
- duct and plenum damaged or deteriorated, especially if air leaking
- duct and plenum air leaks, including ducts disconnected from plenums and fittings
- condensation on ducts and plenums
- stains or condensation on and near supply registers
- duct openings in garage, except if HVAC system serves only the garage
- flexible duct penetrates garage ceiling or wall
- filter dirty, absent, incorrect size
- filter access difficult; makes filter difficult to change/clean

Unit 7: Heating Systems

Topics covered in this Unit include:

- **Knowledge Areas**
- **Heating Systems – General**
- **Theories of Heat Transfer and Combustion**
- **Combustion Air**
- **Gas Forced-air Furnaces**
- **Floor Furnaces and Wall Furnaces**
- **Room Heaters – Vented**
- **Decorative Gas Appliances – Vented**
- **Decorative Gas Appliances – Unvented**
- **Category I Gas Vents and Oil Vents**
- **Special Gas Vents**
- **Oil Forced-ais Furnaces**
- **Electric Forced-air Furnaces**
- **Distributed Electric Heating**
- **Hot Water Heating Systems**
- **Steam Heating Systems**

Knowledge Areas

➤ **Knowledge areas in-scope of a home inspection and in-scope of the exam**

- heating systems
- distribution systems
- vent systems

Heating Systems – General

➤ **Heating systems (permanently installed) common types**

- **central forced-air furnace**: gas, oil, electric
- **floor furnace and wall furnace**: usually gas, oil uncommon
- **room heaters**: vented and unvented, usually gas, oil uncommon
- **fireplaces and log sets**: vented and unvented, usually gas
- **electric baseboard heaters and radiant heaters**
- **boilers**: hot water and steam, usually oil or gas, electric uncommon

➤ **Definitions**

- **backdrafting** (spillage): combustion products flow down vent into appliance and building; potential carbon monoxide hazard
- **chimney**: vertical structure, sometimes with offsets, that contains one or more flues; conducts combustion products from fuel-burning appliance out of building; made from masonry or metal

- **damper (barometric):** draft-control device in oil appliance vent connector that opens and closes to adjust vent system pressure
- **draft – induced:** combustion products pulled through heat exchanger by fan
- **draft – natural:** combustion products rise by being less dense than cooler air (stack effect)
- **flue:** area inside chimney through which combustion products flow
- **hydronic heating:** hot water or steam circulated through pipes to heat building

Theories of Heat Transfer and Combustion

➤ **Heat transfer**
- **conduction:** heat energy flows within a solid material
- **convection:** heat energy flows by movement of a gas or liquid
- **radiation:** heat energy flows by infrared radiation

➤ **Typical heating fuels**
- gas: natural (methane) and propane
- oil: #2 fuel oil, occasionally kerosene
- solid: wood and wood pellets, rarely coal and biomass

➤ **Combustion byproducts**
- complete combustion, gas: carbon dioxide, water vapor
- complete combustion, oil: carbon dioxide, water vapor, nitric acid, sulfuric acid, sulfur dioxide
- incomplete combustion: complete combustion byproducts plus increased water vapor, carbon monoxide, carbon (soot), nitrogen oxides
- most combustion is incomplete to some extent, so incomplete combustion byproducts are possible

Combustion Air

➤ **Combustion air sources**
- outside building: includes ventilated attics and crawlspaces; recommended
- inside building: usually allowed, but not in tightly air-sealed buildings

➤ **Combustion air – general, gas and oil**
- interior spaces measured in cubic feet of volume
  - spaces include other rooms if no doors between rooms
- openings measured in net free area minus obstructions, such as louvers and screens
- opening locations
  - two openings: one within 12 inches from floor, one within 12 inches from ceiling
  - one opening: opening within 12 inches from ceiling
- appliance combustion air measured in Btu/hour (Btu/h) of appliance fuel input
- where combustion air is drawn from outside, room where appliance is located should be insulated as if it were outside
- see fireplace for solid-fuel combustion air

- out of scope to calculate combustion air adequacy

➤ **Combustion air from inside building**
- same rooms as appliance: 50 cubic feet room volume per 1,000 Btu/h
- openings between rooms on same story: 1 square inch per 1,000 Btu/h
- openings between rooms on different stories: 2 square inches per 1,000 Btu/h

➤ **Combustion air from outside building**
- vertical ducts and openings: 1 square inch per 4,000 Btu/h
- horizontal ducts and opening: 1 square inch per 2,000 Btu/h
- one opening or duct near ceiling: 1 square inch per 3,000 Btu/h

➤ **Combustion air ducts**
- minimum 28 gauge galvanized steel
- stud and floor cavities allowed if only one fireblock removed
- duct dimension minimum 3 inches
- screen required at outside opening
- screen prohibited at attic openings
- one duct may not open into more than one room

➤ **Gas/oil appliance prohibited locations**
- bedrooms, bathrooms, closets; many exceptions
- does not apply to direct vent appliances

➤ **Makeup air**
- replaces air exhausted by appliances, such as clothes dryers and exhaust fans
- different from combustion air

➤ **Evidence of possible inadequate combustion air**
- yellow or orange flame, gas
- soot in combustion chamber or at vent termination

➤ **Typical defects**
- inadequate combustion air opening or duct size
- blocked openings, especially by insulation in attic
- fuel-burning appliance in prohibited location
- room where appliance located not insulated when combustion air from outside
- no screen at combustion air outside opening
- screen at combustion air attic opening

Gas Forced-air Furnaces

➤ **Types**
- Category I: hot vent gas, natural draft vent; common type
  - medium efficiency furnace

93

- o usually Type B vent
- o induced draft most common, about 80% efficiency
- o natural draft/draft hood, about 65% efficiency, most have been replaced
- Category II: none available
- Category III: hot vent gas, positive pressure direct vent; uncommon type
  - o stainless steel vent
- Category IV: cool vent gas, positive pressure vent; common type
  - o high efficiency furnace, 90+% efficiency
  - o plastic vent
  - o condensate produced in furnace, sometimes in vent

➢ **Furnace components**
- cabinet: usually one cover for burner compartment, one cover for blower compartment
- blower (fan): usually a circular squirrel-cage fan
  - o permanent split capacitor (PCM) motor: older, single speed, less efficient
  - o electronically commutated motor (ECM): variable speed, more efficient
- heat exchanger: combustion products flow through heat exchanger interior and out to vent; air to be heated flows around heat exchanger exterior and out to distribution ducts
  - o heat exchanger cracks and leaks let combustion products mix with heated air; major safety defects
  - o interior of most modern heat exchangers not accessible or visible for inspection
- gas valve and gas supply connection
  - o modern furnaces use igniter to light gas
  - o old furnaces use pilot light to light gas; most old furnaces have been replaced
  - o flexible gas connectors not allowed to enter cabinet
- safety sensors
  - o flame-rollout: button-shaped sensors near burners, detects if flame leaves combustion chamber
  - o high limit: button-shaped sensor near burners (newer), or contained in box inside burner cabinet (older), detects if furnace gets too hot
  - o draft sensor: tube connected to inducer fan, detects if fan is operating

➢ **Typical defects, important inspection points**
- cabinet supported, intact, minimal rust or other deterioration, access covers in place, clearance to combustibles
- blower compartment interlock switch operating, not bypassed
- no unusual noise or vibration from blower
- blower reasonably clean, minimal rust or other deterioration
- heat exchanger intact, if visible (usually not visible)
- no evidence of flame rollout, scorching, backdrafting, soot, condensation, or water intrusion in vent system
- internal wiring and safety sensors present, in position, not bypassed
- fuel connections proper, gas shutoff valve in same room, no gas odor
- pilot light (if any) on, steady blue flame
- condensate tubes intact, not crimped, slope toward discharge (Category IV furnaces)
- cables enter cabinet through bushing
- vent system intact, properly installed, clearance to combustibles

- minimal air leaks from cabinet or attached plenums
- adequate service access
- ignition point elevated minimum 18 inches in garage
- ignition sequence activates properly using operating controls
  - thermostat calls for heat, draft inducer activates, igniter activates, gas valve opens (click), gas flows, burners ignite, igniter deactivates
  - flame blue with yellow tips, strong and steady, minimal flickering
  - fan operates without unusual noise or shaking
  - no short cycling

Floor Furnaces and Wall Furnaces

➢ **Types**

- Category I gas: provides heat for one or a few rooms by convection and radiation; blowers uncommon; oil-fired uncommon
  - usually older, may be abandoned
  - Type B vent, Type BW for wall furnaces
  - installation and clearances per manufacturer's instructions

➢ **Typical defects, important inspection points**

- cabinet supported, intact, minimal rust or other deterioration, minimal debris in cabinet, minimum 18 inch walkway on at least one side (floor furnaces)
- clearance to combustibles: 6 inches to walls, 12 inches to drapes, swinging doors, and similar combustibles
- heat exchanger intact, if visible (usually not visible)
- framing around furnace intact, no cut joists or studs
- pilot light (if any) on, steady blue flame
- no evidence of flame rollout, scorching, backdrafting, soot, condensation or water intrusion in vent system
- internal wiring and safety sensors present, in position, not bypassed
- fuel connections proper, gas shutoff valve in same room, no gas odor
- cables enter cabinet through bushing
- vent system intact, properly installed, clearance to combustibles
- adequate service access
- ignition sequence activates properly using normal operating controls
  - thermostat calls for heat, gas valve opens (click), gas flows, burners ignite
  - flame blue with yellow tips, strong and steady, minimal flickering
  - no short cycling

Room Heaters – Vented

➢ **Types**

- Category I gas: provides heat for one or a few rooms by convection and radiation; internal blowers possible; oil-fired uncommon
  - Type B vent or single wall vent, direct vented
  - installation and clearances per manufacturer's instructions

- ➤ **Typical defects, important inspection points**
  - cabinet intact, minimal rust or other deterioration
  - clearance to combustibles: 6 – 12 inches sides, 4 – 48 inches rear and top, 60 inches front
  - pilot light (if any) on, steady blue flame
  - no evidence of flame rollout, scorching, backdrafting, soot, condensation or water intrusion in vent system
  - fuel connections proper, shutoff valve in same room
    - ○ exception if valve permanently labeled, readily accessible, serves only the appliance
  - vent system intact, properly installed, clearance to combustibles
  - ignition sequence activates properly using operating controls
    - ○ thermostat calls for heat, gas valve opens (click), gas flows, burners ignite
    - ○ flame blue with yellow tips, strong and steady, minimal flickering

Decorative Gas Appliances – Vented

- ➤ **Types**
  - includes cabinet with logs that look like a fireplace, and gas logs installed in wood-burning fireplaces
  - decorative gas appliance is not a fireplace; not intended to provide the only heat to habitable rooms
  - manufacturer-supplied vent system, or Type B vent if unit listed for this vent system
  - installation and clearances per manufacturer's instructions

- ➤ **Typical defects, important inspection points**
  - cabinet intact, minimal rust or other deterioration
  - clearance to combustibles, typical: 3 – 6 inches side walls and trim, 8 – 16 inches top and trim, 0 – 10 inches front hearth extension
  - pilot light (if any) on, steady blue flame
  - no evidence of scorching, backdrafting, soot, condensation or water intrusion in vent system
  - wood-burning chimney damper permanently opened
    - ○ opening size depends on Btu/hour input
  - fuel connections proper, shutoff valve in same room
    - ○ exception if valve permanently labeled, readily accessible, serves only the appliance
  - vent system intact, properly installed, clearance to combustibles
    - ○ shroud (if any) at vent termination approved by appliance manufacturer
  - ignition sequence activates properly using normal operating controls
    - ○ switch activated, gas valve opens (click), gas flows, burners ignite
    - ○ flame blue with yellow tips, steady

Decorative Gas Appliances – Unvented

➤ **Types**

- room heaters (space heaters, vent-free heaters), decorative fireplaces, logs installed in wood-burning fireplaces
- decorative gas appliance is not a fireplace, not intended to provide the only heat to habitable rooms
- installation and clearances per manufacturer's instructions

➤ **Operating issues**

- air quality: water vapor and carbon dioxide produced; possible carbon monoxide and nitrogen oxides
  - o manufacturers often recommend limited use time and open window for ventilation
  - o oxygen-depletion safety system required

➤ **Combustion air**

- 1 cubic foot room volume per 20 Btu/hour appliance input
- no use in bedrooms and bathrooms
  - o exceptions: maximum 6,000 Btu/hour bathrooms, 10,000 Btu/hour bedrooms
    - ▪ room volume complies with minimum volume

➤ **Typical defects, important inspection points**

- cabinet intact, minimal rust or other deterioration
- clearance to combustibles: varies significantly depending on appliance and manufacturer
- pilot light (if any) on, steady blue flame
- no soot
- fuel connections proper, shutoff valve in same room
  - o exception if valve permanently labeled, readily accessible, serves only the appliance
- ignition sequence activates properly using normal operating controls
  - o switch activated, gas valve opens (click), gas flows, burners ignite
  - o flame blue with yellow tips, steady

Category I Gas Vents and Oil Vents

➤ **Components**

- vent: final vertical section of a vent system
  - o manufactured metal pipe or masonry chimney
- vent connector: component that connects a fuel-burning appliance to a vent
  - o all pipes before the vent are vent connectors
  - o vent connectors have different rules from vents
- vent cap: listed device at termination of vent
- barometric damper, oil: round plate on two hinges installed in vent connector to regulate draft in chimney

- ➢ **Types**
  - Type B double wall: gas, galvanized steel
  - Type L double wall: oil or gas, stainless steel
  - Type B and Type L vents may serve one appliance or multiple appliances (common vents)
  - single-wall pipe: gas or oil, several restrictions
  - masonry chimney: gas or oil

- ➢ **Masonry chimney used as Category I gas vent**
  - chimneys designed for hot gasses from wood-burning fireplace; may be too large for cooler gas appliance gasses
  - requirements to use chimney as Category I gas vent
    - seal flue below vent connector, and area around where vent connector enters chimney
    - chimney enclosed entirely within building walls until roof penetration
    - chimney may be vent for one draft-hood appliance or for multiple appliances
      - may not be vent for one induced draft appliance
    - flue should be at least as large as the vent connector **area**, and not more than seven times the vent connector **area** if vent for one draft-hood appliance
    - vent connector distance to opposite edge of chimney/flue minimum 3 inches

- ➢ **Typical defects**
  - **inadequate clearance to combustibles**
    - Type B, gas: 1 inch; single-wall 6 inches; clearance includes to insulation
    - Type L, oil: 3 inches; single-wall 9 inches; clearance includes to insulation
    - barometric damper: 18 inches
  - **inadequate clearance from sidewalls and windows**
    - Type B, gas: minimum 8 feet horizontal or 2 feet above anything within 10 feet horizontal
    - Type L, oil: minimum 2 feet above anything within 10 feet horizontal
  - **inadequate clearance above roof**
    - Type B, gas: minimum 1 – 4 feet depending on roof slope
  - inadequate clearance from mechanical air intake opening
    - Type B, gas: minimum 10 feet horizontal or 3 feet above
  - gas vent extends too far above roof
  - disconnected or inadequately secured sections, including draft hoods
  - **smaller diameter gas vent connector connected to vent below larger diameter gas vent connector**
  - connect vent sections using minimum 3 screws, or manufacturer's locking connections
  - larger vent section facing up when smaller vent section inserted
  - damaged, deteriorated, rust, mineral or water stains
  - rust, debris, stains at draft hood, flue collar, or barometric damper
    - indicates possible backdrafting of combustion products
  - no listed cap on Type B vent or Type L vent; no cap on single-wall vent
  - vent too small or too large for appliance
  - vent connector slopes down; should slope up minimum ⅛ inch per foot
  - barometric damper absent, not operating deteriorated, damaged

- improper vent material; single-wall gas vent minimum 28 gauge galvanized steel
- flexible Type B vent and single-wall gas or oil vent improperly installed or damaged
  - no installation in attics and crawlspaces and garages (single-wall)
  - no penetration of walls, floors, ceilings
- inadequate, damaged, deteriorated roof or wall flashing
- gas vent or vent connector too long; elbows total more than 180°
- two or more gas appliances connected to a vent connector, connector manifold
  - allowed, but rules complicated
- common vent connectors enter vent at same level; may do so if angle less than 45°
- chimney improperly used as gas vent, see above for requirements
- vent connector loose or not sealed where enters chimney
- unused chimney openings not sealed
- vent contains asbestos materials, sometimes called Transite (a brand name)

Special Gas Vents

> **Types**

- Category III and IV appliance vents
  - vent materials, installation, and termination, as specified by appliance manufacturer
    - Category III usually stainless steel
    - Category IV usually Schedule 40 PVC, CPVC, or ABS pipe
  - termination requirements vary significantly by manufacturer and model
- direct exhaust: combustion air from inside building, combustion products to outside
- direct vent: combustion air from outside building, combustion products to outside

Oil Forced-air Furnaces

> **Components**

- burner/motor: gun (atomizing) most common type in residential
- fuel pump: part of burner, increases oil pressure
- nozzle: inside blast tube, controls air flow in refractory chamber
- flame retention head: part of blast tube, makes flame shape more uniform and efficient
- refractory chamber/fire pot: where oil is burned

> **Safety components**

- flame sensor (cad cell, fire eye): senses flame in refractory chamber, shuts off burner if no flame
- reset switch (red): restarts burner if shut off by flame sensor
- oil line automatic safety valve: installed in oil line, closes to shut off oil flow if fire
- electrical shutoff switch: near entrance to room where furnace located, shuts off burner in emergency

- ➢ **Typical defects, important inspection points**
  - cabinet supported, intact, minimal rust or other deterioration, access covers in place, clearance to combustibles
  - soot and other stains at and around burner, furnace room, vent, supply registers
  - **puffback**: pop or bang when flame ignites if residual oil is not purged from refractory chamber
  - flame not white, touches refractory chamber walls
  - refractory chamber deteriorated, saturated with oil
  - unusual noise or vibration from burner
  - unusual odors in and around burner, furnace room, oil tank
  - excessive smoke in refractory chamber
  - inadequate service access

Electric Forced-air Furnaces

- ➢ **Types**
  - electric heat furnace
  - electric heat and split air conditioner; air handler and evaporator in one cabinet
    - o easy to mistake for a heat pump
  - heat strips (emergency heat) in heat pump air handler

- ➢ **Typical defects, important inspection points**
  - cabinet supported, intact, minimal rust or other deterioration, access covers in place, clearance to combustibles
  - blower compartment interlock switch operating, not bypassed
  - no unusual noise or vibration from blower
  - blower reasonably clean, minimal rust or other deterioration
  - no heat, or insufficient heat from heating elements
  - internal wiring and safety sensors present, in position, not bypassed
  - cables enter cabinet through bushing
  - minimal air leaks from cabinet or attached plenums
  - adequate service access
  - ignition point elevated at least 18 inches in garage

Distributed Electric Heating

- ➢ **Types**
  - baseboard heaters (linear convector, baseboard convector)
  - wall heaters
  - radiant heater (usually under floor); usually supplemental heat
  - unit heater (hung from ceiling); uncommon in residential
  - all produce heat by running electricity through wires designed to become hot without deteriorating

Typical defects, important inspection points

- does not operate, insufficient heat, or excessive heat
- cabinet intact, minimal rust or other deterioration, clearance to combustibles
- electric receptacle above heater, heater could melt plugged-in cord insulation
- heaters not served by dedicated circuit
- heater not GFCI protected where required (in bathrooms)

Hot Water Heating Systems

➢ **Types**
  - also called **hydronic systems**
    - o hot water circulates through pipes into radiators/convectors or pipes in floors or ceilings (radiant system) and returns to heating equipment
  - water circulation systems
    - o closed: sealed system, most common
    - o open: system open to atmosphere on upper story, 1900s vintage, most replaced, uncommon
  - water heating equipment
    - o **boiler:** oil, gas, electric uncommon
    - o **water heater**: oil, gas, electric uncommon
    - o normal operating temperature: 120° - 130° F.
    - o normal operating pressure: 12 – 15 psi
  - domestic hot water (DHW) from hydronic systems
    - o **tankless coil**: DHW heated by coil in boiler tank
    - o **indirect-fired**: DHW heated by water from boiler pumped into coil in separate tank
    - o **range boiler**: water rises by convection from boiler tank to provide DHW, obsolete

➢ **Components**
  - combustion (heating) components, heat exchanger, thermostat: similar to gas and oil furnaces; see these for components and typical defects
  - water shutoff valves: allows water shutoff for service, install on supply and return circulation pipes and on water supply pipe
  - backflow preventer: keeps contaminated water in heater out of drinking water supply
  - automatic fill valve: adds water to tank, when necessary, optional
  - pressure reducing valve: reduces water pressure entering tank
    - o typical range 12 – 15 psi
  - low-water cutoff: shuts off heater if water level in tank too low
  - **aquastat**: controls when heater fires, may control circulation pump activation
    - o typical high limit 200° - 220° F.
    - o typical low limit 120° - 200° F.
  - gauges: allows monitoring of water temperature and pressure in tank, may be one or two gauges
  - pressure relief valve: releases water from tank when pressure in boiler exceeds 30 psi
    - o discharge pipe should be minimum ¾ inch, rated for hot water, terminate not more than 18 inches above floor

- air removal: air entering circulation system can block flow; air removed by air bleeder valves (manual), air scoops and separators (automatic)
- expansion tank: provides place to accept water that expands and contracts when heated and cooled
  - size depends on water volume in system; typical 1 – 4 gallons
- circulation pump: pumps water through distribution system
- water pipe systems
  - one pipe series loop: water circulates from one radiator to the next in series, water returns to heater after last radiator, radiator at end of line gets less heat; older system, obsolete, poor heat distribution
  - one pipe monoflow: water flows through monoflow/diverter fitting in pipe that diverts some water to each radiator, water returns to heater after last radiator
  - two pipes: hot water flows in one pipe, cool water from radiator returns in separate pipe; most efficient and effective; costs more to install
- water pipe types: copper, steel, PEX, polybutylene
- radiators/convectors: distribute heat in rooms by convection and radiation
  - should have shutoff valve on hot water pipe

➤ **Typical defects, important inspection points**
- cabinet supported, intact, minimal rust or deterioration, clearance to combustibles
- water leaks, all components
- rusted, deteriorated, damaged, inoperative, all components
- inadequate or no heat at distribution devices
- circulation pump inoperative or noisy
- backflow preventer installed backwards, installed before water shutoff valve
- pressure relief valve or discharge pipe absent, leaking, wrong size, wrong location
- expansion tank waterlogged, completely filled with water
- dissimilar metals, such as copper and steel, in contact
- inadequate pipe support, see plumbing for support requirements
- excessive dirt on baseboard fins
- absent valves where required
- no control diagram and operating instructions

Steam Heating Systems

➤ **Types**
- also called hydronic systems
  - steam rises and flows by convection through pipes into radiators/convectors, steam condenses into water releasing heat, water returns to boiler by gravity; no pumps in system
- common steam circulation systems
  - low pressure: ½ - 2 psi
  - high pressure: over 15 psi; uncommon in residential
- water heating fuel: oil or gas
- domestic hot water (DHW) from hydronic systems
  - tankless coil: DHW heated by coil in boiler
  - indirect-fired: DHW heated by water from boiler pumped into coil in separate tank

- ➤ **Components**
  - combustion (heating) components and thermostat: similar to gas and oil furnaces, see these for components and typical defects
  - water shutoff valve: allows water shutoff for service; install on water supply pipe
  - backflow preventer: keeps contaminated water in boiler out of drinking water supply
  - automatic fill valve: adds water to boiler, when necessary, optional
  - pressure reducing valve: reduces water pressure entering boiler; 15 psi typical
  - low-water cutoff: shuts off boiler if water level in tank too low
  - **pressuretrol or vaporstat**: controls when boiler fires
  - pressure gauge: allows monitoring of pressure in boiler
  - sight glass: allows monitoring of boiler water level and water condition
  - pressure relief valve: releases water from boiler when pressure in boiler exceeds 15 psi
    - discharge pipe should be at least ¾ inch, rated for hot water, terminate maximum 18 inches above floor
  - **steam pipe systems**
    - one pipe counterflow: steam flows to radiators and water flows from radiators **toward** boiler in same pipe
      - horizontal pipes should slope about 1 inch per 10 feet toward boiler
      - old system, very inefficient
    - one pipe parallel flow: steam flows to radiators and water flows from radiators **away** from boiler in same pipe until after the last radiator
      - horizontal return pipes should slope about 1 inch per 20 feet away from boiler until after last radiator, then toward boiler in dry and wet return pipes
    - two pipes: steam and water flow in different pipes
      - horizonal water return pipes should slope about 1 inch per 20 feet away from boiler until after last radiator, then toward boiler in dry and wet return pipes
      - most efficient and effective; costs more to install
    - dry return pipes: carry water from radiators, and are **above** the normal boiler water level
    - wet return pipes: carry water from radiators, and are **below** the normal boiler water level
    - **Hartford loop and equalizer pipe**: required on wet return systems to avoid draining boiler tank, and avoid the explosion potential if boiler fires with dry tank
      - equalizer pipe connects steam and wet return pipes
      - Hartford loop connects to equalizer pipe 2 - 4 inches below normal boiler water level
  - steam pipe types: usually steel, copper uncommon
    - steam pipes should be insulated; insulation not necessary on return pipes
      - insulation on old pipes is possible asbestos-containing material
  - radiators/convectors: distribute heat in rooms by convection and radiation
  - **vents and traps**: purge air and cool water in distribution system so steam can flow
    - main vent, at least one in all systems; ball float trap or inverted bucket trap
      - locate near end of dry return pipe, minimum 18 inches above normal tank water level and minimum 6 – 10 inches above dry return pipe
    - air vent, one on each distribution device in one pipe systems
    - thermostatic trap, one on each distribution device in two pipe systems
    - float and thermostatic trap (F&T) trap, at least one in two pipe systems
      - locate downstream from last distribution device

103

➢ **Typical defects, important inspection points**
- cabinet supported, intact, minimal rust or deterioration, clearance to combustibles
- water and steam leaks, all components
- rusted, deteriorated, damaged, inoperative, all components
- inadequate or no heat at distribution devices
- banging in pipes or distribution devices (water hammer)
- backflow preventer installed backwards, installed before water shutoff valve
- pressure relief valve or discharge pipe absent, leaking, wrong size, wrong location
- new boiler, old pipes; old pipes may not work properly with new boiler
- inconsistent water level in sight glass
- water dripping from top of sight glass
- rusty/dirty water in sight glass
- dissimilar metals, such as copper and steel, in contact
- inadequate pipe support or slope, see plumbing for support requirements
- excessive dirt on baseboard fins
- no control diagram and operating instructions

Unit 8: Insulation, Ventilation, Moisture Management

Topics covered in this Unit include:

- **Knowledge Areas**
- **Insulation, Ventilation, Moisture Management – General**
- **Theory of Energy Conservation and Moisture Management**
- **Attic Ventilation**
- **Crawlspace Ventilation**

Knowledge Areas

➢ **Knowledge areas in-scope of a home inspection and in-scope of the exam**

- thermal insulation
- ventilation of attics, crawlspace, roof assemblies
- moisture management

➢ **Knowledge areas out-of-scope of a home inspection but in-scope of the exam**

- humidifiers and dehumidifiers

Insulation, Ventilation, Moisture Management – General

➢ **Definitions**
- **air barrier**: materials intended to prevent air flow into or out of conditioned space
- **dew point**: temperature at which water vapor condenses and becomes liquid water
- **humidity, relative**: amount of water vapor in air compared to how much water vapor air could hold; expressed as percentage
- **insulation**: material intended to restrict heat flow into or out of conditioned space
- **permeability**: how much water vapor material will allow to pass through; perms expressed as greater than zero number; higher number, more water vapor passes
- **R-value**: resistance of material to heat flow; higher number, less heat flow; applied to thermal insulation
- **thermal envelope**: heated and cooled areas of a building; should be insulated and air sealed
- **U-value (factor)**: how much heat flow material allows; inverse of R-value; expressed as a greater than zero number; higher number, more heat flow; applied to windows and doors
- **vapor retarder** (barrier): material that restricts water vapor flow
- **water-resistive barrier**: material that restricts liquid water flow; usually an air barrier; may be a vapor retarder

➢ **Insulation types**
- R-values and perm ratings vary by manufacturer and product
- batts (blanket): usually fiberglass (R-3 - 4/inch), or mineral wool (R-3.7/inch)
  - o not an air barrier or vapor retarder unless faced with material, such as Kraft paper

- loose-fill (blown-in): usually fiberglass (R-2.2 - 2.7/inch), cellulose (R-3.5/inch), or mineral wool (R-3.1/inch)
  - not an air barrier or vapor retarder
- rigid sheets: expanded polystyrene (EPS) (R-4/inch), extruded polystyrene (XPS) (R-5/inch), polyisocyanurate, polyurethane (R-6/inch)
  - air barrier, vapor retarder, and water barrier, depending on how installed
- spray foam: polyisocyanurate and polyurethane
  - open cell R-3.7/inch; air barrier, not a vapor retarder
  - closed cell R-6 per inch; air barrier, vapor retarder, water barrier
- vermiculite and perlite: loose-fill; more common before 1950s, vermiculite is possible asbestos-containing material
- urea-formaldehyde: spray foam; more common 1970s and 80s; off-gassed formaldehyde after installation and shrank over time; no longer used

➤ Vapor retarder types
- Class I: 0.1 perms or less, polyethylene sheets
- Class II: .01 – 1.0 perms, Kraft paper
- Class III: 1.1 – 10 perms, paint

➤ Water-resistive barrier types
- asphalt-impregnated Kraft paper, Grade D paper, building paper (felt)
  - air and water barrier, Class II vapor retarder
- house wrap, liquid coatings, some types of wall sheathing
  - air and water barrier, may be vapor retarder

➤ Radiant barriers
- reflects infrared radiation so less heat enters attic; no R-value
- best performance when attached rafters/truss top chords; much less useful on attic floor; some roof sheathing has radiant barrier
- a vapor retarder; possible deterioration of wood if water vapor condenses on barrier

➤ Insulation and fenestration requirements (2021)
- attic: R-30 warm zones; R-49 to R-60 cold zones
- floor: R-13 warm zones; R-19 to R-38 cold zones
- basement walls: none warm zones; R-13 to R-19 cold zones
- windows/doors: none warm zones; R-3.33 (U-0.3) cold zones

➤ Humidifiers
- installed with gas and oil-fired forced-air furnaces to compensate for moisture removed from air by combustion; optional
- water supply required; often by saddle valve on nearby water pipe; saddle valves no longer allowed because of leaks
- should be installed at supply plenum, or as recommended by manufacturer
  - installation at return plenum can damage furnace by excess moisture
- bypass duct between supply and return plenums may be required by manufacturer
  - duct should be metal as specified by manufacturer

o   duct should have damper, close when using air conditioning
- regular maintenance required

Theory of Energy Conservation and Moisture Management

➢ **Theory of energy and moisture flows**
- **heat energy flows from hot to cold**
- **hot air rises** because it is less dense than cold air (stack effect)
- **moisture flows from area with more moisture to area with less moisture** (vapor diffusion)
- **hot air holds more moisture than cold air**

➢ **Theory of thermal insulation**
- **insulation must be in contact with air barrier at conditioned space**
  o   contact gaps leave space uninsulated
    ▪ gaps occur by poor installation, not cutting insulation around obstructions, such as wires and pipes, not securing horizontal insulation against falling
- batt and loose-fill insulation work by trapping air and holding air so it does not move
  o   **air movement around or through these insulation types reduces R-value**
  o   these insulation types should be covered by air barrier on all sides to achieve rated R-value
  o   **compression of these insulation types reduces R-value**
    ▪ compression occurs by poor installation, not cutting insulation around obstructions, such as wires and pipes, foot traffic, wetting, settlement
- **insulation effectiveness depends on entire assembly**
  o   thermal bridging reduces assembly R-value
    ▪ wood (studs, joists, headers) has lower R-value than insulation; more wood, lower assembly R-value
    ▪ metal has much lower R-value than insulation and wood
  o   windows and doors reduce assembly R-value
    ▪ typical windows and doors between R-1 and R-2
    ▪ best windows about R-4.5

➢ **Theory of vapor retarders**
- framed assemblies (especially walls) may get wet
  o   air carries water vapor though visible and invisible openings
  o   water leaks through openings
  o   water vapor diffuses through permeable material
- **one side of framed assembly should be permeable to allow assembly to dry**
  o   no vapor retarder on walls in warm, cool, humid, or dry environments (Climate Zones 1 – 4)
  o   vapor retarder on interior side of walls in cold environments (Climate Zones 5 – 8, and Marine 4)
  o   no vapor retarder required in most ventilated attics
- some common decorating materials can be a vapor retarder, such as wallpaper (especially foil and vinyl) and vinyl floor coverings

- wood-framed assemblies that remain wet will deteriorate, fungi (mold) may grow, and wood-destroying insects may be attracted

➢ **Theory of moisture and air and movement in buildings**
- **air and moisture will not move without a <u>force</u> (<u>pressure</u>) and an <u>opening</u>**
  o pressure can be air pressure or water vapor pressure
  o openings can be visible (a hole), or microscopic
- common air pressure difference causes
  o leaks in HVAC ducts, and unbalanced HVAC air supply and return volumes in rooms
  o exhaust fans, especially clothes dryers, kitchen exhaust hoods, whole-house fans
  o combustion air drawn from inside
  o stack effect
- common openings in walls, ceilings, and floors
  o electrical boxes (lights, switches, receptacles)
  o recessed lights
  o whole-house fans
  o openings between stories (duct and vent chases, pipe and wire penetrations)
  o numerous small holes can add up to several square feet, especially in older buildings
  o air sealing can be more effective than adding insulation
    ▪ air sealing can have unintended air quality reduction, especially when combustion air drawn from inside
    ▪ controlled addition of outside air may be necessary
- common water vapor sources
  o occupants (bathing, cooking, clothes washing, breathing)
    ▪ not using exhaust fans, and exhaust fans improperly installed
  o high moisture levels in crawlspaces and attics

➢ **Typical defects**
- insulation R-value or depth/thickness less than current recommendations, or less than value on insulation card
- insulation absent, compressed, disturbed
- insulation not in contact with air barrier at conditioned spaces
- insulation wet or evidence of having been wet
- insulation blocking ventilation openings
- insulation poorly installed, not cut to fit into space, not cut around obstructions
- chases not fireblocked and not insulated
- insulation too close to heat-generating components, such as combustion vents
- paper vapor retarder exposed, fire hazard
- vapor retarders on both sides of assembly

Attic Ventilation

- ➤ **Attic ventilation – general**
  - most attics are ventilated
    - o attics that should be ventilated include inaccessible attics, rafter bays in vaulted ceilings, attics above unconditioned space
    - o ventilation in winter keeps underside of roof near outdoor temperature; reduces ice dams; reduces water vapor in attic
    - o ventilation in summer may keep attics cooler, may reduce roof covering deterioration from excess heat
  - attics may be unventilated
    - o seal attic as conditioned space
    - o air barrier and insulation located at rafters and gables instead of at ceiling joists
    - o vapor retarder type and location depends on insulation and vapor retarder materials and on installation methods

- ➤ **Attic ventilation installation**
  - ventilation opening ratio 1 square foot net free ventilation opening area per 300 square feet attic floor area, assuming the following
    - o 40 – 50% of opening area within 3 feet vertically of ridge
    - o remaining area at or near eaves
  - openings should be covered by screens, louvers, grilles to restrict vermin entry
    - o net free opening area reduced by covers
    - o opening size maximum ¼ inch
  - baffles should be installed at eaves so insulation does not block ventilation (newer requirement)
  - do not install powered attic ventilation near roof ridge if ridge or gable ventilation openings installed
    - o powered ventilator will disrupt air flow causing hot/cold/moist areas
  - ventilation openings in gables allowed, but subject to wind-blown water intrusion

- ➤ **Typical defects – ventilated attic**
  - eave openings blocked by insulation, paint, other obstructions
  - opening covers absent, damaged
  - ridge openings blocked by roof coverings
  - turbine or powered ventilator inoperative, damaged, deteriorated
  - improper opening distribution (eaves and ridge), or inadequate opening quantity
  - evidence of water intrusion, especially at gables
  - evidence of condensation

- ➤ **Typical defects – unventilated attic**
  - openings to outside not sealed
  - improper vapor retarder location or installation
  - thermal or ignition barrier not present on foam insulation
  - insulation absent, damaged
  - absent or improperly installed vapor diffusion port, if required

Crawlspace Ventilation

➢ **Crawlspace ventilation – general**
- most crawlspaces are ventilated
  - passive crawlspace ventilation is supposed to reduce moisture in crawlspace
  - recent studies show passive ventilation may increase moisture

➢ **Crawlspace ventilation installation**
- ventilation opening ratio 1 square foot net free ventilation opening area per 1,500 square feet crawlspace floor area, assuming the following
  - Class I vapor retarder on crawlspace floor
  - openings maximum 3 feet from each foundation corner, or as appropriate to provide cross-ventilation
- openings should be covered by screens, louvers, grilles to restrict vermin entry
  - net free opening area reduced by covers
  - opening size maximum ¼ inch

➢ **Unventilated (closed) crawlspace installation**
- crawlspaces should be unventilated, not required
- seal crawlspace as conditioned space, including access openings
- air barrier located at crawlspace walls
- vapor retarder on crawlspace floor, minimum 6-mil polyethylene sheets
  - seams lapped minimum 6 inches and sealed
  - turn up walls and piers and seal
- insulation on crawlspace walls or between floor joists
  - leave 2 – 3 inch space at top of wall for termite inspection
- provide ventilation minimum 1 cubic foot per minute per 50 square feet crawlspace floor
  - may be HVAC supply opening, or continuous exhaust fan to exterior

➢ **Typical defects – ventilated crawlspace**
- openings blocked; louvers stuck
- opening covers absent, damaged
- improper opening distribution (no cross ventilation), or inadequate opening quantity
- vapor retarder absent, damaged, disturbed, poorly installed
- evidence of water intrusion, such as liquid water or wet soil on floor, dark areas or efflorescence on walls
- insulation damp or strands hanging down
- fungal growth or deterioration of wood
- evidence of prior repairs, such as interior foundation drains, dehumidifiers, water-resistant coatings

➢ **Typical defects – unventilated crawlspace**
- openings to outside not sealed
- improper vapor retarder installation
- thermal or ignition barrier not present on foam insulation
- insulation absent, damaged
- absent, inadequate ventilation

Unit 9: Mechanical Exhaust Systems

Topics covered in this Unit include:

- **Knowledge Areas**
- **Mechanical Exhaust Systems – General**
- **Clothes Dryer Exhaust Systems**
- **Kitchen Exhaust Systems**
- **Bathroom Exhaust Systems**
- **Indoor Air Management Systems**

Knowledge Areas

➤ **Knowledge areas in-scope of a home inspection and in-scope of the exam**

- mechanical exhaust systems

➤ **Knowledge areas out-of-scope of a home inspection but in-scope of the exam**

- indoor air management systems, such as heat recovery and energy recovery systems

Mechanical Exhaust Systems - General

➤ **Definitions**

- **exhaust**: to remove odors, moisture, and other contaminants from a building using mechanical systems, such as fans
- **ventilate**: to add outside air to a building using mechanical systems in order to maintain air quality

Clothes Dryer Exhaust Systems

➤ **Lint**

- lint is flammable, fires can occur in clothes dryer exhaust ducts
- lint can block ducts and termination fittings, increasing cost of use

➤ **Duct requirements**

- 4 inch diameter duct; too small, not enough air flow; too large, too little air flow, lint can accumulate
- minimum 28 gauge smooth-wall galvanized steel
- secure duct sections with pop-rivets or screws not longer than ⅛ inch
- support ducts for electric dryers minimum every 12 feet; minimum 4 feet for gas dryers
- maximum developed duct length 35 feet (not including transition duct)
  - add 2½ feet for 45° fittings, 5 feet for 90° fittings
- terminate outside building; not in attic or crawlspace
  - backdraft damper on termination fitting
  - no screen on termination fitting

- o no termination within 3 feet from door or operable window
- transition duct connects dryer and exhaust duct
  - o length maximum 8 feet
  - o should not penetrate walls, ceilings, floors
- provide opening at least 100 square inches make up air opening if dryer located in closet with closeable doors

➢ **Typical defects**

- duct not 4 inches diameter
- duct not smooth wall
- duct disconnected, damaged, deteriorated
- duct terminates inside building, or too close to window or door
- screen at termination fitting
- excessive lint near dryer or near termination fitting
- damper at termination fitting stuck
- transition duct too long, penetrates wall, ceiling, floor
- transition duct constricted or damaged

Kitchen Exhaust Systems

➢ **General**

- kitchen exhaust systems not required if window near kitchen area
- types
  - o recirculating hood: located above cooking appliance; "filters" cooking fumes and recirculates them back into kitchen
  - o updraft exhaust hood: located above cooking appliance; exhausts cooking fumes up and outside building
  - o downdraft exhaust: located in cooking appliance; exhausts cooking fumes down and outside building

➢ **Duct requirements**

- duct size and installation per exhaust system manufacturer's instructions
- ducts smooth wall galvanized steel, stainless steel, copper
  - o usually minimum 6 inches diameter round, 3¼ by 10 inches rectangular
  - o corrugated ducts and flexible ducts not allowed
- Schedule 40 PVC allowed for ducts installed under concrete slab
- terminate externally exhausted ducts outside building, not in attic or crawlspace
- screen required at termination fitting
- backdraft damper required at termination fitting or at hood

➢ **Typical defects**

- duct too small
- duct not smooth wall, not approved material
- duct disconnected, damaged, deteriorated, not air tight
- duct terminates inside building
- no screen at termination fitting
- damper at termination fitting stuck

Bathroom Exhaust Systems

➢ **Requirements**

- required if no operable window in bathroom or toilet room
- terminate duct outside building, not in attic, crawlspace, eaves
- fan capacity minimum 50 cfm switched, 20 cfm continuous, uncommon
- duct size depends on fan capacity and material
  - usually minimum 4 inches diameter newer installations, 3 inches diameter common at older installations
- screen required at termination fitting
- backdraft damper required at termination fitting or at fan

➢ **Typical defects**

- duct damaged, deteriorated, crushed
- duct too small
- duct terminates inside building
- no screen at termination fitting
- damper at termination fitting stuck

Indoor Air Management Systems

➢ **Ventilation rates**

- recommended ventilation rate in houses at least 0.35 air changes per hour, and at least 15 cfm per person
  - ventilation required to dilute pollutants including water vapor, volatile organic compounds, combustion byproducts, odors
  - usually accomplished by air leaks through unsealed openings in older houses
  - whole-house mechanical ventilation may be required in newer houses that comply with energy code air sealing requirements, and in older houses that have been air sealed

➢ **Mechanical ventilation system types**

- outside air duct connected to HVAC return plenum
  - problems: too much or too little air enters house; condensation, especially in winter; outside air must be heated or cooled, increasing HVAC operating cost
- **energy recovery ventilation** system (ERV)
  - extracts **heat** from exhaust air and heats incoming ventilation air in heating mode
  - extracts **heat and water vapor** from ventilation air; cools and dehumidifies incoming ventilation air in cooling mode
  - not recommended for cold climates; recommended for warm/humid climates
- **heat recovery ventilation** system (HRV)
  - extracts **heat** from exhaust air and heats incoming ventilation air in heating mode
  - extracts **heat** from incoming ventilation air and cools incoming ventilation air
  - recommended for cold climates; acceptable for warm/humid climates

➢ **HRV and ERV duct configurations**
- fully ducted: operates independently from HVAC system
    - exhaust ducts pull exhaust air from bathrooms, kitchen, other places if necessary
    - supply ducts provide ventilation air to areas of house, as designed
- partially ducted
    - exhaust ducts pull exhaust air from bathrooms, kitchen, other places if necessary
    - ventilation air provided to HVAC supply plenum for distribution
- simplified ducting
    - exhaust air pulled from HVAC return plenum
    - ventilation air provided to HVAC supply plenum for distribution

➢ **HRV and ERV installation**
- installation per manufacturer's instructions
- common termination instructions
    - 18 inches above grade or snow level
    - minimum 6 feet separating ventilation air and exhaust air terminations
- ERV require condensate management system

➢ **Typical defects**
- improper installation, ducts not connected to appropriate systems or locations
- ducts crimped, crushed, damaged
- air intake too close to plumbing vent or combustion vent
- air exhaust too close to air intake openings, such as windows and doors
- blocked intake or exhaust openings; no screen on openings
- lack of maintenance, clogged filters
- condensate management system defects, see air conditioner condensate management

Unit 10: Plumbing and Fuel Distribution Systems

Topics covered in this Unit include:
- **Knowledge Areas**
- **Plumbing Systems – General**
- **Water Service and Distribution Pipes and Valves**
- **Faucets**
- **Bathtubs, Showers, Sinks**
- **Toilets, Clothes Washing Machines, Floor Drains**
- **Backflow Prevention**
- **Water Treatment Devices**
- **Domestic Hot Water Systems**
- **Drain Waste, Vent Pipes**
- **Drain, Waste, Vent Fittings**
- **Traps and Fixture Drains**
- **Plumbing Vents**
- **Private Sewage Disposal Systems**
- **Sewage Ejectors, Sump Pumps, Backwater Valves**
- **Fuel Storage and Distribution Systems – General**
- **Gas Pipes, Connectors, Valves**
- **Oil Pipes, Connectors, Tanks**

Knowledge Areas

➢ **Knowledge areas in-scope of a home inspection and in-scope of the exam**

- water supply and distribution system
- fixtures and faucets
- drain, waste, and vent systems
- domestic hot water systems
- fuel storage and distribution systems
- sump pumps, sewage ejector pumps, related valves and pips

➢ **Knowledge areas out-of-scope of a home inspection but in-scope of the exam**

- septic systems
- water treatment

Plumbing Systems - General

➢ **Definitions**

- **cleanout:** opening in building drainage system that allows access for removing blockages
- developed length (of a pipe): length of a pipe measured from where pipe begins to where it ends, including all fittings
- **drain, waste, vent (DWV) system**: pipes that conduct waste water from plumbing fixtures out of building

- **fitting**: component that connects two or more pipes together
- **functional drainage**: flow out of fixture about equal to flow into fixture
- **functional water flow**: water flow rate from pipes or fixtures equals or exceeds minimum required; some fixtures have flow restrictors that intentionally limit flow
- Schedule 40 and Schedule 80: thickness of pipe walls; Schedule 40 thinner than Schedule 80
- **water hammer arrestor**: device that prevents shock and vibration damage to plumbing components when water stops flowing quickly
- water pressure: the force that water exerts on pipe walls and plumbing fixtures
- water flow: amount of water coming from a plumbing fixture; once a pipe is full, additional water pressure does not increase water flow

Water Service and Distribution Pipes and Valves

➢ **Definitions**
- **water service pipe**: pipe from water meter or well head to building water shutoff valve
- **water distribution pipes**: pipes beginning at building water shutoff valve

➢ **Water pressure**
- maximum: 80 psi
- minimum: none, must be adequate to provide functional water flow

➢ **Water pressure regulator (pressure reducing valve)**
- required when water pressure to building (street pressure) exceeds 80 psi
- may be installed anywhere after building water shutoff valve, and before first fixture or appliance
- adjustable, adjusting screw frequently frozen on older valves

➢ **Protection requirements**
- **freeze**: insulate distribution pipes run outside building thermal envelope, such as in ventilated attics and crawlspaces, and in exterior wall cavities
- puncture: protect pipes with steel shield plates if edge of hole is 1½ inches or less from the edge of the framing member
- corrosion: protect metal pipes run in or through concrete or masonry against corrosion using a pipe sleeve, wrapping with protective material, or other approved method
- breakage: protect pipes run through foundation walls with a pipe sleeve at least two pipe sizes larger than protected pipe

➢ **Copper tubing**
- types: rigid (drawn); flexible coiled (annealed)
- wall thickness: all have same outside diameter
  - o K: thickest, green markings
  - o L: middle thickness, blue markings
  - o M: thinnest, red markings
- use: water service, hot and cold distribution
- history: 1930s – present

- service life: 20 – 50+ years
- known problems: leaks if water has high acid or alkaline content
- support: maximum 6 feet horizontal; 10 feet vertical; no steel supports (galvanic corrosion)
- fittings: soldered; flared or compression (annealed only)
- fittings connecting to other pipe types: threaded, push-connect, press-connect (drawn); no connection to iron or steel pipes unless dielectric fitting used

➢ **Chlorinated polyvinyl chloride (CPVC)**
- use: water service, hot and cold distribution
- history: 1960s – present
- service life: 50+ years
- known problems: none
- support: maximum 3 feet horizontal; 10 feet vertical
- fittings: solvent cement; primer not required
- fittings connecting to other pipe types: threaded, push-connect

➢ **Galvanized steel**
- use: water service, hot and cold distribution
- history: 1860s – 1960s; uncommon since then
- service life: 50 years
- **known problems**: rusting inside pipe; restricted inside diameter due to rust trapping debris, reduced water flow if restricted diameter
- support: maximum 12 feet horizontal; 15 feet vertical
- fittings: threaded
- fittings connecting to other pipe types: no connection to copper pipes unless dielectric fitting used

➢ **Cross-linked polyethylene (PEX); PEX-AL-PEX similar**
- use: water service, hot and cold distribution
- history: 1980s – present; common in many markets
- service life: 40 - 50+ years
- known problems: failure of fitting manufactured 1996 – 2010, type F1807
- support: maximum 32 inches horizontal; 10 feet vertical; manufacturer-supplied talons
- fittings: crimp fittings
- fittings connecting to other pipe types: threaded, push-connect

➢ **Polybutylene (PB)**
- use: water service, hot and cold distribution
- history: 1970s – 1990s; uncommon since then due to significant failure rate
- service life: uncertain
- **known problems**: failure of fittings, especially plastic with aluminum rings
- support: maximum 32 inches horizontal; 4 feet vertical
- fittings: crimp fittings
- fittings connecting to other pipe types: per fitting manufacturer's instructions

➢ **Lead**
- use: water service, hot and cold distribution; no longer allowed, should be removed
- history: Roman era – 1970s; less common since 1930s
- service life: 40 – 50 years
- **known problems**: lead is highly toxic

➢ **Water connectors**
- use: connect water distribution pipes to fixtures and appliances
- typical materials: copper, stainless steel, PEX, polybutylene
  - plastic tubing should be labeled with listing/approval information
- installation: connector not crimped so that internal diameter reduced; not linked together; not penetrate walls, floors, ceilings

➢ **Water valves**
- types
  - **ball**: full open valve, handle control
  - **gate**: full open valve, wheel control, common at many fixtures
  - **angle stop** (fixture shutoff): shuts off water at fixtures for maintenance; can be any valve type; handle or wheel control
  - **stop and waste**: used at hose bibbs to shutoff water for winter, opening in valve body allows draining pipe to hose bibb
- required valves
  - main building shutoff: full open, locate near where water service pipe enters building
  - water heater: full open, on cold water input pipe
  - fixtures and appliances: accessible fixture shutoff valve at cold and hot water pipes, except bathtub, shower

➢ **Hot water circulation systems**
- provides instant hot water by continuously circulating hot water to fixtures
- issue: energy cost of heat loss in pipes and pump operation versus cost of water to get hot water at fixture
- may be required in jurisdictions where water is scarce; timer on pump may be required
- may use return pipes installed during construction; or retrofit using thermal bypass valve at fixture far from water heater

➢ **Typical defects**
- active leaks, usually at fittings and valves
- mineral deposits, corrosion, rust, usually at fittings and valves
- incompatible metals in contact, copper and steel
- inadequate pipe support, improper support materials
- pipes crimped, damaged
- absent insulation on pipes outside of building thermal envelope
- valves stuck, do control water flow, common at fixture shutoff valves
- elevated water pressure
- inadequate water pressure or water flow
- water hammer, usually at clothes washing and dishwashing machines

Faucets

> **Faucet types**
>   - compression: handle turns screw to lift washer and allow water flow; repair by replacing washer
>   - ball: single handle moves ball to allow water flow; repair by replacing O-rings
>   - cartridge: single handle moves cartridge to allow water flow; repair by replacing O-rings and cartridge
>   - disc: similar to cartridge; repair by replacing seals and discs

> **Bathtub and shower faucets**
>   - could be any faucet type
>   - device in faucet should limit water temperature to 120° F.

> **Shower diverter**
>   - diverts water from tub spout to shower
>   - sometimes frozen in place, or does not fully divert water flow

> **Hose connection faucets**
>   - also called hose bibb, hose cock, spigot, sill cock
>   - usually compression faucet
>   - required to have backflow preventer, either screw-on or integrated
>   - should have means to shut off valve and drain pipe if subject to freezing

> **Flow restrictors and aerators**
>   - usually found on sinks; not required
>   - flow restrictor reduces water flow to conform with code flow requirements
>   - aerator adds air to reduce water flow and reduce splashing
>   - low functional flow at sinks can be caused by clogged flow restrictor or aerator

> **Hot/cold control convention**
>   - **hot water flow control on left, cold water flow control on right**
>   - control may be different if indicated on faucet

> **Typical defects**
>   - water leaks, or leak evidence, at spout, handles, faucet base
>   - leak evidence includes corrosion, rust, stains
>   - hot/cold control reversed
>   - faucet does not control water flow or temperature over designed range
>   - shower or bathtub faucet does not limit water temperature to 120° F.
>   - inadequate functional flow or functional drainage
>   - handles absent, loose, damaged, deteriorated, corroded
>   - faucet stuck or difficult to operate
>   - diverter stuck, does not fully divert flow, leaks from diverter control
>   - water leaks from rear of bathtub spout

- faucet or valve loose in wall
- no backflow prevention at hose connections
- leak at sink sprayer or in cabinet under sink sprayer

Bathtubs, Showers, Sinks

➢ **Bathtubs**
- materials: cast iron, steel, fiberglass
- DWV: minimum 1½ inch P trap; maximum 6 feet fixture drain length (both often concealed)
- drain stopper: required; several types
- support: under bathtub; bathtub should not be supported by rim (often concealed)
- overflow drain: not required, but often installed near flood rim level

➢ **Whirlpool bathtubs**
- same as bathtubs; most whirlpool bathtubs are fiberglass
- **pump access**: minimum 12x12 inches; minimum 18x18 inches if pump more than 2 feet from opening
- electrical: pump should be on dedicated GFCI circuit, usually 20 amps; bonding pump motor to metal pipes usually required

➢ **Showers and tub/showers**
- shower pan materials
  - o prefabricated fiberglass
  - o site-built liners: PVC, newer; copper, lead very old; tile usually applied over liners
- shower pan installation
  - o curb no longer required; if installed height maximum 9 inches
  - o slope floor toward drain between ¼ and ½ inch per foot
- wall materials
  - o prefabricated panels: cultured marble, fiberglass
  - o site-built
    - cement panels, lath and mortar
    - water-resistant drywall (green board) no longer allowed
    - tile often applied over site-built materials
    - glass, including windows, should be safety glazing
  - o non-absorbent wall covering to minimum 6 feet above shower floor
- shower size
  - o floor area minimum 900 square inches with minimum dimension 30 inches
    - exception: minimum dimension 25 inches if area at least 1,300 square inches
  - o ceiling height minimum 80 inches over the entire minimum floor area
- doors and openings
  - o door should swing out; okay to swing in if also swings out
  - o clear opening size minimum 22 inches
  - o space in front of opening minimum 24 inches

- DWV
  - minimum 1½ inch P trap; maximum 6 feet fixture drain length (both often concealed)
    - current trap size per International Residential Code, enforcement depends on jurisdiction
  - minimum 2 inch trap, traditional size per Uniform Plumbing Code; maximum 8 feet fixture drain length (both often concealed)

> **Sinks**

- at least one sink in each kitchen and bathroom
- DWV
  - kitchen: minimum 1½ inch P trap; maximum 6 feet fixture drain length (both often concealed)
  - bathroom: minimum 1¼ inch P trap; maximum 5 feet fixture drain length (both often concealed)
  - sink drain outlet maximum 30 inches horizontally and 24 inches vertically from trap inlet
- overflow drain: not required, frequently installed in bathroom sinks
- drain stopper: not required, but strainer or crossbar required
- working space: minimum 21 inches in front

> **Typical defects**

- fixtures, fixture parts, or wall materials loose, damaged, deteriorated, rusted
- caulk absent or deteriorated, especially at tile seams
- whirlpool pump does not operate
- whirlpool pump access absent or too small
- whirlpool return jets do not move, absent; return cover absent
- shower/tub floor does not slope toward drain; puddles exist after water shut off
- shower area or dimensions too small; ceiling height too low
- fixture moves, inadequate support, not level
- DWV active leaks or leak evidence, leak evidence includes corrosion, rust, stains
- DWV slow drain, pipes blocked
- pop-up stopper does not move, does not retain water

Toilets, Clothes Washing Machines, Floor Drains

> **Bidets**

- inspect as a bathroom sink
- backflow preventer required if water source inside bowl

> **Toilets**

- types: gravity flush (common), power flush (uncommon), dual flush (standard water use flushing solids, less water use flushing liquids)
- flush valve assembly: flush arm, flapper valve, overflow tube
- fill valve assembly: float, fill valve(ballcock), fill tube
- water use: 1.6 gallons per flush since 1 January 1994; 5 gallons previous
- DWV

- o internal trap, no separate trap
    - o minimum 3 inch closet flange connection to drain pipe
    - o wax O-ring seals toilet base connection to closet flange
    - o caulk required around toilet base
  - **working space around toilet: minimum 21 inches in front, 15 inches on each side**

➢ **Clothes washing machine connections**
  - water supply: typically compression-type hose connection faucets
  - DWV: laundry sink or standpipe
  - standpipe
    - o minimum 2 inch pipe and trap
    - o pipe length minimum 18 inches, maximum 42 inches

➢ **Floor drains**
  - drain opening in floor, typically in basements; occasionally in bathroom and laundry room
  - DWV: minimum 2 inch P trap; maximum 8 feet fixture drain length (both concealed)

Backflow Prevention

➢ **Definitions**
  - **backflow**: flow of contaminated material into water distribution system
  - **back siphonage**: flow of contaminated material caused when water supply loses pressure and draws contaminated material into water supply by vacuum
  - **cross-connection**: an intentional or unintentional connection between water supply pipes and a contaminate source

➢ **Air gap**
  - vertical distance between water supply fixture and drainage fixture
  - air gap minimum distance: two times the supply fixture opening size

➢ **Backflow prevention device**
  - may be separate device or integrated into supply fixture
    - o device often integrated into clothes washing machines
  - several device types; required type depends on risk of backflow and type of contaminate
    - o example: toilet fill valve should have anti-siphon backflow preventer
      - ▪ locate preventer at least 1 inch above water in tank
  - provide access and protect device from freezing

➢ **Typical required locations in houses**
  - air gaps between: sink faucet and bowl, bathtub spout and tub, shower head and shower pan
  - high loop or vacuum breaker: dishwashing machines

- backflow prevention devices: clothes washing machine, hose connection, landscape irrigation system, swimming pool fill system, water feature fill system, hot water and steam heating fill system, water treatment system, fire sprinkler system, bidet

Water Treatment Devices

➢ **Water softeners**
- exchange minerals, such as iron, magnesium, calcium, with sodium
  - o minerals collect in pipes and appliances; can block pipes, especially galvanized steel, causing blockages
  - o minerals reduce soap effectiveness
- have no effect on water contaminates
- discharge should terminate into drain pipe through air gap or backflow prevention device
- discharge should not terminate into plumbing vent
- install electrical bonding jumper between metal pipes serving water softener

➢ **Water filters**
- types: mechanical filters, activated carbon, reverse osmosis
  - o mechanical filters remove sediment; others remove various types of contaminants, such organic compounds, heavy metals
- discharge termination same as water softeners

➢ **Typical defects, fixtures, backflow, water treatment**
- fixtures or fixture parts loose, damaged, deteriorated, rusted
- fixture moves, inadequate support
- active water leaks or leak evidence; leak evidence includes corrosion, rust, stains
- DWV active leaks or leak evidence; floor damaged under toilet
- flush valve leaks into bowl (ghost flushing)
- slow drain, pipes or traps blocked
- floor drain dry trap, sewer odors
- inadequate working space at fixture
- backflow prevention absent, improperly installed

Domestic Hot Water Systems

➢ **Definitions**
- thermal expansion: 50 gallons of water (size of typical water heater) expands about ½ gallon when heated
- thermal expansion tank/valve: device that gives expanded water in a water heater somewhere to go so the water does not damage plumbing components

➢ **Water heater types**
- storage tank (most common): water heated and stored in tank
- demand (tankless): water heated when needed, no storage tank
- provided by hydronic heating system

➢ **Fuel types**
- electric resistance
- electric heat pump
- gas, oil

➢ **Hot water temperature**
- recommended maximum 120° F.
- higher temperature causes burns, especially for children and elderly; uses more energy

➢ **Storage tank water heaters**
- components, all storage tank water heaters
  - tank: capacity 2½ to 100+ gallons; 40 – 50 gallons common
  - insulation: more insulation required in new units, replacement units may be too large for existing space
  - cold water inlet (dip tube): pipe runs to bottom of tank
  - hot water outlet: at top of tank
  - (sacrificial) anode rod: dissolves to protect tank from corrosion and leaks
  - drain valve: allows tank draining to remove sediment and extend tank life
  - temperature/pressure relief valve opening: at top or side of cabinet near top
- electric resistance water heaters
  - two heating elements
    - lower element activates first (where dip tube deposits cold water)
    - upper element activates when needed
    - lower element usually fails first; both elements can be replaced
    - each element controlled by thermostat; both can be replaced
  - usually 240 volt, 30 amp circuit
    - should have disconnect within sight of water heater
- electric heat pump water heater
  - installation per manufacturer's instructions
  - typical recommended air flow space: 700 – 1,000 cubic feet
  - typical recommended clearance: 2 – 7 inches side, 6 – 8 inches top
- gas and oil-fired water heaters
  - burner: at bottom of tank near center
  - flue: conducts combustion products from burner to vent
  - baffle: in flue, keeps combustion products in flue longer to increase efficiency
  - pilot light (gas)
    - thermocouple: shuts off gas if pilot light out
  - high limit sensor: shuts off gas if water temperature exceeds limit
  - flammable vapor ignition resistant (FVIR) combustion chamber required after 1 July 2003; most open combustion units have been replaced (gas)
  - draft hood (Category I units): see gas furnaces
  - direct vent (Category III and IV units): side vented
    - Category I unit occasionally improperly replaced with side vented unit

- ➢ **Demand (tankless) water heaters**
  - installation and maintenance per manufacturer's instructions
    - ○ regular heat exchanger cleaning/flushing required to maintain water flow rate
  - hot water temperature depends on water demand and input water temperature
    - ○ multiple fixtures simultaneous operation or low inlet water temperature may lower hot water temperature at fixtures below anticipated level

- ➢ **Temperature/pressure relief valves**
  - valve required for all water heaters, including demand and swimming pool heaters
    - ○ usually set to release at 150 psi or 210° F.
  - install valve so sensor is within maximum 6 inches of top of tank; no fittings between valve and tank

- ➢ **Temperature/pressure relief valves discharge pipe**
  - pipe approved for hot water, such as copper, CPVC, PEX
  - minimum diameter ¾ inch
    - ○ flexible water connectors not full ¾ inch, not allowed
  - slope pipe toward discharge point
  - terminate pipe minimum 1½ inches above floor, and maximum 6 inches above floor
  - no tee fittings or valves on pipe

- ➢ **Drain pan**
  - required if water heater leak could damage building components
  - pan should be drained to floor drain or to outside
  - pan not required for replacement unit if not required for original unit

- ➢ **Ignition elevation in garage**
  - ignition source (not bottom of tank) minimum 18 inches above garage floor
    - ○ ignition source includes electric water heating elements
  - elevation of FVIR water heater not required

- ➢ **Impact protection**
  - vehicle impact protection in garage required
    - ○ may be tire stop, bollard, framing

- ➢ **Seismic bracing**
  - bracing or anchoring against movement required in areas subject to earthquakes
  - straps located at upper and lower ⅓ of cabinet and attached to framing

- ➢ **Thermal expansion devices**
  - required at storage tank water heaters if cold water supply closed
    - ○ closing devices include check valve, pressure reducing valve, some water meters
  - may be a tank or a valve drained to receptor, or to outside

➢ **Typical defects**
- active leaks, or leak evidence, at cabinet, pipes, water connectors, valves
  - leak evidence includes corrosion, rust, stains
- cabinet or combustion chamber damaged, deteriorated, rusted, scorched
- cabinet moves, poorly supported; not braced in seismic areas
- water heater not impact protected
- water heater ignition source not elevated in garage when required
- dielectric fitting not installed between copper and steel pipes and fittings
- water temperature exceeds 120° F.
- temperature/pressure relief valve or discharge pipe improperly installed
- plastic pipe connected to gas water heater at fittings
- water heater noisy when operating; possible sediment at bottom of tank
- electric heating elements not operating (usually lower element)
- electric heating element wattage different than wattage on water heater label
- PEX too close to draft hood (less than 6 inches), or too close to top of water heater (less than 18 inches); distances depend on PEX and water heater manufacturer's instructions

Drain, Waste, Vent Pipes

➢ **Protection requirements**
- same as water supply/distribution pipes

➢ **Acrylonitrile Butadiene Styrene (ABS)**
- use: interior DWV, building sewer, water service (uncommon)
- history: 1960s – present, use regional
- service life: 50+ years
- known problems: some pipes made between 1985 – 1990 by some manufacturers split along pipe seams
- support: maximum 4 feet horizontal; 10 feet vertical; mid-story guide 2 inch diameter and smaller
- fittings: solvent cement, primer not required; threaded Schedule 80 (uncommon)
- fitting connections to other pipe types: banded/elastomeric coupling; transition cement (common but not code approved); adapter fitting to PVC (uncommon)

➢ **Cast iron**
- use: interior DWV, building sewer
- history: 1850s – present, uncommon since 1960s
- service life: 50 years
- **known problems**: rusts from inside and leaks; rusts from inside and outside when used as building sewer; rough on inside, traps debris causing more frequent blockage
- support: maximum 10 feet horizontal, 5 feet from fitting; 15 feet vertical
- fittings: hub and spigot with caulked or compression joint, banded/elastomeric coupling
- fitting connections to other pipe types: banded/elastomeric coupling

➢ **Clay sewer pipe**
- use: building sewer
- history: ancient times – present, uncommon since 1950s
- service life: pipe 100 years if not crushed; mortar joint seals 30 years
- known problems: breakage, stoppage by plant roots
- fittings: hub and spigot sealed with mortar

➢ **Galvanized steel**
- use: interior DWV, water service (uncommon)
- history: 1860s – 1960s, uncommon since 1960s
- service life: 50 years
- **known problems**: rusts from inside and leaks; rough on inside, traps debris causing more frequent blockage
- support: maximum 12 feet horizontal, 15 feet vertical; no copper supports
- fittings: threaded
- fitting connections to other pipe types: banded/elastomeric coupling

➢ **Orangeburg sewer pipe**
- use: building sewer, use regional
- history: 1940s – 1970s, mostly 1950s – mid 1960s; many failed, already replaced
- service life: 30 - 50 years
- **known problems**: deterioration and collapse, blockage by plant roots; replacement recommended

➢ **Polyvinyl Chloride (PVC)**
- use: interior DWV, building sewer, water service
  - SDR35 (green) PVC only building sewer; not allowed inside foundation
- history: 1960s – present, use regional
- service life: 50+ years
- known problems: none
- support: maximum 4 feet horizontal; 10 feet vertical; mid-story guide 2 inch diameter and smaller
- fittings: solvent cement, primer usually required, but primer-less type available; threaded Schedule 80 (uncommon)
- fitting connections to other pipe types: banded/elastomeric coupling, transition cement (both common but not code approved); adapter fitting to ABS (uncommon)

➢ **Lead**
- use: DWV, building sewer, water service; no longer allowed, should be removed
- history: Roman era – 1970s; uncommon since 1930s
- service life: 40 – 50 years
- known problems: highly toxic, but lower risk than potable water pipes

➢ **Sewer pipe repair**
- bursting: break existing pipe, pull new pipe behind
- sliplining: coat existing pipe with liquid such as PVC
- cured-in-place: coat existing pipe with epoxy
- typically used with non-collapsed pipe, such as cast iron

Drain, Waste, Vent Fittings

➢ **Pipe slope**
- drain and waste pipes slope toward building sewer, including at fittings
    - 3 inch diameter and smaller minimum ¼ inch per foot
    - more than 3 inch diameter minimum ⅛ inch per foot
    - too much slope may allow solids to accumulate and cause blockages
- vent pipes
    - slope not specified; ⅛ inch per foot recommended to drain rain water and condensation

➢ **Pipe direction change**
- direction change types
    - horizontal to vertical: high water velocity, most fittings allowed
    - vertical to horizontal: lower water velocity, only specific fittings allowed
    - horizontal to horizontal: low water velocity, few fittings allowed

➢ **Pipe fitting types**
- bends, drainage: 90°, 60°, 45°, 22½°; allowed for most direction changes
    - exception: short turn 90° bends not allowed horizontal to horizontal
- bends, vent: not allowed in drainage pipes; very short turn
- sanitary tee: allowed only for horizontal to vertical change
- wyes and tee-wyes: allowed for most direction changes
- 90° bends with inlets: allowed use depends on fitting orientation

➢ **Saddle fittings, drilling pipes**
- saddle fitting: clamps on to pipe; punctures hole in pipe; not allowed
- drilling hole in pipe: drilling holes in pipes not allowed; pipe connections should use approved fitting

➢ **Cleanouts**
- opened to clear pipe blockages
- cleanout openings: capped pipe fittings, traps with slip joints, toilets
- general location rule: not more than 100 feet between cleanout openings
- specific location rules
    - maximum 10 feet from junction of building drain and building sewer, near foundation wall
    - every 100 feet in all horizontal pipes, including building sewer
    - near where horizontal pipe changes direction more than 45°
- access in front of opening minimum 18 inches

Traps and Fixture Drains

➢ **Definitions**
- trap: device that keeps sewer gas from entering the building by maintaining water seal in trap
- fixture drain: pipe between trap outlet and vent connection
- sewer gas: methane and other contaminates; offensive odor; unsanitary; fire hazard
- slip joint: removable connections at trap inlet and outlet

➢ **Trap types**
- allowed: P trap, bottle trap (depends on jurisdiction)
- no longer allowed, but may remain if originally installed
  - S trap, common at sinks in older houses
  - drum trap, common at bathtubs in older houses
  - bell trap, uncommon at floor drains in older houses
  - building trap, uncommon in older houses

➢ **P trap installation**
- water seal minimum 2 inches, maximum 4 inches
- install level so trap does not drain
- trap maximum 30 inches horizontally or 24 inches vertically from fixture drain outlet
- one trap per fixture; no separate trap at toilet
- slip joint connection allowed only at accessible traps

➢ **Fixture drain installation**
- see individual plumbing fixture for trap size and fixture drain length
- fixture drains longer than maximum more likely to siphon trap and lose water seal
- distance between trap and vent minimum 2 pipe diameters, crown venting

Plumbing Vents

➢ **Definitions**
- air admittance valve: valve used in place of atmospheric vent
  - check (cheater) vent: spring-loaded valve that looks like air admittance valve but approved only for manufactured homes
- atmospheric vent: plumbing vent open to air; usually terminates on roof; every building should have at least one
- vent system: equalizes air pressure in DWV pipes to avoid siphoning trap water seal; every trap should be protected by a vent

➢ **Vent terminations**
- minimum 6 inches above roof, or above snow accumulation depth
- minimum 10 feet horizontally from operable window or mechanical air intake opening
- minimum 3 feet above or 4 feet below operable window

- air admittance valve: minimum 4 inches above drain being vented, 6 inches above insulation; maximum 15° from vertical
- vent terminations should not support other components, such as antennae, flags

➤ **Typical defects, pipes, fittings, traps, and vents**
  - trap not level
  - trap water seal less than 2 inches or more than 4 inches deep
  - trap type not allowed
  - active leaks, or evidence of leaks; leak evidence includes corrosion, rust, stains
  - pipe or fittings damaged, deteriorated, rusted
  - pipe or fitting inadequate support, improper support material, or improperly sloped
  - improper fitting used to connect different pipe types
  - check vent installed in building
  - improper vent termination height or location
  - cleanout absent where required
  - inadequate working space at cleanout
  - PVC electrical conduit used as DWV pipe

Private Sewage Disposal Systems

➤ **Definitions**
  - private sewage disposal system: system on private property that accumulates plumbing waste, breaks down waste in tank, disperses liquid waste into earth; solid waste must be removed (pumped) from tank
  - public sewer: system accumulates plumbing waste from many buildings, processes waste in central locations, disperses liquid waste into a body of water
  - percolation (perc): ability of liquid waste to flow through soil; sand percs well, clay percs poorly; septic systems need good percolation to function properly

➤ **Septic system types**
  - gravity: waste flows into below grade drain field by gravity
  - powered: waste pumped into below grade drain field
  - mound: waste flows by gravity into built-up hill of sand and gravel to begin percolation; used where soil does not percolate well

➤ **Septic system components**
  - **tank**: concrete, fiberglass, plastic; microbes in tank begin breaking down waste material
  - **drain (leach, absorption) field**: plastic pipe with holes that distributes liquid waste into soil; pipe placed in trenches filled with gravel; trench length and width depends on tank size and system type
  - **soil:** absorbs liquid waste; microbes in soil remove most remaining contaminates
  - **pump:** used by powered systems to distribute liquid waste into drain field

➤ **Septic system maintenance**
  - put only biodegradable materials into system; chemicals, such as bleach, kill microbes; nonbiodegradables increase pumping frequency

131

- solids in tank must be removed by pumping; pumping frequency depends on system use; filter, if any, must be cleaned or replaced
- drain filed service life 20 – 40+ years, depending on soil type and system use

Sewage Ejectors, Sump Pumps, Backwater Valves

➤ **Definitions**
- backwater valve: check valve installed in building drain to prevent flow from public sewer into building; required when plumbing fixture below nearest upstream public sewer access cover
- sewage ejector: vessel (sump, crock) and pump that pumps liquid and solid waste into DWV pipes; required when building sewer pipe above building drain pipes
- sump pump: vessel (sump, crock) and pump that pumps ground water or storm water away from building

➤ **Sewage ejector**
- fixtures served by ejector: only fixtures below building drain
- sump pit: size minimum 18 inches diameter by 24 inches deep; accessible sealed lid
- discharge pipe type: most DWV pipes; minimum size 2 inches; full open valve and check valve required
- vent pipe (atmospheric): minimum size 1¼ inch; air admittance valve not allowed
- power: per manufacturer's instructions; usually 15 or 20 amp, 120 volt, GFCI circuit

➤ **Sump pump**
- sump pit: size minimum 18 inches diameter by 24 inches deep; lid not required
- discharge pipe: pipe type: most DWV pipes; flexible hoses not allowed, but common; check valve required (newer requirement)
- power: per manufacturer's instructions, usually 15 or 20 amp, 120 volt, GFCI circuit

➤ **Typical defects**
- pump does not operate, operates improperly, unusually noisy, moves when activated
- improper discharge or vent pipe size or type
- absent check valve or full open valve on ejector discharge pipe
- absent check valve on sump pump discharge pipe
- leak or overflow, or evidence of leak or overflow, at pit or pipes
- absent, damaged, poorly sealed ejector pit lid
- absent backwater valve where required

Fuel Storage and Distribution Systems - General

➤ **Fuel types**
- gas, natural (methane): utility provided; meter belongs to utility; fuel gas code applies after meter; US DOT regulations apply before meter
- gas, propane: onsite storage; fuel gas code applies beginning where gas pipe enter building; NFPA 58 applies before pipe entry
- fuel oil: onsite storage; residential code applies to all components

Gas Pipes, Connectors, Valves

➤ **Black steel**
  - wall thickness: minimum Schedule 40
  - support, horizontal: maximum 6 feet ½ inch pipe; 8 feet ¾ and 1 inch pipe; 10 feet 1¼ inch and larger; no copper supports (galvanic corrosion)
  - fittings, threaded: joint compound or **yellow** tape at joints; white tape for water
  - fittings connections to other pipe types: threaded; no connection to copper tubing unless dielectric fitting used

➤ **Copper tubing**
  - types: rigid (drawn); flexible coiled (annealed)
  - wall thickness: all have same outside diameter
    - K: thickest, green markings
    - L: middle thickness, blue markings
    - M: thinnest, red markings; not allowed for gas
  - support, horizontal: maximum 4 feet ½ inch pipe; 6 feet ¾ and 1 inch pipe; 8 feet 1¼ inch and larger; no steel supports (galvanic corrosion)
  - fittings: threaded; braised; flared or compression (annealed); joint compound or **yellow** tape at threaded joints
  - fittings connections to other pipe types: threaded; no connection to iron or steel pipes unless dielectric or brass fitting used; white tape for water
  - labeling: yellow label GAS every 5 feet

➤ **Corrugated stainless steel tubing (CSST)**
  - description: flexible stainless steel in polyethylene sheathing; diameter ½ - 1½ inch
    - common sheathing colors: yellow, black, orange; color usually identifies bonding requirement (yellow usually bond, black usually bonding not required)
  - support: per manufacturer's instructions; typical instructions horizontal maximum 6 feet ½ inch pipe; 8 feet ¾ inch and larger
  - fittings: supplied by manufacturer
  - fittings connections to other pipe types: per manufacturer's instructions
  - bonding: per manufacturer's instructions; typical #6 AWG copper wire from first CSST fitting to grounding electrode system

➤ **Flexible appliance connectors (FAC)**
  - description: flexible stainless steel or brass in polyethylene sheathing; connects gas pipe to appliance
    - 1970s era brass-colored FAC may leak, should be replaced
  - installation: per manufacturer's instructions; typical restrictions, FAC may not
    - enter appliance cabinet
    - pass through walls, floors, ceilings
    - be buried
    - be bent so radius smaller than 1½ inch
    - be too tight, should move 1 – 2 inches
    - be connected together

➢ **Sediment traps and drip legs**
  - sediment trap: keeps debris from entering gas appliance
    - gas leaves trap at 90° angle to trap nipple
    - required at gas appliances, such as water heaters and furnaces
  - drip leg: keeps moisture from entering gas appliance
    - gas leaves trap at 180° angle to trap nipple
    - required at gas appliances only where wet gas is present (very uncommon)

➢ **Gas valves**
  - required valves
    - building shutoff: after gas meter; usually at propane tank
    - appliance shutoff: maximum 6 feet from appliance in same room
      - see gas appliances for exceptions
    - valve should be approved for use with gas

➢ **Protection**
  - same as water pipes, except freeze protection not required
  - installation in floors: run in ventilated sleeve; sleeve often DWV pipe

➢ **Burial**
  - depth minimum 12 inches, except 8 inches for outdoor gas lights and grills

➢ **Prohibited locations**
  - HVAC supply and return ducts, chimneys and chimney chases, laundry chutes

➢ **Gas meters and regulators**
  - installation per utility instructions
  - typical distance to **regulator** minimum 3 feet to: operable windows and doors, ignition sources, such as switches and receptacles, electrical panels, air conditioning condensers

➢ **Propane tanks**
  - types
    - permanent: above ground or buried; 500 – 2,000 gallons
    - cylinder: fixed location; 500 – 1,000 gallons
    - exchange cylinder: portable, 25 gallons or less, no location restrictions
  - location, permanent tank
    - above ground: minimum 10 – 25 feet from building and property line, depends on tank size; minimum 10 feet to ignition source
    - below ground: minimum 10 feet from house and ignition source
  - location, cylinder: minimum 10 feet from ignition source

➢ **Typical defects**
  - active leaks
  - pipe or fittings damaged, deteriorated, rusted

- pipe or fitting inadequate support, improper support material, inadequate protection
- improper fitting used to connect different pipe types
- absent or improper joint sealant at pipe fitting
- absent, damaged, deteriorated shutoff valve
- CSST improperly installed, **not bonded**
- flexible gas connector improperly installed
- copper gas pipe not labeled
- improper propane tank location, support
- propane tank damaged, deteriorated, rusted
- absent, improperly installed sediment trap

Oil Pipes, Connectors, Tanks

➢ **Common pipe/connector types**

- ⅜ copper Types K or L (most common)
- steel or brass allowed (uncommon)
- flexible metallic connectors approved for oil

➢ **Pipe systems**

- one-pipe: oil supply only; best when tank above burner and pipe at or below burner
- two-pipes: oil supply, return pipe for excess oil and air

➢ **Pipe installation**

- accessible manual shutoff valve required; often at tank or where pipe enters building
- automatic fire shutoff valve (Firematic, a brand name) required in some jurisdictions
- pipe should be supported and protected from damage; how undefined

➢ **Oil tanks**

- maximum capacity 660 gallons
- location
  - if inside: minimum 5 feet from burner
  - if buried: minimum 5 feet from property line, 1 foot from foundation, covered by 1 foot of soil
- tank should have oil level gauge
- tank not located under electrical service drop
- tank protected from damage, snow, water, freezing; how undefined
- underground tank fill and vent pipes minimum 2 feet from building openings; fill pipe equipped with tight metal cover
- abandoned underground tanks: out of scope to determine presence; disclaim inspection
  - good practice to look for visible fill or vent pipes near foundation, or patched holes in foundation wall

➢ **Typical defects**

- active leaks or leak evidence, leak evidence includes corrosion, rust, stains, odor
- pipe or fittings damaged, deteriorated, rusted
- pipe or fitting inadequate support, improper support material, inadequate protection
- absent, damaged, deteriorated shutoff valve
- flexible connector improperly installed
- improper tank location, support
- tank damage, deterioration, rust, especially at tank bottom
- evidence of abandoned underground tank
- absent fill or vent caps

Unit 11: Interior Components

Topics covered in this Unit include:

- **Knowledge Areas**
- **Habitable Rooms**
- **Walls and Ceilings**
- **Interior Doors and Windows**
- **Floor Coverings**
- **Stairways, Guards, Handrails**
- **Cabinets and Countertops**
- **Kitchen Appliances**
- **"Smart Home" Technology**

Knowledge Areas

➢ **Knowledge areas in-scope of a home inspection and in-scope of the exam**

- walls, ceilings, floors
- stairways and railings (addressed in Exterior Unit – decks)
- cabinets and countertops
- kitchen appliances

➢ **Knowledge areas out-of-scope of a home inspection but in-scope of the exam**

- "smart home" technology

➢ **Inspection scope – interior**

- in scope: defects that adversely affect ability of component to perform its intended function, and defects likely caused by other in scope defects, such as structural defects
- out of scope: cosmetic defects, such as expected wear and tear

Habitable Rooms

➢ **Definition**

- **habitable rooms**: rooms used for living, sleeping, eating, and cooking
- **not habitable rooms**: bathrooms, hallways, closets, storage rooms, utility rooms

➢ **Habitable room requirements**

- ceiling height minimum 7 feet in habitable rooms and hallways
- ceiling height minimum 80 inches in bathrooms, laundry rooms, and basements without habitable rooms
  - o requirements for habitable rooms in basements same as other habitable rooms
- habitable room dimensions minimum 7 feet and 70 square feet, except kitchen
- habitable rooms should have
  - o operable window, or ventilation air from outside provided by HVAC system

- o light from a window or electric light
- o permanently installed heat source capable of maintaining 68° F.
- closet not required in a sleeping room

Walls and Ceilings

➢ **Drywall**
- also called gypsum board, plasterboard, Sheetrock® (a brand name)
- types
  - o white board: drywall with light grey or cream-colored paper, general use
  - o green board: moisture-resistant drywall; no longer allowed around showers and bathtubs with shower
  - o Type X: fire-resistant drywall, ⅝ inch thick
  - o less common: mold-resistant, sound-resistant
- sheet size
  - o 4 feet wide; 8, 10, 12 feet lengths common
  - o ½ inch thick standard; ¼ and ⅜ inch thick for curved walls
- installation
  - o nailed or screwed to framing; adhesive recommended, not required
  - o corners reinforced with metal or plastic corner bead
  - o finishing: tape and bed seams, corners, and fasteners, skim to smooth, sand
  - o textured finishes (optional): popcorn, knock-down
    - ▪ finishes before 1970s may contain asbestos

➢ **Plaster (interior)**
- more common before 1950s; replaced by drywall
- materials: lime, gypsum, or cement, mixed with sand, binder (such as animal hair or fiberglass), and water; applied over wood or gypsum lath
- installation: three coats, scratch, brown, finish; total thickness about ⅞ inch

➢ **Wood**
- typical 4x8 foot panels about ¼ inch thick; dimensional lumber, various sizes

➢ **Suspended (drop) ceilings**
- most often in basements
- metal grid suspended by wires attached to framing; fibrous tiles (panels) inserted into grid
  - o panels before 1970s may contain asbestos

➢ **Interior trim (molding)**
- conceals space between wall covering and windows, doors, floor coverings
- decorative
- types (many other types and styles)
  - o base: conceals space between wall and floor coverings
  - o quarter-round, shoe molding: conceals space between base and floor coverings

- chair rail: decorative; applied near middle of wall
- casing: conceals space between wall coverings and windows and doors
- stop: applied around wood windows to secure sash, around doors to stop door from further closing
- crown: decorative; applied at intersection of wall and ceiling

➢ **Wall covering and trim defects**
- fastener pops: dimple or exposed fastener, fastener works loose from framing
  - almost always cosmetic; common in new buildings when wood framing shrinks due to wood drying
  - repair by resetting fastener, apply drywall joint compound (mud), sand, paint
- cracks and separation (drywall, plaster, moldings)
  - thin cracks usually cosmetic; caused by building movement and wood shrinking
    - most common locations: at corners of windows and doors, room corners, wall/ceiling intersection, sharp angles, drywall seams
    - repair by applying drywall mud, sand, paint
    - cracks may recur, especially in newer building, or if cause not addressed
  - wide cracks, cracks that increase in width, or cracks that recur after repair may indicate more serious issues
    - especially if accompanied by sticking windows and doors, visibly unlevel floors and ceilings, or walls not plumb or square
    - important to determine and repair crack cause before crack repair
    - cracks at intersection of wall and ceiling that appear in winter and disappear in summer may be caused by truss uplift; a cosmetic issue; difficult to repair
  - separation of moldings from wall usually cosmetic
    - typical causes: normal caulk deterioration, or poor nailing
    - may be more serious if accompanied by other defects, such as moisture stains and wall covering cracks
- moisture stains
  - common causes: roof leaks, leaks around windows and doors, condensation in wall and ceiling cavities, plumbing supply and DWV pipes leaks, condensate pipe leaks and condensation, HVAC evaporator leaks, HVAC duct condensation
  - out of scope to determine cause; report stain and recommend evaluation
- damage, deterioration, waviness, bulging
  - repair, if practical, depends on cause

Interior Doors and Windows

➢ **Doors and windows – general**
- see exterior components for exterior doors and windows, including typical defects for all doors
- interior window inspection includes operation of at least one window per room and visual inspection at and around windows
- safety glazing requirements apply to exterior and interior doors

➢ **Hinge-type doors**

- door swings on hinges, usually at least 90°; usually swings into room, may swing out
- types: single door (slab); double door, one or both slabs operable
- dimensions: usually 80 inches high; widths 12 – 72 inches, 2 inch increments
- typical materials: solid wood, engineered wood with hollow core; fiberglass
- door parts: hinge and lock jambs (vertical), rails (horizontal), mullion (center), hinges
- installation: set door frame plumb and square in rough opening; shim as needed to achieve even ⅛ inch space between door and frame; fasten; seal wood on all sides to reduce shrinking and swelling caused by moisture
- locks: privacy (lockable) and passage (no lock)

➢ **Sliding-type doors**

- doors move horizontally on tracks
- types
  - sliding door: slides on top track; usually two operable slabs
  - pocket door: slides on top track into openings in wall; one or more operable slabs
  - bifold door: moves on top track, rotates on top and bottom supports at cased opening; two operable slabs
- dimensions: usually 80 inches high; widths 12 – 72+ inches
- typical materials: solid wood, engineered wood with hollow core, fiberglass
- door parts: tracks, rollers, support for bottom of bifold door
- installation: set plumb and square in rough opening; shim as needed; fasten; seal wood on all sides to reduce shrinking and swelling caused by moisture
- locks: privacy (lockable) and passage (no lock)

Floor Coverings

➢ **Inspection scope**

- many floor covering defects are cosmetic, out of scope
- some defects, such as cracks through tile and stone and water damage, could indicate structural defects, water intrusion, or other in scope defects
- some defects can create safety issues, such as trip and slip hazards

➢ **Carpet, wall-to-wall**

- types: usually 12 foot wide rolls, sometimes wider; peal-and-stick squares
- installation
  - should be allowed to acclimate in conditioned space before installation; almost never done
  - should be applied over a pad for better wear
- typical problems often due to poor installation or improper cleaning (too much water)
  - shrinkage, pulling away from walls; swelling, ripples; visible seams (difficult to avoid with some carpet types); wear at transitions between floor coverings (no transition piece)

- ➤ **Laminates, engineered wood, natural wood**
  - laminates and engineered wood are manufactured products made to look like other materials, such as wood and tile
    - ○ cannot be sanded and refinished; repair of minor damage sometimes possible
  - natural wood may be hardwood, such as oak or maple, or softwood, such as pine
    - ○ can be sanded and refinished
  - installation per manufacturer's instructions: should be allowed to acclimate in conditioned space before installation; seldom done; usually install over vapor retarder, sometimes over a pad
  - typical problems; may be due to poor installation
    - ○ shrinkage, pulling away from walls or separating at seams between pieces; splitting, too little moisture; swelling, ridges between pieces, cupping, too much moisture, no vapor retarder
    - ○ same problems can be due to poor humidity control in building

- ➤ **Linoleum and vinyl**
  - types: 12 foot wide rolls; peal-and-stick squares
  - these are vapor retarders; installation above damp crawlspace or damp concrete slab may result in discoloration caused by fungi
  - installation per manufacturer's instructions
  - typical problems; often due to poor installation
    - ○ shrinkage, pulling away from walls and separating at seams between pieces; swelling, ridges between pieces; showing subfloor defects, failure to install over smooth subfloor

- ➤ **Tile and stone**
  - types: ceramic tile, Saltillo (terra cotta clay), granite, marble, slate, travertine (limestone); many sizes and shapes
    - ○ some types are slippery and should not be on floors, such as glazed ceramic tile
  - floor framing should deflect less than allowed for other floor coverings because tile and stone can crack if subfloor moves
  - typical problems; often due to poor installation or subfloor deflection
    - ○ grout cracks, cosmetic unless wide spread or grout absent; cracks through tile and stone, will recur unless cause addressed; hollow sound under tile or stone, uneven subfloor or improper application of adhesive

Stairways, Guards, Handrails

- ➤ **General**
  - stairway, guard, and handrail rules vary significantly between jurisdictions and over time
    - ○ decision whether and how to report issues depends on safety concerns
  - interior stairways, guards, and handrails same as for decks

Cabinets and Countertops

➢ **Cabinet types and materials**

- kitchen base: supported on floor, secured to wall; typical depth 24 inches; width between 9 – 36 inches; height 36 inches with countertop
- bathroom base: supported on floor, secured to wall; typical depth 18 – 22 inches; width 18 – 36 inches; height 31 – 36 inches with countertop
- wall: secured to wall; typical depth 12 inches; width 12 – 36 inches; about 18 inches above countertop
- filler strip: often required in corners to allow doors and drawers to open without impacting knobs or handles of perpendicular cabinets or appliances
- drawer guides (slides): various quality from plastic guides to metal with soft closing springs
- door and drawer knobs and pulls: various quality and styles
- typical materials
  - backs, sides, bottoms: plywood, particleboard, MDF
    - all easily damaged by moisture
  - front plate, doors, drawers: wood, plywood with laminate covering, MDF

➢ **Cabinet installation**

- cabinets and countertops should be level and plumb
- secure to walls using typical #8x2½ inches screws; screws should have washer or button head, no drywall screws or nails

➢ **Countertops**

- typical materials
  - laminate: plywood or particleboard with thin plastic cover; easily damaged; difficult to repair
  - solid-surface: acrylic and polyester resins; easily damaged; minor damage repairable
  - granite and marble: resistant to cuts and burns, easy to stain; regular sealing required to avoid staining; minor damage repairable
  - quartz: quartz dust and resins; resistant to cuts and stains, easy to burn; minor damage repairable
  - tile: difficult to keep grout clean; resistant to most damage; cracked tile replacement difficult to match color
  - cultured marble (bathrooms): marble dust and polymers; easily damaged; minor damage repairable

➢ **Countertop installation**

- secure countertop to base cabinet; method depends on cabinet and countertop type
- seams should not be near sink to avoid water damage, especially laminate
- extra support may be required for countertops that cantilever past base cabinet, especially thin granite and marble
- caulk between countertop and separate backsplash, and around sink to avoid water damage

➢ **Typical defects**

- loose cabinets and countertops, especially loose wall cabinets
- improper fasteners, especially wall cabinets
- damage and deterioration, especially water damage in sink base cabinet
- loose doors and drawers
- doors and drawers do not operate as intended
- doors and drawers strike perpendicular cabinets or appliances
- absent door and drawer pulls and handles (not all cabinets have these)
- material seam near sink, especially laminate
- sharp countertop edges
- inadequate support under cantilevered countertops

Kitchen Appliances

➢ **Inspection scope**

- in scope appliances vary between Standards of Practice
- inspection scope applies to appliances listed in the Standard of Practice
  - if appliance not listed, not in scope
- typical in scope appliances, permanently installed: range, cooktop, wall oven, microwave oven, exhaust hood, dishwasher, food waste disposer
- typical out of scope appliances: refrigerator, freezer, clothes washer and dryer, trash compactor (included in some Standards of Practice)
- inspection includes operating primary appliance functions

➢ **Cooktop, range, oven**

- important inspection points
  - condition of interior, burners, heating elements, doors, seals
  - presence of anti-tip bracket on ranges
- typical inspection operation
  - all burners, bake function

➢ **Dishwashing machine**

- important inspection points
  - condition of interior, door, seals, area under machine
  - presence of high loop or air gap device
- typical inspection operation
  - one wash/dry cycle

➢ **Microwave oven and exhaust hood**

- important inspection points
  - condition of interior, door, seals
  - condition and type of visible exhaust duct, filters, lights
- typical inspection operation
  - microwave heats water
  - operation of exhaust fan and light

➢ **Food waste disposer**
  - important inspection points
    o condition of exterior; no rust, leaks, leak evidence
    o discharge pipe above drain connection
    o presence of directional fitting
  - typical inspection operation
    o normal sound while operating, no unusual vibration of disposer or sink

➢ **Typical defects and inspection points, all appliances**
  - nothing inside that could be damaged during operation
  - condition of visible electrical, water supply, drain, and fuel connections
  - unusual movement, not level, not adequately attached to cabinet or countertop
  - does not function, or functions inadequately, using normal controls
  - damaged, deteriorated, missing parts such as knobs, racks, trays
  - door binds, scrapes, strikes cabinets, does not remain open
  - inadequate clearance to combustibles
  - inadequate clearance in front or above for safe use
  - near end of service life

"Smart Home" Technology

➢ **Smart home definition**
  - internet, wi-fi, Bluetooth, ZigBee, or similarly connected devices that allow remote control of devices, remote sensing of devices, and may allow devices to communicate with each other
  - no generally accepted definition of the term "smart home"

➢ **Typical components**
  - reliable high-speed internet connection required for most devices
  - router: connects devices to internet; connection may be wired, 5G wireless, satellite
  - hub: enables devices to communicate; hub may be incorporated into router, or hub may communicate with router
  - cable: connects router to internet service provider network in wired systems; typical RG-6 or better coaxial cable; Cat-5e or better cable
  - antenna: roof-mounted often required for satellite; may be required for reliable 5G service
  - range extender: may be required for devices too far away from router to communicate with router

➢ **Typical devices**
  - security systems, including door and window sensors, cameras, motion detectors, smoke alarms, locks
  - entertainment devices, such as televisions, speakers
  - HVAC thermostats
  - smart speakers, allow voice inquiries and control of some devices
  - appliances, such as refrigerators, coffee makers, ranges
  - receptacles and switches, for control of lights and power to devices
  - sensors, such as water flow

➤ **Issues**

- privacy/hacking: data collection and sale of data by vendors and hackers; identity theft
- interoperability: no accepted protocol for communication between devices
- obsolescence: technology and standards in flux; devices may become obsolete, especially if support for their communication protocol or for the device itself is discontinued

➤ **Inspection considerations and limitations**

- **inspection of "smart home" systems and devices is out of scope of all known home inspection Standards of Practice**
- attempts to inspect these systems and devices in resale homes may be hampered by security codes, lack of access to control devices, and similar limitations
- **some of these devices are personal property and may not convey with the property**
- operating these devices risks changing settings, damaging the devices, and damaging property
- **inspectors should disclaim inspection of these systems** and devices in inspection agreement and in report; recommend evaluation by a specialist

Unit 12: Fireplaces, Fuel-burning Appliances, Chimneys, Vents

Topics covered in this Unit include:

- **Knowledge Areas**
- **General – Solid Fuel Fireplaces and Chimneys**
- **Masonry Fireplaces**
- **Masonry Chimneys**
- **Factory-built Fireplaces and Chimneys**
- **Fireplace Inserts**
- **Wood-burning Stove**

Knowledge Areas

➤ **Knowledge areas in-scope of a home inspection and in-scope of the exam**

- solid-fuel-burning fireplaces, appliances, chimneys, vents
- gas and liquid-fuel-burning fireplaces, appliances, chimneys, vents (see Unit 3, Heating Systems)

General – Solid Fuel Fireplaces and Chimneys

➤ **Definitions**

- corbel: increase masonry chimney width; masonry course above extends past course below
- fireplace: system burns solid fuel, usually wood; system includes firebox, chimney, hearth, and hearth extension
  - ○ applies to site-built and factory-built (prefabricated) fireplaces and chimneys
- hearth: floor of fireplace where fuel burned
- hearth extension: noncombustible area in front of fireplace; protects against fires caused by embers that escape from firebox
- pyrolysis: reduction of wood ignition temperature caused by exposure to high temperature; creates fire risk, even if fireplace/chimney has existed for decades
- racking: decrease masonry chimney width; masonry course below extends past course above
- Rumford fireplace: fireplace with taller opening and narrower hearth than standard fireplaces; uncommon

➤ **Combustion air**

- combustion air opening and duct to outdoors required for masonry fireplaces; newer requirement, many fireplaces do not have these
  - ○ specifications for factory-built fireplaces per manufacturer's instructions
- outdoor opening may be in ventilated attic or crawlspace
  - ○ cover opening with ¼ inch screen

- interior opening located inside firebox or within 24 inches of firebox
- opening size minimum 6 square inches, maximum 55 square inches

➢ **Cricket (saddle)**
- **cricket**: part of roof that diverts water away from an obstruction, such as a chimney
- required when chimney more than 30 inches wide where it intersects roof
    - applies to masonry chimneys and framed chimney chases
- integrate into roof covering and flashed as appropriate for roof covering and chimney materials

➢ **Creosote**
- creosote: combustion product created by burning unseasoned (wet) wood, inadequate combustion air, problems that cause cool chimney temperatures
- types (degrees): first degree, black or brown soot; second degree, black flakes; third degree, tar-like substance
    - all degrees are fire hazards, third degree most serious

➢ **Rain cap and spark arrestor**
- rain cap limits water intrusion into chimney
- spark arrestor limits escape of embers from chimney
- neither required, except spark arrestor in some wildfire-prone areas

➢ **Abandoned chimneys**
- present water intrusion and maintenance issues; recommended removal to below roof line, removal not required

➢ **Draft issues**
- smoke stains above and around firebox opening could indicate issues causing combustion gasses to fall into building instead of being expelled by chimney
    - typical causes: inadequate combustion air, chimney too cool; flue too large; chimney too short or not far enough above roof; room where fireplace located depressurized

➢ **Inspection limitations**
- inspection limited to visible areas; many areas not visible
- NFPA Level II inspection recommended when building sold

Masonry Fireplaces

➢ **Components**
- footing (fireplace and chimney): solid concrete or masonry; minimum 12 inches thick, extends minimum 6 inches beyond all parts of firebox and chimney
- hearth: solid concrete or masonry; minimum 4 inches thick, 20 inches deep; no combustible materials under hearth

- hearth extension: solid concrete or masonry; minimum 2 inches thick; no combustible materials under hearth extension; no space between hearth and hearth extension
  - dimensions if opening less than 6 square feet: minimum 16 inches in front and 8 inches on each side of firebox opening
  - dimensions if opening 6 square feet or more: minimum 20 inches in front and 12 inches on each side of firebox opening
- firebox walls: solid or fully grouted masonry, concrete, or stone; minimum 8 inches thick if lined with 2 inch thick firebrick, or 10 inches thick if no firebrick
  - refractory mortar thickness maximum ¼ inch
- doors: required at firebox opening; should fit tightly and open and close freely; newer requirement, many fireplaces do not have these
- lintel: spans firebox opening, supports material above opening; usually steel
  - should extend minimum 4 inches on each side of firebox opening
- damper: closes flue to prevent air entry when fireplace not used; locate in throat or at top of flue; should fit tightly, open and close freely
- throat: opening between firebox and smoke chamber; locate minimum 8 inches above lintel
  - minimum 4 inches deep and minimum area same as flue area
- smoke chamber: directs combustion products into flue; should be covered with mortar and be smooth
- cleanout (ash dump): opening in fireplace floor where ashes can be disposed; cleanout door minimum 6 inches tall, noncombustible, tight seal; no combustible material in cleanout area

➢ **Clearances to combustibles**

- framing and wall coverings: minimum 2 inches fireplace sides, 4 inches rear
- **combustible trim (such as mantel): minimum clearance above and at sides of firebox opening**
  - minimum 6 inches, all trim
  - trim between 6 and 12 inches, minimum 1 inch clearance for each ⅛ inch of trim thickness or depth
    - example: maximum mantel leg thickness at 10 inches from firebox opening 1¼ inches (10 x ⅛)

Masonry Chimneys

➢ **Materials**

- solid masonry (bricks), cored masonry with grout-filled cores, concrete, stone
- chimney thickness minimum 4 inches
- minimum one wythe masonry between multiple flues in same chimney

➢ **Construction**

- corbel: use solid or grout-filled core masonry
  - maximum corbel: ½ masonry height and ⅓ masonry depth
- racking: no limits

- no size or shape change within 6 inches above or below where chimney passes through floor, ceiling, or roof
- flue liner: typical clay liner manufactured for masonry chimneys
  - extend liner minimum 4 inches, maximum 6 inches above chimney cap
  - leave about ¾ inch space between liner and chimney wall
  - fill joints between liner sections with refractory mortar; mortar should not protrude into flue
  - liner should be smooth, no cracks or gaps
  - old chimneys not required to have clay liner; use may continue if safe, NFPA Level II (minimum) inspection recommended
- relining flues: use liner approved for intended use, such as burning wood, gas, oil; install per manufacturer's instructions; post a permanent notice if flue relined
- flue may not be shared with another fireplace, or with any appliance
- seismic reinforcing required in earthquake-prone areas

➢ **Chimney height above roof**

- **terminate masonry and factory-built chimneys minimum 3 feet above roof and minimum 2 feet from any obstruction within 10 feet horizontally**
  - measure at high side of roof

➢ **Chimney cap (crown)**

- materials: concrete, metal, stone; mortar not allowed (but frequently used)
- slope to drain water
- thickness minimum 2 inches at any point
- extension beyond chimney walls minimum 2½ inches
- leave bond break between liner and cap; fill with flexible sealant

➢ **Typical defects masonry fireplaces and chimneys**

- chimney inadequate clearance to roof or obstructions
- chimney or fireplace masonry or mortar absent, deteriorated, spalled, cracked, efflorescence
- chimney cap improperly built, absent, deteriorated, cracked, rusted, holding water
- clay chimney liner absent, cracked, gaps between sections, not smooth
- manufactured chimney liner improperly installed
- chimney or firebox inadequate clearance to combustible framing and trim
- smoke stains around chimney or firebox
- chimney or firebox active water intrusion or evidence of water intrusion
- creosote, especially second and third stage
- chimney supports structural loads, such as antennas
- firebox doors damaged, deteriorated, do not operate freely
- masonry with open cores
- absent fireblocking
- absent or improperly installed outside air (newer requirement)
- more than one appliance or fireplace connected to a flue
- chimney leaning

Factory-built Fireplaces and Chimneys

➢ **General**

- more common than masonry fireplaces since 1970s
- components intended to work as a system; not allowed to mix components from different manufacturers
- installation per manufacturer's instructions, which vary between manufacturers and models

➢ **Components**

- cabinet, metal: typical clearance to combustibles 0 – ½ inch
- refractory panels, metal: at sides and rear of firebox
  - o hairline cracks in panels normal
  - o cracks ¼ inch or wider, run through the entire panel, or panel deterioration may be reportable
- damper: should open and close easily
- hearth extension: same rules as masonry fireplace

➢ **Clearances to combustibles**

- combustible trim (such as mantel) minimum 6 inches sides, 12 inches above
- typical minimum 12 inches to perpendicular walls, 48 inches to wall in front

➢ **Chimney**

- chimney: double wall galvanized steel
- typical minimum 2 inches clearance to combustibles, including insulation
- typical height minimum 15 feet
- typical non-vertical offset maximum 20 feet long at maximum 30° angle to vertical
- unsupported projection above roof or chase maximum 6 feet
- height above roof: same as masonry chimneys
- shrouds (covers): should be approved by fireplace manufacturer for use with specific chimney and fireplace

➢ **Typical defects, factory-built fireplaces and chimneys**

- defects that are not masonry-specific apply to factory-built fireplaces and chimney
- framed chase not strapped to framing; moves when pushed
- chimney too short; offset too long or too shallow
- fireplace visible from attic; absent or inadequate fireblocking

Fireplace Inserts

➢ **General**

- appliance installed in masonry fireplace; typically burns wood or wood pellets
- installation per manufacturer's instructions, which vary between manufacturers and models
- vented using manufacture-approved metal vent system
  - may be vented directly into chimney if approved by insert manufacturer

➢ **Typical defects**

- refractory panels cracked or deteriorated; hairline cracks normal
- door or gasket damaged or deteriorated; does not close or latch as intended
- inadequate clearance to combustibles
- vent or vent connector, if any, damaged, deteriorated, rusted, improperly installed
- soot around insert or at vent termination
- creosote build up

Wood-burning Stove

➢ **General**

- free-standing appliance that burns wood or wood pellets (pellet stove)
- installation per manufacturer's instructions, which vary between manufacturers and models
- installation information, including clearances to combustibles, should be available on stove label, if present and visible
- flue (stove) pipe single-wall steel; typical instructions
  - minimum 26 gauge for 6 inches or smaller diameter; minimum 24 gauge for larger than 6 inches
  - secure using minimum 3 sheet metal screws or similar
  - slope horizontal sections up minimum ¼ inch per foot
  - do not penetrate floors or ceilings; do not run in attic
  - minimum 18 inches clearance to ceilings horizontal sections
  - height above stove minimum 15 feet
  - maximum non-vertical offset includes two 90° elbows
  - unsupported projection above roof or chase maximum 6 feet
  - height above roof: same as masonry chimneys

➢ **Typical defects**

- same as fireplace inserts

Unit 13: Life Safety Equipment and Systems

Topics covered in this Unit include:

- **Knowledge Areas**
- **Fire Safety and Occupancy Separation**
- **Smoke Alarms and Carbon Monoxide Alarms**

Knowledge Areas

➤ **Knowledge areas in-scope of a home inspection and in-scope of the exam**

- egress requirements (see Unit 2, Exterior Components)
- fire safety and occupancy separation requirements
- smoke alarms and carbon monoxide alarms

➤ **Knowledge areas out-of-scope of a home inspection but in-scope of the exam**

- fire suppression systems

Fire Safety and Occupancy Separation

➤ **Fireblocking**

- **slows vertical spread of fire** in walls and horizontal spread of fire in concealed open spaces; improves energy efficiency by reducing air flow between conditioned and unconditioned spaces
  - not same as draftstopping
- required in concealed vertical spaces, such as wall cavities, and chases for HVAC ducts, appliance vents, and chimneys
- required in concealed horizontal spaces longer than 10 feet, such as double framed walls, drop soffits, and large framed openings
- required where pipes and wires penetrate top plates
- common fireblocking materials: nominal 2 inch thick lumber, ¾ inch wood panels ½ inch thick drywall, mineral wool or fiberglass batts, fire-resistant caulk and foam

➤ **Draftstopping**

- **slows horizontal spread of fire** in open area between usable spaces
  - not same as fireblocking
- required when open area more than 1,000 square feet has usable space above and below
  - most common open areas are floor trusses and suspended ceilings
  - most common usable spaces are stories above basements, first stories, habitable attics; not first stories above crawlspaces
- most common draftstopping materials are ½ inch thick drywall and ⅜ inch thick plywood or OSB
- divide draftstopped areas in approximately equal areas not more than 1,000 square feet

152

➢ **Fire separation between garage and house**
- minimum ½ inch thick drywall on garage side of wall and garage attic ceiling
- minimum ⅝ inch thick Type X drywall on garage side of ceiling if habitable space above garage
- minimum 20-minute fire-rated door between garage and house, with self-closing hinges and self-latching lock
- metal or duct board HVAC ducts between garage and house; no flexible duct
- no HVAC supply or return openings in garage, unless HVAC system serves only garage
- fire-rated door required on pull-down stairs to attic above garage
- door from garage to house may not open into a bedroom

➢ **Fire separation between townhouse units**
- townhouse: a single family attached dwelling with all of following: public area on at least two sides, three or more dwellings in one building, dwelling goes from foundation to roof
- minimum 2 hour firewall between dwellings extending from foundation to roof
- parapet wall extending minimum 30 inches above roof, or non-combustible roof covering plus fire-retarding material minimum 4 feet on each side of firewall

➢ **Foam plastic materials**
- foam plastic materials: foam plastic sheet insulation, such as XPS and EPS, and spray foam insulation
- exposed materials most often in attics, crawlspaces, and unfinished garages
- thermal barrier covering exposed foam plastic may be required if equipment, such as a furnace or water heater, present
  - thermal barrier materials include ½ inch thick drywall
- ignition barrier covering exposed foam plastic may be required where no equipment is present
  - ignition barrier materials include ⅜ inch thick drywall and ¼ inch thick wood panels
- numerous additional requirements and exceptions

Smoke Alarms and Carbon Monoxide Alarms

➢ **Smoke alarm types**
- photoelectric: best at detecting smoky fires; slightly less responsive to flaming fires
- ionization: better at detecting flaming fires; much less responsive to smoky fires
- combination: combines photoelectric and ionization in one unit

➢ **Smoke alarm installation requirements**
- inside every sleeping room
- near every sleeping room (distance not defined)
- minimum one alarm on each story, including basement and habitable attic
- not recommended in attics, crawlspaces, garages, near combustion appliances, and high humidity areas, such as laundry rooms and bathrooms, near windows and fans
- alarm located minimum 10 feet from cooking appliance

- minimum 4 inches from wall when installed on ceiling
- maximum 12 inches from ceiling when installed on wall
- minimum (typical) 3 feet from air movement device, such as ceiling fan or HVAC supply register
- interconnection of alarms required; may be wired or wireless
- connection to building power and battery backup required

> **Carbon monoxide alarm installation**
- minimum one alarm in house with fuel-burning appliance, including fireplace, or attached garage
- inside sleeping room with fuel burning appliance in room or in attached bathroom
- not recommended in attics, crawlspaces, garages, near combustion appliances, and high humidity areas, such as laundry rooms and bathrooms, near windows and fans
- interconnection of alarms required; may be wired or wireless
- connection to building power and battery backup required

Section 1 Test: Property and Building Inspection

Select the BEST answer

1.1.1   Which components are used to reduce retaining wall rotation?

    a. 60d nails
    b. Concrete footings
    c. ½ inch diameter lag screws
    d. Deadmen and tiebacks

1.1.2   Soil should slope away from the foundation at least

    a. ¼ inch per foot within the first 20 feet.
    b. 6 inches within the first 10 feet.
    c. ½ inch per foot within the first 12 feet.
    d. 10 inches within the first 15 feet.

1.1.3   What provides the primary support for a driveway?

    a. Reinforcing steel
    b. Welded wire mesh
    c. Soil
    d. Control joints

1.1.4   A fence surrounding a swimming pool should be at least ___ inches above the walking surface.

    a. 40
    b. 45
    c. 48
    d. 52

1.1.5   Construction of a retaining wall may require a building permit under which condition?

    a. Wall is more than 4 feet tall.
    b. Wall retains material other than soil.
    c. Wall is not supported by a concrete footing.
    d. Wall is made from concrete blocks.

1.1.6   Which is an example of a vegetation condition that a home inspector should report?

    a. Plant that may grow too large for the space where it is located
    b. Plant not recommended for the climate zone where it is located
    c. Tree branches hanging over the building
    d. Dead tree that is far from the building

1.1.7   Which insect is attracted when moisture is near a building foundation?

    a. Wasps
    b. Bedbugs
    c. Hornets
    d. Termites

1.2.1   Wood-based siding should be installed at least how many inches above soil?

a. 2
b. 4
c. 5
d. 6

1.2.2   Which component provides the primary barrier to water intrusion into an exterior wall?

a. House wrap
b. Extruded polystyrene sheathing
c. Hardboard panel siding
d. Adhered masonry veneer

1.2.3   The building egress door should have how many inches of clear opening width?

a. 30
b. 32
c. 36
d. 40

1.2.4   Safety glazing is required in a window when one single piece of glazing is more than 9 square feet, the glazing is within 36 inches horizontally of a walking surface, and the bottom of the glazing is less than ___ inches above the walking surface.

a. 12
b. 18
c. 24
d. 30

1.2.5   A handrail is required at deck stairs when there are ___ or more risers.

a. 2
b. 3
c. 4
d. 5

1.2.6   While the vehicle door is operating, a garage door operator pressure reverse sensor should cause the vehicle door to open when

a. the door strikes a 1 inch thick object.
b. the door strikes someone's hands.
c. someone walks under the door.
d. a 4 inch wide object is placed under the door.

1.2.7   Weep holes in brick veneer should be located how many inches apart?

a. 29
b. 33
c. 37
d. 41

1.3.1   Some roofs are described as flat roofs. A flat roof should slope at least __ inch per foot toward water discharge points

   a. 0
   b. $^1/_{16}$
   c. ⅛
   d. ¼

1.3.2   Which is a waterproof roof covering?

   a. Standing seam metal panels
   b. Asphalt shingles
   c. Metal shingles
   d. Wood shakes

1.3.3   Which is a likely cause of ice dams?

   a. More than two layers of roof covering
   b. Leaks in attic HVAC ducts
   c. Inadequate insulation in walls below the attic
   d. Type B gas vent is too long

1.3.4   When are gutters required?

   a. Annual rainfall exceeds 20 inches.
   b. Roof slope exceeds 8/12.
   c. Expansive soil is present.
   d. Foundation is a basement.

1.3.5   Water may remain on a low slope roof up to ___ hours.

   a. 24
   b. 30
   c. 42
   d. 48

1.3.6   Where is kick out flashing required?

   a. A wall extends past a roof
   b. A chimney penetrates a roof
   c. At the end of a roof valley
   d. On both sides of a shed roof

1.3.7   What is the recommended way to apply counterflashing at a brick wall above a roof?

   a. Fasten the counterflashing to the bricks with roofing nails
   b. Adhere the counterflashing to the mortar with roofing cement
   c. Fold the counterflashing into a groove cut into mortar
   d. Install the base flashing and counterflashing behind the brick wall

1.3.8   What must be done to a polyurethane foam roof covering within three days after applying the foam?

a. Cut grooves into the foam toward water drainage points
b. Apply an ultraviolet-resistant coating on the foam
c. Sand the foam to remove high spots
d. Wash the foam with a weak acid solution

1.4.1   A building on the United States south Atlantic coast should be built to resist _____ that may be applied.

a. wind forces
b. earthquake forces
c. flooding forces
d. any forces

1.4.2   Which moisture management components are required if basement space is usable?

a. Dmpproofing and a foundation drain
b. Waterproofing and a foundation drain
c. Dampproofing and a sump pump
d. Waterproofing and an ejector pump

1.4.3   A notch at the end of a dimensional lumber floor joist should not be larger than_____

a. ⅛ of the nominal joist depth.
b. ¹/₆ of the actual joist depth.
c. ¼ of the actual joist depth.
d. ⅓ of the nominal joist depth.

1.4.4   A soffit at a kitchen ceiling creates an open area that is 25 feet long. This soffit should be_____ within the open area.

a. draftstopped at 12½ feet
b. fireblocked at 10 and 20 feet
c. draftstopped at 15 and 22 feet
d. fireblocked at 12½ feet

1.4.5   What should be installed on the garage ceiling if there is habitable space above a garage?

a. ½ inch thick drywall
b. ½ inch thick plywood
c. ⅝ thick Type X drywall
d. ¾ inch thick drywall

1.4.6   A hole drilled in a non-load-bearing stud should be not more than _____

a. 25% of the nominal stud depth.
b. 40% of the actual stud depth.
c. 50% of the nominal stud depth.
d. 60% of the actual stud depth.

1.4.7   Which roof style is triangle-shaped with rafters and ceiling joists forming the triangle?

    a. Gable
    b. Hip
    c. Shed
    d. Mansard

1.4.8   What is the minimum size of a purlin if the rafter it supports is a 2x8?

    a. 2x4
    b. 2x6
    c. 2x8
    d. 2x10

1.5.1   Why is a building's electrical system grounded?

    a. System will not function without a connection to the earth
    b. Provides an alternate return path for electricity
    c. Electricity flows through the earth
    d. Prevents electric shock during a ground fault

1.5.2   What is a characteristic of multiwire branch circuits?

    a. Arc fault circuit interrupter protection is required
    b. They are required on 240 volt circuits
    c. Two energized wires share one neutral wire
    d. They originate from at least two overcurrent devices

1.5.3   Service drop wires should be at least ___ feet above a walking surface.

    a. 7
    b. 10
    c. 12
    d. 18

1.5.4   Where is a ground fault circuit interrupter protected circuit required?

    a. Crawlspace
    b. Attic
    c. Finished basement
    d. Bedroom

1.5.5   What action is required when installing a neutral wire as an energized wire?

    a. Increase the neutral wire size by one AWG number
    b. Install a neutral wire at receptacles
    c. Provide ground fault circuit interrupter protection on the circuit
    d. Label the wire as energized at accessible locations

1.5.6   A light switch is required at the top and bottom landings of a stairway with ___ or more risers.

    a. 2
    b. 4
    c. 6
    d. 8

1.5.7   What is a function of the equipment grounding wire?

   a. Provides an additional path for normal current flow
   b. Connects devices to the earth
   c. Prevents electric shock during a ground fault
   d. Conducts static electricity away from devices

1.5.8   What is required when a subpanel in a detached building is supplied by a four-wire feeder?

   a. Install a grounding electrode system
   b. Bond neutral and equipment grounding wires together
   c. Use a subpanel rated at least 50 amps
   d. Provide electricity to the subpanel using UF cable

1.5.9   Where is the first place an inspector should look to find the maximum allowed overcurrent device for a 5 ton air conditioning condenser?

   a. In the National Electrical Code
   b. On the condenser label
   c. At the condenser's appliance disconnect
   d. In the homeowner's instruction manual

1.6.1   A ton of refrigeration is how many Btu?

   a. 2,000
   b. 8,000
   c. 12,000
   d. 16,000

1.6.2   What is the component in which only gas flows between the evaporator and compressor?

   a. Suction tube
   b. Condensate tube
   c. Capillary tube
   d. Condenser fin tube

1.6.3   The inspector observes icing at the evaporator. Which is the most likely cause?

   a. Circuit breaker ampacity too high
   b. Deteriorated suction line insulation
   c. Refrigerant overcharged
   d. Blocked air filter

1.6.4   Condensate from an evaporator may be discharged into a plumbing _____

   a. fixture drain.
   b. floor drain.
   c. vent.
   d. trap.

1.6.5   Which is a prohibited HVAC return location?

    a. Kitchen
    b. Bedroom
    c. Habitable attic
    d. Dining room

1.6.6   A compressor is part of _____

    a. an evaporator.
    b. a condenser.
    c. a furnace.
    d. hot water boiler.

1.7.1   Which is produced when natural gas burns completely?

    a. Carbon
    b. Nitric acid
    c. Carbon monoxide
    d. Water vapor

1.7.2   Which is the most likely cause of a yellow flame in a natural gas-fired water heater?

    a. The vent system is too long
    b. There is insufficient combustion air
    c. The anode rod has deteriorated
    d. The temperature/pressure relief valve is not working

1.7.3   Which is a safety system in a gas furnace?

    a. Draft sensor
    b. Aquastat
    c. Fire eye
    d. Pressuretrol

1.7.4   What is the required distance between a Type L vent and insulation?

    a. 1 inch
    b. 2 inches
    c. 3 inches
    d. 4 inches

1.7.5   Which is a safety system for a steam boiler?

    a. Air scoop
    b. Aquastat
    c. Expansion tank
    d. Hartford loop

1.7.6   Which is a normal operating pressure for a hot water boiler?

    a. 2 psi
    b. 8 psi
    c. 12 psi
    d. 16 psi

1.8.1   The U-value of a material is the amount of ___ that can pass through a material.

   a. water vapor
   b heat
   c. light
   d. electricity

1.8.2   Which is a type of thermal insulation?

   a. Polyisocyanurate
   b Polyvinyl chloride
   c. Polyethylene
   d. Ethylene propylene diene terpolymer

1.8.3   Batt and loose-fill insulation must be in contact with _____ in order to achieve its rated R-value.

   a. a vapor retarder
   b gypsum board
   c. Kraft paper
   d. an air barrier

1.8.4   Which is a common source of water vapor inside a house?

   a. Electric water heaters
   b Occupant smoking
   c. Occupant breathing
   d. Hot water radiators

1.8.5   What percentage of attic ventilation openings should be near the ridge?

   a. 30 – 39%
   b 40 – 50%
   c. 51 – 60%
   d. 61 – 70%

1.8.6   Which is required in an unventilated (closed) crawlspace?

   a. A dehumidifier
   b Insulation between floor joists
   c. An air barrier at crawlspace walls
   d. A vapor retarder on the bottom of floor joists

1.9.1   Which is a risk posed by clothes dryer exhaust ducts?

   a. Fire
   b Water damage
   c. Carbon monoxide poisoning
   d. Mold exposure

1.9.2   Which material may be used when installing a kitchen exhaust duct under a concrete slab?

   a. Galvanized steel
   b PEX
   c. Copper
   d. PVC

1.9.3   A bathroom exhaust duct may terminate ____

   a. inside the eaves.
   b above the roof.
   c. in a ventilated crawlspace.
   d. in a ventilated attic.

1.9.4   A clothes dryer exhaust duct should terminate ___ feet from an operable window.

   a. 2
   b 3
   c. 5
   d. 6

1.9.5   An energy recovery ventilation system extracts ___ from ventilation air in cooling mode.

   a. water vapor
   b oxygen
   c. carbon dioxide
   d. ozone

1.9.6   What is the maximum developed length of a clothes dryer exhaust duct?

   a. 25 feet
   b 30 feet
   c. 35 feet
   d. 40 feet

1.10.1   The maximum allowed water pressure in a house is ___ psi.

   a. 60
   b 70
   c. 80
   d. 90

1.10.2   Which is a common problem with galvanized steel water distribution pipe?

   a. Galvanic corrosion
   b Conducts electricity
   c. Lead poisoning
   d. Low water flow

1.10.3   What is the minimum dimension of a shower with an area of 1,000 square inches?

a. 25 inches
b   30 inches
c. 32 inches
d. 34 inches

1.10.4   Which type of backflow prevention would one typically find at a lavatory?

a. vacuum breaker
b   reduced pressure
c. air gap
d. check valve

1.10.5   What component in a water heater dissolves to protect the water tank?

a. Anode
b   Dip tube
c. Baffle
d. Thermocouple

1.10.6   A 3 inch diameter drain pipe should slope at least how many inches per foot?

a. $^1/_{16}$
b ⅛
c. ¼
d. ⅜

1.10.7   Which is a currently permitted type of plumbing trap?

a. P
b   S
c. Bell
d. Drum

1.11.1   Which is a habitable room?

a. Hallway
b   Storage room
c. Bathroom
d. Kitchen

1.11.2   A dark brown stain is observed at a wall/ceiling intersection under a bathroom. The most likely cause of this stain is _____

a. a plumbing water supply leak.
b   a leak at the roof.
c. a leak at a window.
d. unknown.

1.11.3   In which situation is safety glazing required in or near an interior door?

a. A transom above the door
b   A divided light door
c. Stained glass in the door
d. Cut glass in the door

1.11.4   When inspecting a range, which component should be inspected?

a. Self-cleaning function
b Clock operation
c. Anti-tip bracket operation
d. Oven temperature accuracy

1.11.5   Which is a typical component in a "smart home?"

a. A set-back thermostat
b A hub
c. Category 2 wiring
d. RG-58 coaxial cable

1.12.1   Where would one find the fireplace hearth?

a. On the floor of the firebox
b In front of the firebox
c. At the sides of the firebox
d. At the top of the firebox

1.12.2   A chimney should terminate at least ___ feet above any obstruction within 10 feet.

a. 1
b 2
c. 3
d. 4

1.12.3   How many inches should a hearth extension extend in front of a fireplace with a firebox opening of 5 square feet?

a. 12
b 14
c. 16
d. 20

1.12.4   Which is the most likely cause of creosote in a chimney?

a. Providing too much combustion air
b Burning preservative-treated wood
c. Using a flue that is too small
d. Burning unseasoned wood

1.12.5   Combustible trim should be at least how many inches from a masonry fireplace opening?

a. 6
b 8
c. 10
d. 12

1.12.6 Which is a defect in a masonry fireplace or chimney?

    a. A 21 inch deep hearth
    b An unlined chimney
    c. Bricks with open cores
    d. A 20 inch deep hearth extension

1.12.7 One flue may serve how many fireplaces or appliances?

    a. 1
    b 2
    c. 3
    d. 4

1.13.1 A window opening should be limited to 4 inches if the bottom of the window opening is how many inches above the floor?

    a. 18
    b 24
    c. 30
    d. 32

1.13.2 How many egress doors are required in a house?

    a. 1
    b 2
    c. 3
    d. All doors

1.13.3 A landing on the exterior side of a 32 inch wide door should be how many inches deep in the direction of travel?

    a. 30
    b 32
    c. 36
    d. 42

1.13.4 The roof sheathing of a townhouse should be covered by a fire-retarding material for at least ___ inches on each side of the common wall between units?

    a. 36
    b 42
    c. 48
    d. 54

1.13.5 Type X drywall is required on a garage ceiling when ___

    a. a gas furnace is above the garage.
    b a flexible HVAC duct penetrates the garage ceiling.
    c. a combustion appliance vent penetrates the garage ceiling.
    d. habitable space is above the garage.

1.13.6 An attic access opening in a garage should be covered with at least ___

    a. ¾ inch thick oriented strand board.
    b ½ inch thick drywall.
    c. ⅝ inch thick plywood.
    d. 1 inch thick medium density fiberboard.

1.13.7 Where are carbon monoxide alarms required to be installed?

    a. Inside a sleeping room containing a fuel-burning appliance
    b Inside every sleeping room
    c. One on each story of a house
    d. In an attached garage

Section II: Analysis of Findings and Reporting

Unit 1: Inform Client What Was Inspected

Unit 2: Inspection Limitations

Unit 3: Reporting Defective Systems

Unit 4: Reporting Systems That Need Additional Evaluation or Action

Unit 1: Inform Client What Was Inspected

Topics covered in this Unit include:
- **Knowledge Areas**
- **Information Required in Inspection Reports**
- **Description Statements**
- **Inspection Methods and Procedures**
- **Test Instruments**

Knowledge Areas

➢ **Knowledge areas in-scope of a home inspection and in-scope of the exam**

- information required in inspection reports
- description statements
- inspection method descriptions
- common instruments and proper use

Information Required in Inspection Reports

➢ **Standards of Practice (SoP)**
- **required inspection procedures, report contents, and ethics code governed by the SoP used by inspector**
  - ○ requirements in different SoPs similar, but vary in details
- home inspectors in states **that license** home inspectors should use the SoP and ethics code specified by the state license authority
- home inspectors in states **that do not license** home inspectors should use the SoP and ethics code adopted by the professional association to which they belong, if any

➢ **Home inspection definition**
- **visual inspection** of specified systems and components, such as roof coverings
- **operation** of specified systems and components, such as HVAC systems
- **written reporting** inspection findings and recommendations to client

➢ **Home inspection objective**
- provide client with information about the condition of inspected systems and components at the time of inspection
  - ○ provide information so that a reasonable person may understand it

➢ **Home inspection report required contents**
- defect statements
  - ○ what was defective; implication of the defect; what action should client take
- descriptions of components and systems mandated in the SoP
- descriptions of methods used to inspect attic, crawlspace, roof

- limitation statements
  - report the reason why a required system, component, or procedure was not inspected or performed

Description Statements

- ➤ **Description statement purposes**
  - help client know about systems and components that were present
  - help client know how attics, crawlspaces, and roofs were inspected

- ➤ **Description statement general contents**
  - **describe in sufficient detail that allows reader to distinguish between described system, component, and inspection method and similar systems, components, and inspection methods**
  - describe all types and materials present and inspection methods used if more than one

- ➤ **Structural component descriptions**
  - foundation type and materials
    - typical types: slab on grade, slab on stem wall, crawlspace, basement
      - describe post-tensioned slab if present and visible
    - typical materials: concrete masonry units (blocks), concrete, precast concrete panels, bricks, stone
  - floor, ceiling, roof materials; describe materials for each system
    - typical materials: dimensional lumber (wood), wood trusses; I-joists, plywood, oriented strand board (OSB)
      - describing material size not required

- ➤ **Exterior wall covering materials descriptions**
  - typical materials: adhered masonry veneer, stucco, brick, natural stone, concrete masonry units (blocks), hardboard siding, plywood panel, fiber cement, wood plank (board and batten), wood shingles and shakes, EFIS, aluminum, vinyl

- ➤ **Roof covering materials descriptions**
  - typical materials: asphalt (fiberglass) shingles, concrete or clay tile, metal panels, metal shingles, slate, wood shingles and shakes, modified bitumen, mineral-surfaced roll roofing, built-up (BUR), spray foam, EDPM

- ➤ **Plumbing descriptions**
  - water distribution pipe materials
    - typical materials: copper, CPVC, PEX, galvanized steel, polybutylene
  - DWV pipe materials
    - typical materials: ABS, PVC, cast iron, galvanized steel, clay sewer
  - domestic hot water equipment type and energy source
    - typical types: storage tank, demand (tankless), tankless coil

- o typical energy sources: natural gas, propane, electricity, oil
- building water shutoff and fuel shutoff valve locations
  - o describe in sufficient detail to allow client to locate valves
    - do not test or operate valves; may leak or break

> **Electrical descriptions**
- service current
  - o typical service current (amps): 100, 125, 150, 200, 400
    - do not speculate; recommend electrician evaluation if uncertain
- predominant branch circuit wiring method
  - o typical wiring methods: NM cable, UF cable, AC (armored) cable, SE (service entrance) cable, LFC (liquidtight) conduit, ENT (non-metallic) tubing, PVC conduit, IMC (metal) conduit, knob-and-tube
    - recommended reporting cloth-covered NM cable and knob-and-tube because both are at end of service life, and because of insurance issues
- service panel and subpanel locations
  - o describe in sufficient detail to allow client to locate panels
- presence or absence of smoke alarms and carbon monoxide alarms
  - o inspecting and testing not required

> **Heating descriptions**
- heating equipment type and energy source
  - o typical types: forced-air furnace, split heat pump, package heat pump, mini split heat pump, through-wall heat pump, hot water, steam, floor furnace, wall furnace
  - o typical energy sources: natural gas, propane, electricity, oil

> **Cooling descriptions**
- cooling equipment type and energy source
  - o typical types: air conditioner, split heat pump, package heat pump, mini split heat pump, through-wall heat pump, evaporative cooler
  - o typical energy sources: natural gas, propane, electricity, oil

> **Insulation and vapor retarder type descriptions**
- report absence of insulation or vapor retarder where required
- typical insulation types: loose fill fiberglass, cellulose, mineral wool, vermiculite, perlite; batts, fiberglass, cellulose, mineral wool; EPS, XPS sheets; spray foam
- typical vapor retarder types: Kraft paper, polyethylene sheets, building paper (felt), paint

> **Fuel-burning appliance type descriptions**
- typical types: masonry or prefabricated wood-burning fireplace; wood-burning stove; wood pellet-burning stove; vented or unvented decorative gas or oil appliance (fireplace); gas logs installed in wood-burning fireplace; log lighter; fireplace insert

Inspection Methods and Procedures

➤ **Definitions**

- dismantle: procedure or action that a homeowner would **not** take during normal operation or maintenance
- inspect: **visually** examine required systems and components that are **installed** and **readily accessible**, operate required systems and components using **normal operating controls**, open **readily openable access panels**
- installed: set in position, ready for use, removal requires tools
- normal operating controls: devices intended for homeowner use, such as switches, faucets, and thermostats
- readily accessible: available for visual inspection without dismantling, or requiring procedures that may harm people or property
- readily openable access panel: panel provided by the manufacturer that homeowner would open or remove during normal maintenance, that is within normal reach, and not sealed
- shut down: system or component operation not possible using normal operating controls, such as closed fuel supply valve or electricity supply turned off
- technically exhaustive: procedures that involve dismantling, or use of techniques, instruments, measurements, or specialized knowledge

➤ **Typical inspection methods and procedures**

- operate exterior doors and a representative sample interior doors and windows
- operate water faucets and valves, such as at sinks and hose bibbs
  - exceptions: not required to operate manual stop valves and fixture shut-off valves
- operate water heating equipment by running hot water at faucets
- operate sewage ejectors and sump pumps using normal operating controls, if any
- operate a representative sample of electrical switches, lights, receptacles
- open readily openable HVAC equipment access panels
- operate HVAC equipment
- operate garage vehicle doors and operators
- operate specified kitchen appliances
- operate exhaust fans
- operate fuel-burning appliances that do not require manual ignition, such as using a match

➤ **Inspection methods and procedures descriptions**

- typical attic and crawlspace inspection methods: attic/crawlspace entered, inspected from service platform, inspected from access hatch, not inspected (and why not)
  - describe areas not inspected
- typical roof covering inspection methods: walked on roof, inspected from ground using binoculars, inspected from ladder, inspected using a drone, not inspected (and why not)
  - describe areas not inspected
  - describe all methods used

Test Instruments

➢ **Use of test instruments**

- home inspections are visual; use of test instruments is not required by SoPs
  o test instrument use may increase risk by setting client expectations beyond a visual inspection
    ▪ set client expectations in writing in report and inspection agreement
  o test instrument use may be common practice
    ▪ local standard of care could determine if and how inspector should use a test instrument; and if and how inspector should report findings

➢ **Three-light receptacle tester**

- common in all markets
- detects some electrical receptacle wiring defects, such as hot/neutral reversed, ungrounded, no power
- entering and removing tester can detect physically loose receptacles
- limitations
  o cannot detect multiple wiring errors, such as neutral and ground terminals connected (bootleg ground)
  o GFCI test button may not provide accurate test of GFCI receptacle function; use of test button on receptacle recommended

➢ **Circuit analyzer**

- uncommon in most markets
- detects multiple receptacle and branch circuit defects; defect types detected depend on device design and cost

➢ **Voltage detector**

- also called voltage sniffer, tick tracer (from ticking sound made when voltage present)
- common in most markets
- detects presence of voltage; used as safety device to avoid contact with energized wires
- limitation: does not determine if device or circuit is functioning properly

➢ **Multimeter (clamp on)**

- common in many markets
- measures voltage, current, resistance, other circuit characteristics depending on device design and cost
- used to measure current draw at air conditioning condensers and electric water heater
- limitation: condenser amp draw does not, by itself, demonstrate that system is functioning properly

➢ **Moisture meter**

- common in many markets
- measures moisture content of wood; may measure moisture content of other materials depending on device design and cost
- types

- o pin: measures resistance between pins to determine moisture content of wood
- o pinless: uses radio frequency energy to determine moisture content of materials
- o probe: similar to pin; long probes measure moisture content of materials deeper inside of walls, especially EFIS
  - limitations
    - o measurement depth of pin and pinless 1 inch or less
    - o inaccurate results possible if meter improperly calibrated or used
    - o best used to confirm visual evidence of moisture

➤ **Infrared thermometers and cameras**
- thermometers common in most markets; cameras uncommon
- measures temperature of object without contact with object
- thermometers commonly used to measure temperature at HVAC supply and return water temperature
- cameras commonly used to determine presence of moisture, lack of insulation, hot electrical components
- limitations
  - o measures temperature at object surface; does not detect temperature inside the object; cannot see inside objects
  - o thermometer accuracy declines with distance from object
  - o accuracy affected by object's infrared emissivity
    - more accurate with dull black objects; less accurate with shiny bright objects
  - o inaccurate results possible if device improperly calibrated or used
  - o training required to use an infrared camera, and to interpret the findings

➤ **Probe thermometers**
- common in most markets
- measures temperature when in contact with object
- commonly used to measure temperature drop across evaporator coil

➤ **Combustible gas detectors**
- uncommon in many markets
- detects presence and/or amount of combustible gasses, usually methane and propane
- commonly used to detect gas leaks

➤ **Carbon monoxide (CO) detectors**
- uncommon in many markets
- detects presence and/or amount of carbon monoxide
- commonly used to detect defects such as heat exchanger leaks, combustion defects, vent system defects

➤ **Metal detector**
- uncommon in most markets
- detects presence of metal inside materials such as wood
- commonly used to detect roof sheathing fasteners when performing wind mitigation inspections

➢ **Drones (unmanned aerial vehicles)**
- uncommon in most markets
- detects defects where it is difficult or dangerous for inspector to go
- commonly used to inspect roofs, upper stories of multi-story buildings
- limitations
  - FAA license required to use drone on inspection
  - weather, especially wind, can restrict safe use
  - fine detail can be difficult to see; important details may go undetected

Unit 2: Inspection Limitations

Topics covered in this Unit include:

- **Knowledge Areas**
- **Inspection Limitations**

Knowledge Areas

➢ **Knowledge areas in-scope of a home inspection and in-scope of the exam**

- common situations that limit inspections
- visual inspection limitations
- limitations when inspecting emerging technologies (See Section 1, Unit 11 "Smart Home" Technology)

Inspection Limitations

➢ **Limitation statement required contents**

- report systems, components, or procedures required in SoP used by inspector, but were not inspected or performed
- explain why the system, component, or procedure was not inspected or performed

➢ **Reasons for limitation statements**

- inform client about services included and excluded, and set client expectations
- reduce inspector liability

➢ **Scope limitations**

- SoPs identify specific systems, components, and inspection procedures inspector is required to inspect or perform, and are in scope of a home inspection
- SoPs identify specific and general limitations that are not in scope
- if not required by the SoP, or if excluded by the SoP, inspector is not required to inspect system or component, or perform procedure
- inspector may inspect out of scope systems and components and perform out of scope procedures
  - o if out of scope systems and components inspected or procedures performed, best practice to report that inspection scope not increased
- system and component inspection and procedures may be limited by **written** agreement with client
  - o include agreed-upon limitations in inspection agreement and report
- most clients do not read SoPs
  - o best practice to include common scope limitations in report and inspection agreement

➤ **Visibility, access, and procedure limitations**
  - limitations include systems, components, procedures, and defects that are
    o behind finish materials, such as drywall, floor and wall coverings
    o underground
    o in areas that are unsafe or impractical to enter, such as crawlspaces with low clearances, attics with ceiling joists covered by insulation, and interior of some electrical panels
    o inaccessible, such as interior of chimneys, vents, and heat exchangers
    o concealed by occupant belongings, such as furniture and boxes
      ▪ inspectors should not move occupant belongings
    o concealed by environmental conditions, such as snow and plants
    o not present during the inspection, such as intermittent and latent defects
    o unwise or impractical to perform, such as operating equipment during adverse conditions, including low or high temperatures
  - best practice to report inspection-specific limitations, such as unusual quantity of owner belongings, and presence of snow and other obstructions or conditions
  - best practice to report specific areas that were not accessible if parts of an inspected area were not inspected, such as parts of a crawlspace with low clearance

➤ **Shutdown limitations**
  - systems may be shut down because building is vacant (utilities off), system is not operating properly, or shut down may be unintentional
  - **shut down condition affects only the operation procedure of the inspection; visual inspection requirement remains**
  - **inspector should not activate a shut down system**
    o inspector may contact parties, such as the selling real estate agent, regarding the situation
  - inspector should report systems that were shut down (reason why not inspected) and recommend that systems be inspected

➤ **Not ready for inspection limitations**
  - systems and components may not be fully installed and ready for inspection at time of new construction inspections, and inspections of buildings undergoing remodeling
    o report incomplete systems and components, and report incomplete condition as reason for not inspecting

➤ **Environmental hazard limitations**
  - SoPs exclude environmental hazards from home inspection scope
    o examples: mold, radon, asbestos, animals and their excrement
  - **best practice to disclaim environmental hazards** in inspection agreement and report

➤ **Common limitations**
  - inspector not required to report or perform: defect correction methods and costs; service life prediction; code compliance; engineering services, including structural and soil; recalls; inspection of detached structures, except garage and carport; move property, snow, insulation, debris; ignite fires, pilot lights

Unit 3: Reporting Defective Systems

Topics covered in this Unit include:
- **Knowledge Areas**
- **Expected Service Life**
- **Common Potential Failure Indications**
- **Deficiency and Implication Statements**
- **Common Safety Issues**

Knowledge Areas

➢ **Knowledge areas in-scope of a home inspection and in-scope of the exam**

- expected service life of components
- common indicators of potential failures
- common deficiency descriptions
- common safety issues
- implications of deficiencies

Expected Service Life

➢ **Determining expected service life and age**

- some SoPs require reporting if system or component (system) is near end of its expected service life (near end of life)
  - o no known SoP requires reporting system age
- date of manufacture often encoded in serial number of appliances, such as HVAC equipment, water heaters, kitchen appliances
  - o serial number on permanent label affixed to appliance
- system condition can be more important than age when determining if a system is near end of life
- **factors determining system condition**
  - o **environment,** such as exposure to damp soil, rain and snow, sunlight, extreme temperatures, salt water, acidic or alkaline water
  - o **maintenance,** such as failure to perform recommended service, change filters, maintain paint and other protective coatings, repair damage
  - o **installation,** such as failure to follow manufacturer's instructions
  - o **use,** heavy use versus occasional use
  - o **quality,** such as "builder-grade" versus top of the line

➢ **Reporting near end of expected service life**

- report that system may be near end of life, if required by the SoP
- being near end of service life is not necessarily a deficiency
- **do not estimate remaining service life**

178

Common Potential Failure Indications

➢ **Specific indications of potential system or component failure**

- refer to Typical Defects in each unit for specific failure indications

➢ **General indications of potential system or component failure**

- **deterioration**: soft (rotted) wood; wood splitting or cupping; masonry spalling; absent or worn coatings (paint), or sealants (caulk, gaskets); rust; corrosion
- **deformation or deflection**: rotated, bowing, bulging, sagging, not level or plumb
- **cracks**: wide; long; non-uniform width; through material, such as brick
- **evidence of moisture infiltration**: standing water, moisture stains, efflorescence, condensation, mineral deposits
- **water leaks** (plumbing and HVAC): standing water, moisture stains, mineral deposits
- **components damaged, loose, disconnected, melted, crimped**
- systems or components near **end of service life**
- evidence of **inadequate maintenance**
- **unusual sounds or vibrations** during operation
- evidence of **prior repairs**
- **inadequate drainage** (plumbing): standing water, stains, mineral deposits
- **components absent or improperly installed**: flashing; air, vapor, and water-resistant barriers; incompatible metals in contact; deck ledgers and guards; electrical wires; plumbing and fuel pipes
- **inadequate clearance to combustibles**: combustion vents and flues, heating appliances, fireplaces
- **inadequate clearance to moisture**: wood to soil and roof covering
- **improper operation**: doors, windows, appliances and equipment, electrical devices
- **improper operation, combustion devices**: soot, stains, scorching, rust, corrosion, creosote

Deficiency and Implication Statements

➢ **Types of deficiencies**

- **not functioning properly** (as intended): system or component is not performing its intended function at time of inspection
    - o it is not working now
- **significantly deficient**: system or component is likely not to perform its intended function at some future time
    - o it may be working now, but it may fail when exposed to adverse conditions, or at some future time
    - o a system or component that has functioned properly for many years could fail when exposed to certain adverse conditions, such as pyrolysis
    - o not all SoPs require reporting this deficiency, or may use different terms or definitions
- **unsafe**: use of system or component presents significant risk of personal injury when used as intended
    - o not all SoPs require reporting unsafe conditions, or may use a different definition

- reporting an unsafe condition based on the inspector's judgment about what is unsafe at time of inspection
- a condition once considered safe or code-compliant may now be considered unsafe
  - example: guard height and baluster spacing
- unsafe does not include risk of property damage

➢ **Deficiency statements**
- **identify the deficient component and describe the nature of the deficiency**
  - what characteristics make the component deficient?
    - be specific and accurate
  - do not speculate about deficiency cause
- deficiency statement examples
  - We observed cracks in the mortar and in the bricks that are wider or longer than normal cracks found in brick veneer.
  - We observed significant displacement of the insulation under the home; the crawlspace is effectively uninsulated. Most of the insulation is no longer in contact with the floor sheathing.
  - We observed that ground fault (GFCI) protected receptacles located in the kitchen did not operate when tested.
  - We observed that a vent connector does not have the recommended clearance to combustible material.

➢ **Implication statements**
- **for every identified deficiency, explain what could happen if the deficiency is not addressed** (unless the implication is self-evident)
  - why should the client take the recommended action?
  - no need to state all implications
  - avoid being unnecessarily alarming or dramatic
- implication statement examples
  - These cracks may indicate structural deficiencies.
  - This will cause increased energy consumption, decreased comfort, and increased wear on HVAC components.
  - This is an electrical shock safety hazard.
  - This is a fire safety hazard.

Common Safety Issues

➢ **Common safety issue examples**
- **slip hazards**: depressions in walkways where water could accumulate, especially if it could freeze; glazed wall tiles installed on floors
- **trip hazards**: one part of a walkway higher than the adjacent part
- **fall hazards**: guards and handrails absent, loose, not graspable; narrow stair treads; high stair risers; large difference between stair tread depth or riser height
- **electrocution hazards**: lack of required bonding of metal; GFCI protection not functioning; exposed energized electrical components; receptacle hot/neutral reversed
- **burn hazards**: high water temperature; exposed heat sources

- **fire hazards**: heat source clearance to combustibles
- **cut hazards**: absent safety glazing
- **carbon monoxide hazards**: inadequate combustion air, improperly adjusted combustion appliance flame; combustion product backdrafting

Unit 4: Reporting Systems That Need Additional Evaluation or Action

Topics covered in this Unit include:
- **Knowledge Areas**
- **Type of Person to Perform Recommended Actions**
- **Relationships Between Building Components**
- **Immediate Action Situations**

Knowledge Areas

➤ **Knowledge areas in-scope of a home inspection and in-scope of the exam**

- identify type of person to perform further actions
- relationships between building components
- situations that warrant immediate action

Type of Person to Perform Recommended Actions

➤ **Types of action recommendations**

- **correct**: repair or replace defective system or component
  - repair or replace decision made by qualified specialist
  - best used when clear evidence of a defect exists
- **further evaluate**: more information needed to determine if a defect exists, if so, what action is appropriate
  - best used when clear evidence of a defect does not exist, a question exists about the extent or cause of the possible defect, or if system or component is beyond inspector's competence
- **monitor**: defect does not exist, but may exist in the future; defect exists but no current action required

➤ **Action recommendation general issues**

- no SoP requirement to recommend type of person to perform an action
  - many inspectors do
- recommendation should stipulate that person is licensed (if license required in the jurisdiction), otherwise qualified, or both
- **do not recommend specific person or company in report**

➤ **Type of person to perform recommended action**

- **contractor**: best used when action requires a permit, requires specialized knowledge, or when repair/replacement may require more than one specialist or trade
  - includes specialized contractors, such as electrician, plumber, HVAC
  - contractor responsible for selecting and scheduling appropriately qualified specialists and for obtaining permit

- **engineer**: best used when structural defect requires further evaluation to determine cause and remedy
- **tradesperson**: best used when action does not require a permit and does not require specialized knowledge
- **specialist**: general term; best used when appropriate type of person is not clear

Relationships Between Building Components

➢ **A building is a system**

- building components affect other building components
- defect causes may come from seemingly unrelated components

➢ **Common building component relationships**

- **grade/drainage/gutter/downspout defects place moisture near foundation**: moisture near foundation causes moisture-related defects in crawlspaces, basements, floors, walls, ceilings, and attics; **causes structural defects**, such as cracks, settlement, uplift, and movement of foundations
- **structural defects**, such as settlement, uplift, and movement of foundations, walls, and roofs: may **cause cracks in finish materials**; binding and rubbing of doors and windows; movement of walls, floors, and ceilings
- **HVAC air leaks in ducts**, plenums, and cabinets located outside of conditioned space: may cause pressure differences in rooms; **allow moisture to enter**, condense, and damage attics, crawlspaces, basements, wall and floor cavities
- **combustion air** drawn from inside the building: depressurizes building or individual rooms; **draws moist air into wall and floor cavities**, allows condensation and moisture damage
- **improper exhaust duct** terminations and duct leaks: may **cause condensation** and moisture damage in attics, crawlspaces, basements, wall and floor cavities
- **failure to use and maintain exhaust systems: allows moisture to accumulate** in air; causes HVAC system to run longer; allows condensation and moisture damage in attics, and wall, floor, and rafter cavities
- **improper vapor retarder** installation, air-sealing, and firestop installation: **allows moisture to enter**, condense, and damage attics, crawlspaces, basements, wall, floor, and rafter cavities
- **improper flashing** and water-resistive barrier installation: **allows water leaks** and moisture damage that could affect any part of the building, possibly far distant from the leak source
- **improper installation**, settlement, movement, damage, **of insulation: increases HVAC system run time**, increases maintenance cost, reduces service life

Immediate Action Situations

➤ **Inspection and report disclosure rule**

- **inspector should disclose report, findings, and recommendations only to client,** unless client gives permission to disclose to others
    - o includes all real estate agents, attorneys, mortgage companies

➤ **Exception to disclosure rule**

- situations presenting imminent and significant risk of injury or property damage
- inspector decides whether and how to disclose based on situation
    - o disclosure to fuel provider if fuel leak involved
        - ▪ evacuate building if imminent life-safety event occurs
    - o disclosure to seller usually appropriate, if present at inspection
    - o disclosure to seller's real estate agent usually appropriate, if seller not present at inspection
- **inspector could be judged negligent** if a reasonable inspector would have disclosed in a similar situation
- examples of possible immediate disclosure situations
    - o fuel leaks (discovered by sight or smell; no duty to test for leaks)
    - o active fire
    - o exposed energized electrical wires subject to likely contact
    - o presence of carbon monoxide (no duty to test for CO)
    - o presence of dangerous animals, such as poisonous snakes and spiders
    - o active water leaks from plumbing distribution pipes and hot water heat pipes, especially in vacant buildings
    - o water in plumbing water distribution pipes and no heat when temperature below freezing

Section 2 Test: Analysis of Findings and Reporting
Select the BEST answer

2.1.1   Which is a required element of a home inspection report deficiency statement?

a. Estimate of the component's remaining service life
b   Location of the deficient component
c. Action that the client should take
d. Reference to building code section that was violated

2.1.2   Which is a typical required system or component description in a home inspection report?

a. Type of interior wall covering
b   Type of roof covering material
c. Type of service drop wires
d. Type of water service pipe

2.1.3   The heating equipment description must include the heating equipment ___

a. type.
b   age.
c. model number.
d. distribution system materials.

2.1.4   Which statement is TRUE about infrared cameras?

a. Their accuracy increases when more infrared radiation is reflected.
b   They determine the type of material inside a wall cavity.
c. They measure the amount of moisture inside an object.
d. They measure temperature at the surface of an object.

2.1.5   A moisture meter is best used to _____

a. determine if a moisture stain is wet.
b   scan for hidden moisture.
c. find improper window flashing.
d. determine if a toilet O ring is properly installed.

2.2.1   Which is a required part of a home inspection limitation statement?

a. Explain why a system was not inspected
b   Report the location of the system that was not inspected
c. Recommend that a specialist inspect the system
d. Warn that defects could exist in the system that was not inspected

2.2.2   A system that is present, accessible, and functioning during a home inspection may be excluded from the inspection if requested and agreed to by the ___?

a. code official
b   seller
c. client's real estate agent
d. client

2.2.3   Inspector determines that a system required to be inspected and operated is shut down. What is the inspector's best course of action?

   a. Text the client's real estate agent
   b Activate the system
   c. Visually inspect the system
   d. Determine the cause of the system shut down

2.2.4   Inspector sees that the garage is full of moving boxes. What is the inspector's best course of action?

   a. Move the boxes
   b Report that the garage was not inspected
   c. Recommend continuing the inspection when the boxes are removed
   d. Ask the client to move the boxes

2.2.5   Inspectors are required to _____

   a. light pilot lights.
   b estimate remaining service life of HVAC systems.
   c. move small amounts of snow.
   d. inspect detached garages.

2.3.1   The date of manufacture of a heat pump condenser is usually found in the ____

   a. the condenser's serial number.
   b the compressor's serial number.
   c. the condenser's model number.
   d. the reversing valve's model number.

2.3.2   Which is most likely to experience reduced service life?

   a. A package heat pump installed 3 inches above soil
   b Plywood panel siding on an east-facing wall
   c. A gas water heater in a garage
   d. Asphalt shingles on a south-facing roof

2.3.3   Which is a required part of a deficiency statement?

   a. State the location of the deficiency
   b Describe the nature of the deficiency
   c. Identify the cause of the deficiency
   d. Recommend how to repair the deficiency

2.3.4   Which is likely to be considered an unsafe condition?

   a. Leak in the water tank of an electric water heater
   b A gas furnace with a blue flame
   c. ½ inch difference between stair riser heights
   d. PVC conduit buried 18 inches below grade

2.3.5   Which is likely to be considered a deficient condition?

a. A concrete driveway that slopes away from the garage at ½ inch per foot
b A 2x6 wood stud with a hole drilled ¾ inch from the edge of the stud
c. A kitchen countertop with receptacles spaced every 4 feet
d. A 12 foot long 2x10 floor joist with a ¼ inch deep notch 5 feet from the end

2.3.6   The decision to report an unsafe condition is based on ___

a. the inspector's judgment
b applicable building code at the time of the inspection
c. applicable building code when the building was built
d. current authoritative best practice

2.4.1   In which situation would it be best to recommend monitoring a situation?

a. Temperature drop across an evaporator coil is 10° F.
b Plant leaves are 1 inch from the house wall
c. Crack in a concrete block wall is narrow near the floor and wider near the ceiling
d. A brown stain appears under a window

2.4.2   When recommending that action be taken to address a defect, the inspector should advise that the person taking the action be_____

a. available.
b competent.
c. licensed.
d. local.

2.4.3   A hole is present in a direct vented gas furnace return duct located in a ventilated attic. Which is a potential consequence of this defect?

a. Vent system backdrafting
b Rust on nails in the attic
c. Ice dam
d. Condensation in a wall cavity

2.4.4   Inspector observes widespread moisture stains on roof sheathing and rafters in a ventilated attic. Which is the best place to look for the cause?

a. Plumbing vent flashing
b Recessed light fixtures
c. Bathroom exhaust duct terminations
d. Kraft paper-faced batt insulation

2.4.5   Which is the best example of when immediate disclosure of a defect is appropriate?

a. Oil puddle at an oil tank vent tube
b Water flow at a clothes washing machine valve
c. Rotten egg smell at a gas meter regulator
d. Exposed active electrical wire in the crawlspace

2.4.6   An engineer is the best person to address a situation that involves ___

    a. damaged roof trusses.
    b dimensional lumber floor joists with a large notch.
    c. rafters spanning a longer distance than allowed.
    d. deck ledger attached with nails.

2.4.7   The sashes of a double hung vinyl window do not align evenly where the sashes meet; and there is a diagonal crack in the wall at the upper right corner of the window. Which is the most likely cause of this situation?

    a. The window has been warped by heat
    b Shims were not installed where the sashes meet
    c. The wall has moved due to inadequate bracing
    d. The window is not properly flashed.

Section III: Professional Responsibilities

Unit 1: Inspection Agreements

Unit 2: Inspection Process Integrity

Unit 1: Inspection Agreements

Topics covered in this Unit include:
- **Knowledge Areas**
- **Inspection Contract: Purpose**
- **Inspection Contract: Required Elements**
- **Inspection Contract: Optional Elements**
- **Privacy and Disclosure of Inspection Findings**
- **Contract Timing and Signature**

Knowledge Areas

➤ **Knowledge areas in-scope of a home inspection and in-scope of the exam**

- inspection contract purpose
- inspection contract elements
- privacy and disclosure considerations
- inspection contract delivery and signatures

Inspection Contract: Purpose

➤ **Contracts**
- inspection contract definition: __agreement__ **between inspector and client about inspection terms and conditions**
  - agreement means **meeting of the minds, mutual assent** about what each party commits to do, or not to do
    - in exchange for inspection fee, and other client promises, (consideration) inspector promises to perform inspection, and possibly other services
- **written contract protects inspector and client by documenting expectations**
- **written contract reduces ambiguity about contract terms**
- written contract not required, unless required by state law
  - proving existence of contract and contract terms very difficult without signed written contract
- should have separate contract, or contract addendum, for each ancillary service, such as radon and mold/air quality

➤ **Establishing a contract**
- offer: promise to do something, or not to do something
- acceptance: assent to all terms of offer, without exceptions
  - exceptions establish new offer, a counteroffer
- consideration: exchange of value; not necessarily an exchange of money or other assets; promises have value, and can be consideration
- agreement: mutual assent

Inspection Contract: Required Elements

➢ **State law governs contracts**
- required contract elements governed by state law; different laws in each state
- laws of state where home is located are default governing laws
- state inspector license authority may require additional contract elements, and may require written contract

➢ **Contracting party identification**
- inspector name
  - use company name; not personal name, unless a sole proprietor
  - include type of company, such as LLC or corporation (Inc.)
  - include license number, if required by state law
- client name(s)
  - ideally, all parties with interest in property; one client name usually adequate

➢ **Inspection location and date**
- location specific enough to identify property; usually mailing address
- inspection date; time not necessary unless required by state law

➢ **Inspection fee**
- state fee for inspection, and separate fee for each ancillary service

➢ **Description of inspection services**
- **identify inspection SoP, only one SoP**
  - establishes inspector responsibilities
  - use state SoP if state-mandated SoP applies
- state inspection purpose and objective
  - wording may be specified by state law
- list important limitations and exclusions
  - examples: concealed and latent defects, incidental and consequential damages, cosmetic defects, environmental hazards, pests and wood-destroying organisms, wells and septic systems

➢ **Signature(s)**
- client: ideally, all parties with interest in property; signature of identified party usually adequate
- inspector: sign as company representative; not personally, unless a sole proprietor

Inspection Contract: Optional Elements

> **Limitation of liability**
>> - limits client's remedies if dispute arises about inspection
>> - usual limit is refund of inspection fee
>> - state law or state court decisions may restrict availability and wording of liability limits
>> - does not limit claims by those not named in contract
>> - may not limit claims based on negligence or other legal theories

> **Alternative dispute resolution**
>> - arbitration: a formal process similar to a court hearing; an independent, neutral arbitrator acts like a judge, evaluates evidence, renders a decision/award
>>   - binding: winner may go to court to enforce decision
>>   - non-binding: decision advisory, not enforceable
>> - mediation: facilitated negotiation; mediator helps parties try to reach agreement
>>   - often required before court will hear lawsuit
>>   - no decision or award; arbitration or court next step if mediation unsuccessful

> **Other common optional terms**
>> - warranty disclaimer: no express or implied warranties regarding inspection
>> - time limit to file claims: must be reasonable, usually one year from inspection date
>> - disclosure: defines to whom inspector can send inspection report and discuss findings

Privacy and Disclosure of Inspection Findings

> **Inspection and report disclosure rule**
>> - inspector should disclose report, findings, and recommendations **only to client**, unless client gives permission to disclose to others
>>   - includes all parties, such as real estate agents, builders, mortgage companies, government inspectors, attorneys
>> - general permission to disclose can be part of inspection agreement, with option for client to deny permission

> **Use of reports by third parties**
>> - third parties not involved in inspection may obtain report and attempt to use it
>> - do not discuss report or inspection with third parties; recommend new inspection and new report
>>   - conditions in building can change after inspection date; updated inspection is warranted to determine if conditions changed

Contract Timing and Signature

- ➤ **Contract timing**
  - • **present contract to client before date of inspection**
    - ○ ideally, as soon as possible after scheduling inspection
    - ○ gives client time to read agreement and negotiate terms
    - ○ **avoids client alleging adhesion contract**
      - ▪ **adhesion contract**: client has little practical alternative to signing contract
      - ▪ no mutual assent, a contract requirement
      - ▪ court may void all or part of adhesion contract
    - ○ presentation before inspection may be required by state law; if so, failure to do so may subject inspector to license board discipline even if no client complaint
    - ○ easy to do using automated document delivery and signature service

- ➤ **Contract signature**
  - • client signature: ideally, all parties with interest in property should sign contract
    - ○ signature of identified party usually adequate
  - • signature by client's real estate agent may be valid
    - ○ validity depends on whether client gives agent permission to sign
    - ○ agent's signature adds uncertainty about contract validity

Unit 2: Inspection Process Integrity

Topics covered in this Unit include:
- **Knowledge Areas**
- **Legal Concepts**
- **Conflicts of Interest**
- **Insurance**
- **Duty to Client**

Knowledge Areas

➢ **Knowledge areas in-scope of a home inspection and in-scope of the exam**

- legal concepts
- conflicts of interest
- insurance
- duty to client

Legal Concepts

➢ **Litigation procedures**
- litigation procedures, processes, rights, and responsibilities governed by state law in state courts
  - home inspectors unlikely to be involved in Federal court
- basic litigation procedure
  - **complaint filed with court by plaintiff**: alleges wrongs by defendant
    - summons: notifies defendant of complaint
  - **answer filed by defendant**: response to complaint; usually denies plaintiff's allegations
    - counterclaim by defendant (optional): alleges wrongs by defendant
  - **discovery**: exchange of information between parties so that each party is aware of evidence possessed by the other
    - document production, physical materials possessed by parties; interrogatories, written questions; depositions, verbal questions
  - **arbitration/mediation**: often required by court before scheduling trial
  - **trial**: bench trial, case heard by judge; jury trial, case heard by jury
  - **judgment:** judge or jury decides who wins, and amount of damages
  - **collection**: additional steps may be required to collect judgment

➢ **Inspector liability risks**
- **breach of contract**: alleges inspector **did not comply with contract terms**
  - did not comply with SoP, did not properly report defects
  - plaintiff proves allegations and damages by preponderance of evidence (50.1%)
  - plaintiff awarded money damages

- compensatory damages: cost to repair unreported defects, loss of building value, loss of use
- **negligence**: alleges inspector **did not perform as a reasonable inspector would have under similar conditions**
  - defendant had **duty** to plaintiff; **breached** duty; breach **caused** plaintiff's **physical injury** (damages)
    - plaintiff awarded money damages for physical/emotional injury, usually not for property damages
  - plaintiff proves allegations and damages by preponderance of evidence (50.1%)
- **fraud**: alleges inspector made significant **false** statement, and **knew** it was false; plaintiff **did not know** statement was false, reasonably **relied** on statement, suffered **damage**
  - plaintiff proves allegations and damages by clear and convincing evidence
  - plaintiff awarded money damages; may be awarded punitive damages and attorney fees
- **negligent misrepresentation**: similar to fraud, except plaintiff not required to prove defendant knew statement was false

Conflicts of Interest

➢ **Professional integrity**

- inspectors, and the inspection profession, rely on public perception that home inspectors provide reliable and independent information for client's benefit
- inspector should avoid actual or perceived conflicts of interest that might jeopardize the perception
- inspector should fully disclose all potential conflicts of interest to all parties with interest in the inspected property
  - disclosure may not shield inspector from liability
- home inspector conflicts of interest are regulated and interpreted by law in some states
- some states and professional associations do not enforce all of these conflicts of interest

➢ **Conflicts of interest**

- **financial interest in property**: includes direct or indirect ownership, liability for debt on property
  - inspecting a house the inspector is purchasing usually acceptable
- **financial interest in property sale**: includes express or implied promise of future referrals from real estate agents, direct or indirect benefit from commissions on sale
- **payment to referral sources**: includes cash, gifts, and services to referral sources; payment for inclusion on preferred provider lists
  - minor gifts and contributions to professional associations and charities usually acceptable
- **payment from referrals**: includes accepting payment from parties to whom inspector refers clients, such as contractors and alarm companies
- **repair of inspected property**: includes being paid to perform services at property for one year after inspection

- ➢ **Reporting issues**
  - report findings and recommendations based on inspector's experience and expertise
    - o disclaim inspection and recommend evaluation by someone else if system, component, or situation is beyond ability to provide accurate information
  - **do not understate or overstate findings and recommendations**

Insurance

- ➢ **Insurance purpose**
  - transfer risk from policyholder to insurance company
  - business or person may retain risk by self-insuring
  - state license authority may require some insurance types as condition of license

- ➢ **Insurance types**
  - **errors and omissions** (professional liability): defends inspector against allegation that inspector did not properly report defects; pays to settle claim regardless of whether inspector at fault
    - o claims made policy: covers claims filed while policy is active, and that result from inspections performed while policy is active; most common type, least expensive
    - o occurrence policy: covers claims filed while policy is active regardless of when inspection occurred; uncommon, more expensive
    - o tail coverage may be available to cover claims and inspections occurring outside policy active period
    - o coverage for ancillary services may require rider and additional premium
  - **general liability**: defends inspector against allegation that inspector damaged inspected property, or caused injury to someone during inspection; may cover business risks, such as libel
    - o covers injuries at inspector's place of business, with endorsements
  - **worker's compensation**: pays inspector's employee who is injured on the job
    - o pays medical expenses and lost income regardless of fault
    - o business owners may exempt themselves from coverage
  - **inland marine**: covers inspector's tools and equipment
  - **homeowner insurance**: may cover inspector tools and equipment and client injury while at inspector's residence
    - o additional endorsements and premiums usually required
  - **vehicle insurance**: may cover inspector's personal vehicle if used during inspections
    - o additional endorsements and premiums usually required
  - **bond**: pays client if inspector does not pay judgment awarded to client
    - o client must win judgment first
    - o bond company usually tries to collect payment to client from inspector

Duty to Client

➢ **Inspector relationship with client**

- inspector has duty to act in client's best interest

➢ **Value of inspector findings and recommendations**

- inspector findings and recommendations have value during negotiations about financial responsibility for defects
- inspector should make reasonable efforts to ensure confidentiality of discussions with clients
  - o assume recording devices are active at inspected property

Section 3 Test: Professional Responsibilities

Select the BEST answer

3.1.1   Which is required in order to create a valid inspection contract?

   a. Mutual assent
   b Payment of inspection fee
   c. Written document
   d. Review by an attorney

3.1.2   If there is a dispute about the inspection, what is the benefit of a written contract?

   a. Contract must be in writing to be enforceable
   b Inspector's insurance is void without a written contract
   c. Judge has a better understanding of party's intentions
   d. Attorneys cannot be involved without a written contract

3.1.3   John Doe is the president of John Doe Inspections and More, Inc. What name should identify the contracting party of this organization?

   a. John Doe, President
   b John Doe Inspections
   c. John Doe Inspections, Inc.
   d. John Doe Inspections and More, Inc.

3.1.4   If governing law is not specified in a home inspection contract, the contract is governed by the ____

   a. Uniform Commercial Code.
   b laws of the state where the home is located.
   c. Federal Department of Housing and Urban Development.
   d. laws of the state where the inspector lives.

3.1.5   Arbitration of a dispute about an inspection is best described as a ___

   a. trial without a jury.
   b facilitated negotiation.
   c. hearing before a neutral party.
   d. consultation with a judge in private.

3.1.6   A home inspector may discuss the inspection with the client and the client's ___

   a. real estate agent.
   b spouse.
   c. attorney.
   d. mortgage company.

3.1.7   A home inspector lives in a state that licenses home inspectors and performs an inspection in a nearby state that also licenses home inspectors. Which Standard of Practice should the home inspector use, if any?

a. Standard of Practice where the home inspector lives
b   Standard of Practice where the home is located
c. Standard of Practice from a professional association
d. Standard of Practice selected by the inspector

3.2.1   A home inspector found liable for breach of contract would likely be awarded _____

a. compensatory damages.
b   attorney fees.
c. punitive damages.
d. court costs.

3.2.2   A home inspector might be found liable for negligence if the inspector did not ____

a. report truthfully about a defect.
b   explain the implication of a defect.
c. disclose a conflict of interest.
d. perform like a reasonable inspector.

3.2.3   A home inspector would likely have conflict of interest in which situation?

a. Refers a friend's company to a client without compensation
b   Remodel an inspected property eighteen months after the inspection
c. Pays a real estate broker for inclusion on a preferred provider list
d. Receives regular referrals from a real estate agent

3.2.4   Which insurance covers damage caused by the inspector during an inspection?

a. Errors and omissions
b   General liability
c. Surety bond
d. Worker's compensation

3.2.5   A claims made errors and omissions insurance policy covers an inspector in which situation?

a. Claim made while policy is active, inspection occurred before policy active
b   Claim made while policy is active, inspector is not at fault
c. Inspection occurs while policy is active, inspector is at fault
d. Inspection occurs after policy expires, inspector is not at fault

3.2.6   A lawsuit begins with _____

a. discovery.
b   answer.
c. cross-claim.
d. complaint.

Home Inspector License Practice Exam

Select the BEST answer

1. The type of preservative treatment applied to wood may be determined by ___.

    a. reading the label attached to the wood
    b. observing the color of the wood
    c. feeling the raised wood grain
    d. observing the cut ends of the wood

2. Which component is often buried in the soil behind a wood retaining wall to help the wall resist rotation?

    a. Steel rods
    b. Gravel
    c. Tiebacks
    d. Concrete

3. Which type of soil is known to expand when wet?

    a. Sand
    b. Clayey gravel
    c. Inorganic silt
    d. Fat clay

4. A home inspector should report vegetation issues when the plant __.

    a. may grow and touch the building
    b. is in the shade and needs full sun
    c. may adversely affect the building
    d. may attract dangerous animals

5. Which is the best alternative if it is impractical to slope grade away from the foundation?

    a. Upgrade foundation waterproofing
    b. Place gravel next to the foundation
    c. Enlarge gutters and downspouts
    d. Install a French Drain

6. The gate latch that is accessible from the side away from a swimming pool should be at least ___ inches above the walking surface.

    a. 44
    b. 48
    c. 54
    d. 60

7. What should be installed between a concrete driveway and the building foundation?

    a. A control joint
    b. An isolation joint
    c. A construction joint
    d. An expansion joint

8. Adhered masonry veneer is installed in a manner similar to which wall covering?

   a. Stucco
   b. Natural stone
   c. Vinyl siding
   d. Brick

9. A rectangular window with hinges at the two top corners and that opens outwards is called a (an) ___ window.

   a. hopper
   b. casement
   c. single hung
   d. awning

10. According to the International Residential Code, when a cantilevered balcony does not support a roof, what is the recommended ratio of floor joist backspan to cantilever?

    a. 2 to 1
    b. 2.5 to 1
    c. 3 to 1
    d. 3.5 to 1

11. According to the International Residential Code, which is an approved size for a deck handrail (inches)?

    a. 2 by 2
    b. 2 by 4
    c. $^5/_4$ by 4
    d. 1 by 6

12. Garage vehicle door operator safety sensors should be located not more than __ inches above the floor.

    a. 2
    b. 4
    c. 6
    d. 8

13. The bottom edge of an escape window opening should be not more than __ inches above the interior finished floor.

    a. 40
    b. 44
    c. 48
    d. 52

14. The minimum slope of a roof covered by fiberglass shingles is __ inches in 12 inches.

    a. 1
    b. 2
    c. 3
    d. 4

15. Which is considered a reportable defect on fiberglass shingles?

    a. Algae
    b. Stains
    c. Moss
    d. Mold

16. Which is considered a low slope roof covering?

    a. Standing seam metal panels
    b. Slate shingles
    c. Metal shingles
    d. Wood shakes

17. A low slope roof that is completely surrounded by parapet walls may drain water off of the roof through a ___.

    a. downspout
    b. leader
    c. gutter
    d. scupper

18. A gutter should slope toward a downspout at a minimum rate of ___ inch per foot.

    a. $^1/_{16}$
    b. ⅛
    c. ¼
    d. ⅜

19. The transition between a roof and a brick veneer sidewall should be flashed using ____.

    a. angle iron
    b. underlayment
    c. a thimble
    d. step flashing

20. What should be installed where a 31-inch wide chimney penetrates the roof?

    a. A hip
    b. A shed
    c. A cricket
    d. A mansard

21. How many consecutive roof truss top chords may be cut in order to install a skylight?

    a. 0
    b. 1
    c. 2
    d. 3

22. An inspector observes soft sheathing where a plumbing vent penetrates the roof. Which is the most likely cause of this condition?

    a. Condensation around the plumbing vent
    b. Deteriorated vent flashing
    c. Vent pipe is too short above the roof
    d. Vent pipe diameter is too small

23. Which method is most likely to be used to address a ¼ inch wide horizontal crack through the mortar of a concrete block foundation wall?

    a. Sister wall
    b. Carbon fiber mats
    c. Plate anchors
    d. Epoxy

24. A diagonal crack in a poured-concrete basement wall is wider near the floor and narrower near the ceiling. What is the most likely cause of this condition?

    a. Hydrostatic pressure against the wall
    b. Inadequate waterproofing
    c. Footing settlement
    d. Improper vibration of the concrete

25. Which technique is intended to prevent liquid moisture from entering into a basement through the foundation wall?

    a. Waterproofing
    b. Hydraulic sealing
    c. Foundation draining
    d. Dampproofing

26. An excessively notched dimensional lumber floor joist may be repaired by installing ___

    a. bridging.
    b. blocking.
    c. a web stiffener.
    d. a telescoping column.

27. Which is necessary to determine the maximum span of a dimensional lumber floor joist?

    a. The joist length
    b. Where the joist lumber was grown
    c. The joist moisture level
    d. The joist species

28. Using the International Residential Code span tables, what is the minimum lumber grade that may be used to assemble a dimensional lumber beam?

    a. #1
    b. #2
    c. #3
    d. Utility

29. What is installed to keep the wall from racking during high winds?

a. Blocking
b. Stiffeners
c. Bracing
d. Anchors

30. What is the minimum width of an oriented strand board panel used as roof sheathing?

a. 18 inches
b. 22 inches
c. 24 inches
d. 28 inches

31. What is the minimum service current for a single-family dwelling?

a. 60 amps
b. 100 amps
c. 125 amps
d. 150 amps

32. A subpanel in an accessory building is served by a 4-wire feeder. If the subpanel should have a grounding electrode connection, where should the connection be located?

a. At the service equipment
b. At the service point
c. At the subpanel
d. A grounding electrode connection is not required

33. A ground fault circuit interrupter functions by sensing a____.

a. current difference between energized and grounded wires
b. voltage drop on the energized wire
c. resistance decrease on the grounded wire
d. reactance difference between energized and grounding wires

34. A service drop extends 10 feet across a roof with a 3/12 slope. The service drop should be at least ___ inches above the roof.

a. 18
b. 36
c. 42
d. 48

35. Which wiring method may be buried?

a. Nonmetallic sheathed cable
b. Service entrance cable
c. Armored cable
d. Metal-clad cable

36. Which wiring method might be found as original wiring in a house built in 1910?

a. Metal-clad cable
b. Cloth-covered cable
c. Knob-and-tube
d. Liquidtight conduit

37. Which is a problem panelboard the presence of which usually should be reported?

a. Zinsco
b. Cutler Hammer
c. General Electric
d. Siemens

38. No location on a kitchen counter top should be more than __ feet from a receptacle.

a. 1
b. 2
c. 3
d. 4

39. What is the recommended method for testing an arc-fault circuit interrupter (AFCI)?

a. Use a clamp-on multimeter
b. Use a circuit analyzer
c. Use the test button on a 3-light circuit tester
d. Use the test button on the AFCI

40. What is the best term to describe a heat pump that exchanges energy with the earth through buried pipes or tubes?

a. Geo source
b. Water source
c. Ground source
d. Air source

41. Refrigerant flows through this device immediately before it enters a heat pump evaporator coil operating in cooling mode?

a. Expansion device
b. Dryer
c. Compressor
d. Reversing valve

42. Which cooling system blows air through a wet mesh medium before sending the air into the building?

a. Absorption cooler
b. Evaporative cooler
c. Ductless mini-split
d. Chiller

43. The amount of water vapor in the air that an air conditioner must deal with is called the ___ load.

   a. sensible
   b. dynamic
   c. dew point
   d. latent

44. The primary condensate disposal tube should be at least ___ inch diameter.

   a. ⅜
   b. ½
   c. ¾
   d. ⅞

45. After the thermostat calls for heat, which component activates next in the operating cycle of a modern medium efficiency (Category I) gas furnace?

   a. Draft inducer fan
   b. Igniter
   c. Gas valve
   d. High limit switch

46. The tendency of hot gasses to rise is called the ____ effect.

   a. density
   b. stack
   c. convection
   d. pressure

47. Which is a defect that may occur if an air conditioner Btu capacity is too large for the area it serves?

   a. Thermostat malfunction
   b. Evaporator coil icing
   c. Expansion valve clogging
   d. Short cycling

48. Which is a safety system in an oil furnace?

   a. Draft sensor
   b. Aquastat
   c. Fire eye
   d. Pressuretrol

49. Which is a common operating problem with a one pipe series loop hot water distribution system?

   a. The last radiator in the system runs cool.
   b. The distribution pipes become blocked by debris.
   c. The boiler has a reduced service life.
   d. The expansion tank becomes waterlogged.

50. Which component is required in an oil furnace vent connector that uses a masonry chimney as the vent?

   a. Pressuretrol
   b. Draft inducer
   c. Backflow valve
   d. Barometric damper

51. Which is an indication that a gas appliance vent system is not functioning properly?

   a. Soot at the vent cap
   b. White stains at vent fittings
   c. Yellow flame in the combustion chamber
   d. High limit switch activation

52. Heat flow in a liquid or gas primarily occurs by ___.

   a. convection
   b conduction
   c. thermocline
   d. radiation

53. Which is a type of thermal insulation?

   a. Mineral wool
   b Kraft paper
   c. Thermoplastic polyolefin
   d. Acrylonitrile butadiene styrene

54. For maximum effectiveness, insulation must be in contact with ____.

   a. a vapor retarder
   b gypsum board
   c. Kraft paper
   d. an air barrier

55. In a warm/humid climate zone, on which side, if any, of an exterior wall should a vapor retarder be installed?

   a. Either side of the wall
   b The interior side of the wall
   c. Neither side of the wall
   d. The exterior side of the wall

56. Assuming 50% of attic ventilation openings are in the eaves, and the remaining openings are at the roof ridge, what is the minimum ratio of attic ventilation opening area to the number of square feet of attic floor space?

   a. 1/150
   b 1/300
   c. 1/500
   d. 1/1,500

57. Which is required in an unventilated (closed) attic in Climate Zone 2 that is insulated with air permeable insulation?

   a. A Class I vapor retarder under the ceiling joists
   b A thermal barrier at the insulation
   c. A vapor diffusion port
   d. A source of conditioned air

58. The air intake opening of a heat recovery ventilator should be at least __ feet horizontally from a gas appliance vent.

   a. 2
   b 5
   c. 8
   d. 10

59. What is the minimum diameter flexible duct serving a 50 cfm bathroom exhaust fan?

   a. 3 inches
   b 3 ½ inches
   c. 4 inches
   d. 4 ½ inches

60. The exhaust duct serving an over the range hood may be constructed using ___.

   a. Schedule 80 PVC pipe
   b flexible galvanized steel HVAC duct
   c. copper duct
   d. cast iron DVW pipe

61. What is the maximum length of the transition duct between a clothes dryer exhaust duct and the clothes dryer?

   a. 6 feet
   b 8 feet
   c. 10 feet
   d. 12 feet

62. The distance between a bathtub spout with a 1-inch diameter opening should be at least __ inch(es) from the flood rim level of the bathtub.

   a. 1
   b 2
   c. 3
   d. 4

63. A common reason for premature failure of copper water distribution tubing is ___.

   a. acidic water
   b lead solder
   c. hard water
   d. rough edges of tubing cuts

64. What is the minimum working distance on each side of a toilet?

   a. 10 inches
   b 12 inches
   c. 15 inches
   d. 18 inches

65. What is the minimum number of vents that are open to the atmosphere in a sanitary drainage system?

   a. 0
   b 1
   c. 2
   d. 3

66. A draft hood-equipped gas water heater may NOT be located ____.

   a. in a crawl space
   b outdoors
   c. in an attic
   d. in a bedroom

67. Annealed copper gas tubing should be ___.

   a. labeled GAS
   b Type M
   c. supported every 10 feet
   d. not be installed in exterior walls

68. A sewage ejector is necessary when ___.

   a. plumbing fixtures are in a basement
   b the building drain pipe is too small
   c. plumbing fixtures are below the public sewer tap
   d. a backwater valve is installed

69. Safety glazing is required in a window where the glazing is less than 36 inches above a walking surface and within ___ inches from the bottom tread of a stairway.

   a. 48
   b 54
   c. 60
   d. 72

70. A handrail is required at a flight of stairs with ___ or more risers.

   a. 3
   b 4
   c. 5
   d. 6

71. What may need to be installed where cabinets meet at perpendicular corners to keep drawers and doors from interfering with operation of the drawers and doors of the perpendicular cabinets?

a. Stile
b Stop
c. Mullion
d. Filler strip

72. A kitchen overhead exhaust hood with a capacity of 425 cubic feet per minute must be provided with ___ air.

a. makeup
b dilution
c. exhaust
d. cooling

73. The opening directly above a masonry fireplace damper is called the ____.

a. flue
b throat
c. breast
d. lintel

74. A masonry chimney footing should extend __ inches past all sides of the chimney.

a. 2
b 4
c. 6
d. 8

75. A system that is designed to burn processed wood is called a ____.

a. Rumford fireplace
b fireplace insert
c. pellet stove
d. firebox

76. A masonry chimney cap should be constructed using what material?

a. Refractory mortar
b Cement
c. Type S mortar
d. Concrete

77. Bricks that are subjected to water and to repeated freeze/thaw cycles are often deteriorated. This deterioration is called ___.

a. spalling
b flaking
c. weathering
d. racking

78. What is the minimum air space between a chimney that is located within a building and combustible framing?

   a. ½ inch
   b 1 inch
   c. 2 inches
   d. 3 inches

79. Black stains are present at the vent termination of a gas fireplace. Which is the most likely cause of this condition?

   a. Debris in the gas
   b Inadequate combustion air
   c. Operating the fireplace too long
   d. Improperly installed vent system

80. How deep should a hearth extension be in front of a prefabricated wood-burning fireplace?

   a. 12 inches
   b 14 inches
   c. 16 inches
   d. 18 inches

81. How many risers may be on the exterior side of the egress door if the door swings over the exterior landing?

   a. 0
   b 1
   c. 2
   d. 4

82. Which is an approved fireblocking material?

   a. $^7/_{16}$-inch thick oriented strand board
   b 1 x 6 dimensional lumber
   c. ⅜-inch thick Type X gypsum board
   d. ¾-inch thick plywood

83. The door from an attached garage may not open into __.

   a. an egress hallway
   b a room containing a combustion appliance
   c. a bedroom
   d. a room with a closet

84. Fire separation for the attic above townhouse units may be accomplished by installing ____.

   a. ⅝-inch thick Type X gypsum board on the roof sheathing
   b a parapet wall at least 24 inches above the roof
   c. a 3-hour firewall in the attic terminating at the roof sheathing
   d. a fire suppression system in the attic

85.	A carbon monoxide alarm is required ___.

a. inside all bedrooms
b on every story
c. in a house with a fireplace
d. in an attic containing a fuel-burning appliance

86.	Which may be installed at the egress door?

a. A latch on the inside that requires a combination to release
b A screen door with a keyed lock on both sides
c. A lock with a knob on the inside
d. A slide bolt with a hidden release mechanism

87.	If an inspector elects not to enter a crawl space, the inspector must state ___.

a. that there may be defects in the crawl space
b that someone should inspect the crawl space
c. the inspection was incomplete
d. the reasons why the crawl space was not entered

88.	An inspector observes a type of exterior wall covering that is known to have been the subject of product defect litigation. The inspector is required to report ___.

a. that the wall covering is defective
b the type of wall covering
c. where the client can find information about the litigation
d. the allegations involving the wall covering defects

89.	An inspector entered and walked in an attic, but could not inspect a vaulted ceiling with the wall covering applied to the rafters. How should an inspector report about the attic inspection?

a. The attic was inspected by entering the attic.
b The vaulted ceiling area was not inspected because there is no accessible attic.
c. Report both a and b
d. The attic was inspected from the access opening.

90.	Which is out of scope of a home inspection?

a. High voltage electric power wires in the back yard
b A tree with limbs overhanging the roof
c. A retaining wall next to the house
d. A 28-inch wide back door to the house

91.	Twelve months after the home inspection, the client remodels the kitchen. Water damage was discovered behind the cabinets after they were removed. What, if any, is the inspector's responsibility in this situation?

a. The inspector is responsible because water damage is a reportable defect.
b The inspector is not responsible because the damage was not visible during the inspection.
c. The inspector is responsible because of failure to use an infrared camera to locate the damage.
d. The inspector is not responsible because the statute of limitations has lapsed.

92. An inspector did not inspect the interior of a Federal Pacific electrical panel. Which is the best way for an inspector to report this situation?

   a. The electrical panel interior was not inspected because it is unsafe to do so.
   b Federal Pacific electrical panels are defective and should be evaluated by an electrician.
   c. The electrical panel interior was not inspected.
   d. Federal Pacific electrical panels are past the end of their service lives.

93. Which is a required part of a home inspection report defect statement?

   a. Estimate the cost to address the defect
   b State the location of the defect
   c. Recommend a contractor to evaluate the defect
   d. State the implication of the defect

94. A fiberglass shingle roof covering presents significant granule loss. The best way to report this situation is that the roof covering ___ .

   a. is deteriorated and should be replaced
   b will need replacement soon
   c. is near the end of its service life
   d. is defective and should be evaluated

95. A deck stairway has a typical 2 x4 handrail. Which, if any, is the best way to report this situation?

   a. The handrail is not graspable and may result in a fall injury.
   b The handrail shape is a building code violation.
   c. The stairway does not have an acceptable handrail.
   d. The handrail is dangerous and should be replaced.

96. An inspector notes a low temperature drop across an air conditioner evaporator coil. How should the inspector address this situation?

   a. Report that the air conditioner is not functioning
   b Recommend evaluation by a qualified contractor
   c. State that the air conditioner condenser should be replaced
   d. Advise the seller to have routine air conditioner maintenance performed

97. An inspector notes thin dark lines regularly spaced on a wall under a vaulted ceiling. Which is the most likely cause of this condition?

   a. Roof leaks
   b Absent insulation between the studs
   c. Condensation on the wall at the studs
   d. Backdrafting combustion appliance

98. The procedure in which a private third party agreed upon by both parties considers evidence and renders a binding decision is called __ .

   a. mediation
   b arbitration
   c. intercession
   d. reconciliation

99. Which is a required element of an inspection contract?

   a. A written document
   b An identification of the Standard of Practice
   c. A limitation of liabilities
   d. An agreement between the parties

100. One of the primary purposes of an inspection agreement is to protect the ___.

   a. inspector
   b real estate agent
   c. mortgage company
   d. public

101. Under what conditions may a real estate agent provide a home inspection report to third parties?

   a. When requested by the seller
   b When agreed to by the client and the inspector
   c. When required by the mortgage company
   d. When needed by a contractor

102. Why should an inspection agreement be presented to the client before the inspection?

   a. Provides the real estate agent time to advise the client about the agreement
   b Presentation is required by the Uniform Commercial Code
   c. Provides an opportunity for the client to negotiate the agreement
   d. Presentation is required by the Department of Housing and Urban Development

103. Which type of insurance provides legal representation for an inspector who fails to report a defect in a system covered by the Standard of Practice?

   a. Homeowners
   b General liability
   c. Performance bond
   d. Errors and omissions

104. A home inspector's spouse is the client's real estate agent. The inspector may inspect a property for this client if the relationship is disclosed to the ___.

   a. client
   b seller
   c. parties involved in the transaction
   d. state inspector license board

Answer Key: Section 1

1.1.1 (d) deadmen and tiebacks
These components are installed in the material behind the retaining wall. Deadmen are installed parallel to the wall, and tiebacks connect the deadmen to the wall. Friction with the material is the force that helps tiebacks and deadmen resist wall rotation.

1.1.2 (b) 6 inches within the first 10 feet
This is a requirement of the International Residential Code (IRC). Drainage of storm water away from the foundation is essential to keep the building dry and to reduce the chance of infestation by wood destroying organisms.

1.1.3 (c) soil
Cracks in driveways are often caused by soil subsiding or by soil uplift. Subsidence can occur because of poor soil compaction or by erosion by water. Uplift is often caused by tree roots.

1.1.4 (b) 45 inches
This is a requirement of the International Swimming Pool and Spa Code. Fences reduce the chance of children drowning in swimming pools

1.1.5 (a) Wall is more than 4 feet tall.
This is a requirement of the International Residential Code. Tall walls may be subjected to loads that could cause the wall to fail if the wall is not properly designed to resist the imposed loads.

1.1.6 (c) Tree branches hanging over the building
Common home inspection standards of practice limit the requirement to report vegetation defects to those that may adversely affect the building.

1.1.7 (d) termites
Moisture near a foundation provides an attractive environment for some termite species.

1.2.1 (d) 6 inches
This is a requirement of the International Residential Code (IRC) and of most siding manufacturer's instructions. Clearance between soil and wood products is necessary to avoid deterioration due to water.

1.2.2 (a) house wrap
House wrap is an example of a water-resistive-barrier (WRB). A WRB and flashing are the primary components that resist water intrusion into building walls. Wall coverings shed water; they do not prevent water from entering the wall cavity.

1.2.3 (b) 32 inches
This is a requirement of the International Residential Code. Measurement is between the door in the open position and the door frame (usually the stop). In standard door widths, this width is provided by a 36 inch wide door.

1.2.4 (b) 18 inches
This is a requirement of the International Residential Code. Falling into a large piece of glass could cause serious injury.

1.2.5 (c) 4 risers
This is a requirement of the International Residential Code. Graspable handrails are for the safety of all users, especially those with reduced mobility or reduced grip strength.

1.2.6 (a) the door strikes a 1 inch thick object.
This has been a federal government requirement since 1 January 1993. Refer to 16 FR 1211

1.2.7 (b) 33 inches
The International Residential Code 24, R703.8.6, requires weep holes spaced not more than 33 inches on center.

1.3.1 (d) ¼ inch per foot
A completely flat roof is likely to retain water. This can deteriorate the roof covering. Water is heavy, and if enough water collects it can cause the roof to collapse.

1.3.2 (a) standing seam metal panels
The seams of standing seam metal panels are crimped so that water entry is less likely. This allows standing seam panels to be used on low slope roofs. Crimped seams differentiate standing seam metal panels from other type of metal roofs, such as lapped seam panels and metal shingles.

1.3.3 (b) leaks in attic HVAC ducts
Leaky HVAC supply ducts provide warm air in the attic that can increase the temperature of the roof sheathing and melt snow on the roof. Water flows down the roof, freezes at the cold eaves, and forms an ice dam.

1.3.4 (c) expansive soil is present
The International Residential Code (Chapter 8) requires gutters only when collapsable or expansive soil is present.

1.3.5 (d) 48 hours
Small amounts of water that remain on a roof for a short time are unlikely to cause damage. The 48 hour exception allows for the fact that it is difficult to achieve perfect drainage off of a low slope roof.

1.3.6 (a) a wall extends past a roof
Kick out flashing turns water from the roof so it is less likely to flow down the wall below and cause damage. Damage to wall coverings at and below a roof/wall intersection is a common issue.

1.3.7 (c) fold the counterflashing into a groove cut into mortar
Folding the counterflashing into a groove physically anchors the counterflashing and makes it less likely to move and to leak. Applying sealant into the groove helps further reduce water intrusion.

1.3.8 (b) apply an ultraviolet-resistant coating
Polyurethane foam degrades rapidly when exposed to sunlight. An ultraviolet-resistant coating must be applied soon after the foam sets, and must be reapplied as needed.

1.4.1 (d) any forces
Buildings should be designed and built to resist any forces that may be applied. Some forces, such as gravity and wind, are universal. Others, such as earthquake, only occur in specific areas, such as Charleston, South Carolina.

1.4.2 (a) dampproofing and a foundation drain
A foundation drain is required if basement space is usable. Waterproofing is recommended, but only dampproofing is required by the International Residential Code.

1.4.3 (c) ¼ of the actual joist depth
Limits on notches and holes in joists are based on the actual joist depth. A notch may be up to $\frac{1}{6}$ of the actual joist depth, except at the ends of the joist where up to ¼ of the actual joist depth is allowed. Refer to the International Residential Code Chapter 5.

1.4.4 (b) fireblocked at 10 and 20 feet
Fireblocking limits the spread of fire in enclosed vertical and horizontal spaces. Fireblocking is required every 10 feet in horizontal open areas, such as drop soffits and multiple-stud walls.

1.4.5 (c) ⅝ thick Type X drywall
Type X drywall is more fire-resistant than regular drywall. ⅝ thick Type X drywall provides extra protection for habitable space if there is a fire in the garage.

1.4.6 (d) 60% of the actual stud depth
Limits on notches and holes in studs are based on the actual stud depth. Refer to the International Residential Code Chapter 6.

1.4.7 (a) gable
A gable roof is a simple roof with rafters as the triangle legs and a ceiling joist as the triangle base.

1.4.8 (c) 2x8
A purlin should be the same depth as the rafter it supports. A purlin brace may be a 2x4 if the brace is not more than 8 feet long.

1.5.1 (b) provides an alternate return path for electricity
Electricity returns to its source. In utility systems, the primary return path to the generating station is the utility grounded wire. The grounding electrode system provides an alternate return path in case the primary path is disconnected.

1.5.2 (c) two energized wires share one neutral wire
Multiwire branch circuits reduce cost by allowing one electrical cable to serve two circuits, such as the two, 20 amp, kitchen countertop circuits. While multiwire branch circuits frequently originate from two separate circuit breakers, one double-pole circuit breaker can be used.

1.5.3 (b) 10
Ten feet above walkways and similar areas that are intended for pedestrian use is high enough to prevent accidental contact with energized wires.

1.5.4 (a) crawlspace
Ground fault interrupter protected circuits are required in areas where electricity and water are close to each other. Electricity can flow more easily through water.

1.5.5 (d) label the wire as energized at accessible locations
Wires that are used for a purpose inconsistent with their insulation color should be permanently labeled to indicate their actual use to avoid confusion and danger when working on the circuit.

1.5.6 (c) 6
Stairways should be well lit to avoid falls. This requirement helps ensure occupant safety by being able to control stairway lighting before and after using the stairway.

1.5.7 (c) prevents electric shock during a ground fault
The equipment grounding conductor is really part of the electrical bonding system. Electricity flows in this system when non-current-carrying metal becomes energized and trips the overcurrent device, preventing an electric shock.

1.5.8 (a) install a grounding electrode system
Electrical systems in detached buildings are effectively separate systems. A grounding electrode system is necessary for the same reasons as other systems.

1.5.9 (b) on the condenser label
The maximum overcurrent device size and the minimum circuit ampacity are provided on the manufacturer's label affixed to the condenser. While it is possible to find this information elsewhere, the first, and usually the easiest, place is on the label.

1.6.1 (c) 12,000 Btu
Cooling appliance capacity is often encoded in the model number, and is displayed in Btu without the zeros. For example, the cooling capacity of a model number with 36 for the capacity is 36/12=3 tons.

1.6.2 (a) suction tube
Cool gas flows from the evaporator to the compressor after absorbing heat from the building when operating in cooling mode.

1.6.3 (d) blocked air filter
A blocked air filter reduces air flow through the evaporator. This can cause less heat absorption, reduce air temperature at the evaporator coil, and allow ice formation.

1.6.4 (b) floor drain
This is one of several locations where the primary condensate drain may terminate, including outdoors and before a plumbing trap.

1.6.5 (a) kitchen
A return in the kitchen could draw cooking odors, grease, and moisture into the HVAC system, and could reduce the effectiveness of the kitchen exhaust system.

1.6.6 (b) a condenser.
A compressor is located inside an air conditioner/heat pump condenser unit. In cooling mode, a compressor receives cool gas from the evaporator and condenses it into a hot gas and sends it to the condenser coils to discharge heat.

1.7.1 (d) water vapor
Complete combustion of natural gas produces water vapor and carbon dioxide.

1.7.2 (b) there is insufficient combustion air
A natural gas flame should be blue with a yellow tip. Any other color indicates a combustion problem.

1.7.3 (a) draft sensor
The draft sensor in a gas furnace ensures that the draft inducer fan is operating so that combustion products will be pulled through the heat exchanger so they can flow into the vent system.

1.7.4 (c) 3 inches
Type L vents are typically used for oil-burning appliances, which burn hotter than gas appliances. The vent gets hotter, so more clearance to combustibles and insulation is required for fire safety.

1.7.5 (d) hartford loop
A hartford loop helps prevent boiler explosions caused by firing a boiler with no water in the boiler. The loop connects 2-4 inches below the boiler normal water level. This prevents draining all water from the boiler if a leak occurs in the wet return pipe.

1.7.6 (c) 12 psi
The normal operating pressure for a hot water boiler is between 12 psi and 15 psi.

1.8.1 (b) heat
The U-value of a material is the amount of heat that can flow through the material. U-value is the inverse or R-value. U-value is used when describing the thermal properties of windows and doors.

1.8.2 (a) polyisocyanurate
Polyisocyanurate is a spray foam and a sheet insulation. Open cell polyisocyanurate has an R-value of about 3.7 per inch. Closed cell polyisocyanurate has an R-value of about 6 per inch.

1.8.3 (d) an air barrier
Batt and loose-fill insulation work by trapping air so that it does not move. Any air movement through these insulation types reduces their R-value. These insulation types should be in contact with an air barrier on all sides.

1.8.4 (c) occupant breathing
Occupant activities, such as bathing, cooking, washing clothes, and just breathing can contribute to water vapor levels in a house. Using kitchen and bathroom exhaust fans can reduce water

vapor.

1.8.5 (b) 40 – 50%
Too much or too little ridge ventilation can disrupt the air flow in an attic creating dead areas where moisture and heat can accumulate.

1.8.6 (c) an air barrier at crawlspace walls
An unventilated crawlspace is considered semi-conditioned space. The crawlspace should be sealed from outside air intrusion, just like any other conditioned space.

1.9.1 (a) fire
Lint is flammable.

1.9.2 (d) PVC
Schedule 40 PVC may be used when installing a downdraft kitchen exhaust system. This material is likely to function as intended over time when buried.

1.9.3 (b) above the roof
A bathroom exhaust duct may terminate anywhere outside the building. Outdoors does not include eaves, crawlspaces, and attics.

1.9.4 (b) 3 feet
Separation of operable windows and doors from a clothes dryer exhaust duct reduces the chance that the exhaust gas may reenter the building.

1.9.5 (a) water vapor
An energy recover ventilation system provides ventilation and improves air conditioning efficiency by extracting heat and water vapor from the incoming air.

1.9.6 (c) 35 feet
Long clothes dryer exhaust ducts are more likely to become blocked by lint because exhaust velocity slows and deposits lint in the duct.

1.10.1 (c) 80 psi
Water pressure must be adequate to provide functional flow, but not so high as to damage pipes and fixtures.

1.10.2 (d) low water flow
Galvanized steel water pipe rusts on the inside. The rough surface traps debris, eventually reducing the interior pipe diameter, limiting water flow through the pipe.

1.10.3 (b) 30 inches
The minimum dimensions of a shower are 30 inches with a total area of at least 900 square inches. This is a safety requirement. The minimum dimension is 25 inches if the total shower area is at least 1,300 square inches.

1.10.4 (c) air gap
The air gap distance should be at least twice the faucet opening size. The distance between the sink flood rim level and the faucet makes flow from the sink into the faucet difficult.

1.10.5 (a) anode
A very small electric current can occur in a water heater which can corrode the water tank. The anode reacts with this current and dissolves so the water tank does not.

1.10.6 (c) ¼ inch per foot
Drain pipes 3 inches and smaller diameter should slope at least ¼ inch per foot so that liquids and solids will flow. Larger drain pipes may slope at least ⅛ per foot.

1.10.7 (a) P trap

The P trap is currently permitted. S, bell, and drum traps are no longer permitted, but may remain if the trap was permitted when installed.

1.11.1 (d) kitchen

Kitchen is defined in code as a habitable room. Habitable rooms have requirements for size, ceiling height, heat, and light.

1.11.2 (d) unknown

All of the options are possibilities. It is difficult to determine the cause of a defect without further evaluation to determine the exact cause.

1.11.3 (b) a divided light door

Safety glazing is required in each pane of doors with multiple panes, such as French Doors. Decorative glazing, such as cut glass and stain glass, are not required to be safety glazing. A transom is above the 60 inches vertical limit where safety glazing is required.

1.11.4 (c) anti-tip bracket operation

An anti-tip bracket is required to reduce burn injuries caused when someone steps on the oven door and causes the range to tilt forward.

1.11.5 (b) a hub

A hub is a device in a "smart home" communication system that allows the "smart home" devices to communicate with each other.

1.12.1 (a) on the floor of the firebox

The hearth is on the floor of the firebox where the fuel is burned. It should be at solid concrete or masonry least 4 inches thick and 20 inches deep, except for Rumford fireplaces.

1.12.2 (b) 2 feet

A chimney should terminate at least 3 feet above where it intersects the roof and at least 2 feet above any obstruction within 10 feet. This helps ensure that the chimney has enough draft to expel combustion products.

1.12.3 (c) 16 inches

The hearth extension should extend at least 16 inches in front of a fireplace with an opening less than 6 square feet. This reduces the chance that embers escaping from the firebox could ignite nearby materials.

1.12.4 (d) burning unseasoned wood

Burning unseasoned wood is a common cause of creosote accumulation, in part because the fire burns cooler.

1.12.5 (a) 6 inches

Combustible trim, such as a mantel, should be at least 6 inches from the firebox opening to avoid igniting the trim.

1.12.6 (c) bricks with open cores

Fireplaces and chimneys should be built using solid masonry (bricks) or cored masonry with filled cores. Open core masonry may not provide enough protection against heat dissipation. Unlined chimneys may not be built, but may continue to be used if safe.

1.12.7 (a) 1

One flue may serve only one fireplace or appliance. Combustion products from different appliances could disrupt the draft in the flue and interfere with expelling all combustion products.

1.13.1 (b) 24 inches

Window opening size is limited if the opening is 24 inches or lower above the floor and if the opening is 6 feet or more above exterior grade. This is to prevent children from falling out of windows.

1.13.2 (a) 1 door

A house must have at least one egress door that meets the egress door requirements; usually the front door. Other doors do not need to comply with the egress door requirements.

1.13.3 (c) 36 inches

All landings at doors should be at least 36 inches deep in the direction of travel regardless of the size of the door served by the landing.

1.13.4 (c) 48 inches

The roof of a townhouse should be covered with non-combustible roof covering and have fire-retarding material for at least 48 inches on both sides of the common wall. This helps keep fire from spreading between townhouse units.

1.13.5 (d) habitable space is above the garage

Minimum ⅝ inch thick Type X drywall is required on the garage ceiling if habitable space is above the garage. This helps protect the living area from fire in the garage.

1.13.6 (b) ½ inch thick drywall

½ inch thick drywall is the minimum fire separation material between a garage and the house.

1.13.7 (a) inside a sleeping room containing a fuel-burning appliance

Carbon monoxide alarms are required outside of sleeping rooms and inside sleeping rooms where a fuel-burning appliance is in the room or in an attached bathroom.

Answer Key: Section 2

2.1.1 (c) action that the client should take
A home inspection report should guide the client about how to address the reported deficiency, such as have the component evaluated by a qualified specialist.

2.1.2 (b) type of roof covering material
The type of roof covering material is important information because it informs about roof covering potential service life and maintenance procedures.

2.1.3 (a) type
Home inspectors must report the types of installed heating equipment because it informs about potential service life and maintenance procedures.

2.1.4 (d) They measure temperature at the surface of an object.
Infrared cameras and thermometers can only measure the temperature at the surface of the object. Condition of material below the surface may affect the object's surface temperature; however, it is possible for defects to be present that do not affect the object's surface temperature.

2.1.5 (a) determine if a moisture stain is wet.
A moisture meter is best used as a tool to confirm a visual indication of a possible moisture problem. An inspector may wish to confirm an observation in order to avoid reporting a defect that has been addressed. Inspectors are not required to confirm or determine the cause of a defect.

2.2.1 (a) explain why a system was not inspected
Options b, c, and d are recommended parts of a limitation statement. Only option a is required by SoPs.

2.2.2 (d) client
A home inspector's contract is with the client; so the client is the only party that can agree to exclude a system, component, or procedure from a home inspection.

2.2.3 (c) visually inspect the system
Inability to operate a system does not relieve the inspector from the duty to perform other inspection procedures, such as the visual inspection of the system and its components. Often, defects in shut down systems can be determined by visual inspection.

2.2.4 (b) report that the garage was not inspected
Inspectors, clients, and real estate agents should not move occupant belongings because of the liability risk. Insignificant property can become a priceless heirloom if damaged. It is usually best to complete an inspection and arrange for additional inspections after the building has been made fully accessible.

2.2.5 (d) inspect detached garages.
Inspectors are not required to inspect detached structures, except for garages and carports.

2.3.1 (a) the condenser's serial number.
Many manufacturers encode the month and year of manufacture into the serial number, which is usually found on the label affixed to the condenser and air handler. A few manufacturers put the date as month and year on the label.

2.3.2 (d) asphalt shingles on a south-facing roof

South and west-facing roofs are usually exposed to longer and more intense sunlight, which can degrade asphalt shingles at a more rapid rate than identical shingles on the north and east sides.

2.3.3 (b) describe the nature of the deficiency

Explaining the criteria that the inspector used to determine that a system or component is deficient helps the client understand the situation, and may help motivate the client to take the recommended action.

2.3.4 (c) ½ inch difference between stair riser heights

The difference between riser height in a flight of stairs may not be more than ⅜ inch. A larger difference is a fall hazard.

2.3.5 (d) a 12 foot long 2x10 floor joist with a ¼ inch deep notch 5 feet from the end

Notches are not allowed in the center one-third of a dimensional lumber floor joist. This condition would be considered significantly deficient, even if the joist were currently functioning properly.

2.3.6 (a) the inspector's judgment

An unsafe condition depends on the situation at the inspection, so the inspector must make a judgment about safety based on many factors. Failure to comply with current building code does not make a condition unsafe, nor does compliance with past building code make a condition safe.

2.4.1 (b) plant leaves are 1 inch from the house wall

Plants that scrape walls and roofs can damage them. The plant in this example is not touching the wall, but may do so in the future. Client should monitor the plant and take action if it scrapes the wall.

2.4.2 (c) licensed

While all of the options are possible ways to evaluate a contractor, a license is an independent indication that a contractor may have appropriate skills. A license is usually required to obtain a building permit, if one is necessary.

2.4.3 (d) condensation in a wall cavity

A return duct leak means that the furnace injects more air into the building than it removes. This pressurizes the building and can force warm, moist air into the wall cavities. In the winter, the temperature inside the wall cavity can fall below the dewpoint, water vapor can condense into liquid water and cause damage.

2.4.4 (b) recessed light fixtures

Air leaks through and around recessed light fixtures can allow warm, moist air into attics and rafter cavities. Moisture in the air may condense on rafters and roof sheathing resulting in stains. Flashing leaks and exhaust duct termination issues are usually confined to the area round the leak or the termination.

2.4.5 (b) water flow at a clothes washing machine valve

Active water leaks can cause significant damage in a short period of time. Gas smell at a gas meter regulator is not unusual; the regulator is supposed to release small amounts of gas to relieve pressure. A puddle at an oil tank vent tube is usually caused by the technician overfilling the tank.

2.4.6 (a) damaged roof trusses

Trusses are engineered systems. An engineer must design the repair. While the other options are structural defects, standard methods exist to repair the defect. The contractor should engage an engineer if the situation requires one.

2.4.7 (c) the wall has moved due to inadequate bracing
Window sashes that do not close evenly at the meeting rail (where the two sashes meet) could be caused by poor installation or damage during transport, or by wall movement that moves the window out of square. The drywall crack at the window corner suggests that wall movement as a more likely cause.

Answer Key: Section 3

3.1.1 (a) mutual assent
A contract is an agreement between parties. All parties must agree (assent) to all terms.

3.1.2 (c) judge has a better understanding of party's intentions
Interpreting and enforcing a written contract is difficult enough. Accurately determining the terms of an unwritten contract is almost impossible. A written contract documents the party's intentions, and makes it easier to reach an outcome that is consistent with those intentions.

3.1.3 (d) John Doe Inspections and More, Inc.
The name on a company's inspection contract should be exactly as it appears in the company's organizing documents, and as filed with state authorities that register businesses and issue business licenses.

3.1.4 (b) laws of the state where the home is located
Contracts are governed by state law, which differ between every state. It is better to specify governing law in the inspection contract, but if no law is specified, the default is usually the state law where the home is located.

3.1.5 (c) hearing before a neutral party
Arbitration is a formal process whereby independent neutral person(s) are selected by the parties to evaluate the evidence and render a decision and award.

3.1.6 (b) spouse
The named client and spouse are considered one client, unless expressly agreed to in the inspection contract. The home inspector may not discuss the inspection with any other party without the client's permission.

3.1.7 (b) Standard of Practice where the home is located
A home inspector who practices in multiple licensed jurisdictions should use the Standard of Practice, and have a license, in the state where the inspection occurs

3.2.1 (a) compensatory damages
Breach of contract awards are intended to put the plaintiff in a position that would have occurred if defendant had not breached the contract.

3.2.2 (d) perform like a reasonable inspector.
Negligence is defined as failure to perform as a reasonable person would have under similar conditions.

3.2.3 (c) pays a real estate broker for inclusion on a preferred provider list
Payment for inclusion on a preferred provider list is often considered a conflict of interest because of a lack of independence between the broker and the inspector. Such payments violate some state regulations.

3.2.4 (b) general liability
This insurance covers risks, such as damage caused by the inspector and injury to someone during the inspection.

3.2.5 (b) claim made while policy is active, inspector is not at fault
A claims made errors and omissions policy covers inspectors for claims that occur while the policy is active for inspections that occur while the policy is active, regardless of whether the inspector is at fault.

3.2.6 (d) complaint
A lawsuit begins with a complaint by the plaintiff alleging wrongs committed by the defendant.

HILEP Practice Exam Answer Key

1. (a) reading the label attached to the wood
There is no reliable way to determine the type and level of wood preservative treatment without reading the label that should be attached to each piece of preservative-treated wood. If the label is removed, which it often is, then the inspector should disclaim knowledge of whether and how the wood was treated.

2. (c) tiebacks
Tiebacks and deadmen are often used to help wood retaining walls resist rotation. The friction of the soil helps the wall resist rotation by the load behind the wall.

3. (d) fat clay
Unstable (expansive) clay soils expand when wet and contract when dry. These changes can cause significant foundation damage.

4. (c) may adversely affect the building
This is a requirement of the ASHI, and most other, Standards of Practice.

5. (d) install a French Drain
A French Drain is an underground drainage system that uses catch basins to collect water, and pipes to conduct the water to a point where safe disposal is possible.

6. (c) 54 inches
This is a requirement of the International Swimming Pool and Spa Code, and of many local regulations. The purpose is to reduce pool access by children.

7. (b) isolation joint
Concrete driveways and walkways move at different rates with respect to building foundations. An isolation joint allows for this differential movement without damaging either component.

8. (a) stucco
Adhered masonry veneer and stucco are called adhered veneers. They are installed using wire lath attached to the building over a water-resistive barrier.

9. (d) awning
Awning windows are similar to casement (side hinged) and hopper (bottom hinged) windows in that they open outward. Awning windows can be opened when it is raining because the window protects the opening from the rain.

10. (a) 2 to 1
Cantilevered floor joists extend beyond a supporting wall. They must resist the downward load created by occupants and their belongings, and they must resist the upward load created when the cantilevered joists pivot at the wall. The joist backspan into the building helps resist this upward load.

11. (a) 2 by 2 inches
A handrail must be graspable. The International Residential Code (IRC, Chapter 3) specifies allowed profiles and dimensions that most stairway users can grasp. While most of the options presented are commonly used as handrails, only the 2 by 2 is approved by the IRC.

12. (c) 6 inches
This is a requirement of manufacturer's instructions and industry guidelines. The distance helps avoid injury and damage that could occur if the door closes on a child or an object.

13. (b) 44 inches
This is a requirement of the International Residential Code, Chapter 3. The intent is to allow occupants to reach the opening, and to allow first responders to enter through the opening.

14. (b) 2 inches

The International Residential Code Chapter 9, and most shingle manufacturers, do not allow fiberglass shingles to be installed on a roof with a slope less than 2 inches in 12 inches. Double underlayment is usually required for roof slopes between 2 inches and 4 inches in 12 inches.

15. (c) moss

Moss can loosen fiberglass shingle granules and hasten shingle deterioration. The other options are considered cosmetic issues.

16. (a) standing seam metal panels

A low slope roof is defined as having a slope of less than 2 inches in 12 inches. Standing seam metal panels are considered a low slope roof covering. Lapped seam metal panels are not a low slope roof covering.

17. (d) scupper

A scupper is an opening in a parapet wall that allows water to flow through it. A scupper may drain directly to the ground, or it may drain into a downspout.

18. (a) $^1/_{16}$ inch per foot

Gutters should slope toward the discharge point, usually a downspout. Not much slope is necessary. $^1/_{16}$ per foot is a commonly accepted guideline.

19. (d) step flashing

Stepped base flashing should be covered with stepped counterflashing in order to make a low-maintenance seal between the roof covering and the brick veneer.

20. (c) cricket

A cricket (saddle) is a small gable-shaped roof the diverts water around the chimney. The cricket should be flashed as appropriate for the chimney wall material.

21. (a) 0

Trusses are engineered systems. An engineer must design modifications to truss members, including cuts to install components.

22. (b) deteriorated vent flashing

Inexpensive plumbing vent flashing boots, such as those made from neoprene, may not last as long as the roof covering. They may leak before the roof covering is replaced.

23. (d) epoxy

Epoxy is a common method for addressing non-structural cracks in foundation walls. Epoxy seals against water intrusion, and may provide a minor structural benefit.

24. (c) footing settlement

A crack that is wider near the floor than near the ceiling suggests some sections of the footings are settling at a different rate than other sections. Cracks where the footings are settling more will be wider than where the footings are settling less.

25. (a) waterproofing

Waterproofing prevents water vapor and liquid water under some pressure from penetrating the foundation wall. Bituminous coating and polyethylene sheeting is one method of waterproofing.

26. (b) blocking

Blocking installed between a damaged floor joist and adjacent joists helps spread the load to the adjacent joists. Structural repairs require a permit and inspections.

27. (d) the joist species

Lumber species have different characteristics, such as strength and resistance to bending. Lumber span tables list spans for different species and other characteristics, such as joist depth and joist spacing.

28. (b) #2
The International Residential Code Chapter 5 beam span tables assume #2 grade or better lumber. An engineer may specify beams made from other lumber grades.

29. (c) bracing
Wall braces are installed in walls at required locations to help keep the wall from bending out of its usual rectangular shape, a process called racking. Racking causes cracks in building materials, and may contribute to door and window operating problems.

30. (c) 24 inches
The International Residential Code Chapter 8 requires that wood structural panels be at least 24 inches wide. This is necessary to maintain the ability of the panel to resist applied loads.

31. (b) 100 amps
This is required by the National Electrical Code and the International Residential Code Chapter 36 for new construction, and when service equipment is replaced.

32. (c) at the subpanel
Subpanels in accessory buildings should be connected to a separate grounding electrode system. This is an exception to the general rule that there should be no grounding connections downstream from the building service equipment.

33. (a) current difference between energized and grounded wires
Return current in the grounded (neutral) wire should be equal to the supply current in the energized wire. If there is a difference (only about 5 milliamps), there may be a ground fault.

34. (b) 36
Service drop conductors should be at least 36 inches above most roofs. A common exception is where 6 feet or less of the service drop extends above the roof. This usually occurs at the eaves.

35. (d) metal-clad cable
This wiring method may be buried if listed for burial and corrosion protected. This wiring method is a flexible metal jacket with factory-installed conductors. It appears similar to armored cable.

36. (c) knob-and-tube
Knob-and-tube wiring was one of the original wiring methods. It consists of two wires supported by ceramic knobs and protected by ceramic tubes when run through framing members. It is considered obsolete, but may be used if in good condition.

37. (a) Zinsco
These panelboards are most common in houses built between 1940 and 1970. A common alleged problem is the failure of breakers to trip when current is above the designed value.

38. (b) 2 feet
This is required by the National Electrical Code and the International Residential Code Chapter 39 for new construction, and when remodeling a kitchen if electrical work is performed.

39. (d) use the test button on the AFCI
Manufacturers recommend using the test button on the device to test AFCI and GFCI devices. Other test methods may not produce accurate results.

40. (c) ground source
Ground source describes energy exchange with the earth. Geothermal describes using heat from the earth, such as from a hot spring or heat source that relies on heat from within the earth. Although technically incorrect, geothermal is often used to describe ground source heat pumps.

41. (a) expansion device

In modern systems, the high-pressure liquid refrigerant passes through a thermal expansion valve or an electronic expansion valve that causes the liquid to expand into a gas as it enters the evaporator coil. The gas absorbs heat causing it to boil and become a cool gas.

42. (b) evaporative cooler

Evaporative coolers are older technology systems that were common in areas where the humidity is low, such as the Southwest. Most evaporative coolers have been replaced by central air conditioning, although some remain in use because they are far less expensive to operate and maintain.

43. (d) latent load

When an air conditioner removes heat from the air passing over the evaporator coil, part of the energy is used to condense water vapor in the air. Latent load is a factor used to determine the recommended air conditioner Btu cooling capacity.

44. (c) ¾ inch

This is a requirement of the International Residential Code Chapter 14. The pipe is usually PVC. It should drain by gravity to the discharge point.

45. (a) draft inducer fan

The draft inducer fan pulls combustion products through the heat exchanger. The fan must activate before the furnace allows gas to flow. A sensor confirms fan operation, the igniter activates, then the gas valve is allowed to open.

46. (b) stack effect

Hot gas is less dense and more buoyant than surrounding cooler gas; therefore, the hot gas rises and displaces the cooler gas. The stack effect occurs anywhere there are gasses of different temperatures, such as buildings and vent systems.

47. (d) short cycling

An air conditioner that has more Btu capacity than is necessary may rapidly cool the space and shut off. This is called short cycling. Short cycling is inefficient, and often does a poor job of dehumidification.

48. (c) fire eye

The fire eye is located in the oil burner blast tube. It detects the flame and shuts off the burner if the flame is not present. This keeps oil from flowing, which could collect in the blast tube and refractory chamber, and which can explode when exposed to a spark.

49. (a) The last radiator in the system runs cool.

In a one pipe series loop system, each radiator receives water from the nearest upstream radiator. The first radiator gets the hottest water, and each subsequent radiator gets cooler water because the heat was released in the upstream radiators.

50. (d) barometric damper

A barometric damper is a fitting in an oil furnace vent connector that has a hinged flap that opens and closes to help adjust the pressure in the vent system so that combustion products are completely expelled at the top of the vent system.

51. (b) white stains at vent fittings

White stains at vent fittings indicate that moisture is condensing in the vent system. The stains are minerals left when the water leaks out of the vent fittings.

52. (a) convection

Convection is the process by which warmer, more buoyant gas or liquid rises and displaces cooler, denser, gas or liquid. The stack effect is an example of convective movement.

53. (a) mineral wool
Mineral wool insulation comes in batts and loose fill. R-value is around 3.7 per inch for batts and 3.1 per inch for loose fill.

54. (d) an air barrier
Batt and loose-fill insulation work by trapping air so that it does not move. Any air movement through these insulation types reduces their R-value. These insulation types should be in contact with an air barrier on all sides.

55. (c) neither side of the wall
Enclosed exterior wall cavities should be allowed to dry in at least one direction. In a warm/humid climate zone, moisture can enter the wall cavity from the inside or the outside, thus, the wall should be able to dry from either direction. Not installing a vapor retarder allows this drying.

56. (b) 1/300
This is a requirement of the International Residential Code, Chapter 8. The ratio is 1/150 if less than 40% of the ventilation opening area is near the roof ridge.

57. (c) a vapor diffusion port
Water vapor can accumulate in a closed attic in warm climate zones. Air permeable insulation can allow the water vapor to flow through it and condense on the roof sheathing. A vapor diffusion port allows the water vapor to escape, but does not allow air to enter the attic.

58. (d) 10 feet
A closer location could allow combustion gasses from the vent, including carbon monoxide, to be drawn into the building by the heat recovery ventilator.

59. (c) 4 inches
Recent editions of the International Residential Code Chapter 15 have effectively eliminated 3-inch diameter ducts for bathroom exhaust fans Three-inch ducts are common in older buildings and may remain in service. Four-inch diameter and larger ducts allow exhaust gasses to flow through the duct with less resistance.

60. (c) copper duct
Galvanized steel is the most common exhaust duct material for range hoods, but copper and stainless steel may also be used. Schedule 40 or thicker PVC pipe may be used only for downdraft exhaust systems, and only if the pipe is installed in the foundation slab.

61. (b) 8 feet
The clothes dryer transition duct should be not more than 8 feet long. This is a requirement of the International Residential Code Chapter 15.

62. (b) 2 inches
An air gap is a common type of backflow prevention between the potable and waste water systems. The minimum air gap distance is twice the supply fixture opening size, in almost all cases.

63. (a) acidic water
Water with an abnormally high or low pH can erode the protective patina that forms inside of copper water tubing. Once the patina is eroded, the tubing deteriorates, resulting in pinhole leaks. This situation is common in areas with hydrogen sulfide in the water, such as Florida, and in areas where water is drawn from wells.

64. (c) 15 inches
This is a requirement of the International Residential Code Chapter 3. It provides a minimum safe and convenient space for most people.

65. (b) 1
Every sanitary drainage system must have at least one atmospheric vent in order to equalize both positive and negative pressure in the vent system. The remaining vents may be air admittance valves.

66. (d) in a bedroom
This is a requirement of the International Residential Code Chapter 20. It is a safety precaution against oxygen depletion by combustion, or poisoning by backdrafting of combustion products.

67. (a) labeled GAS
Copper gas tubing could be mistaken for water distribution tubing, thus, it must be labeled with GAS in black letters on a yellow background at least every five feet.

68. (c) when plumbing fixtures are below the public sewer tap
Ideally, waste material drains by gravity from the plumbing fixture to the sewer or the septic tank. If a house, or its basement is far below street level, it may be necessary to pump the waste material up to where the material can drain to the sewer or septic tank by gravity.

69. (c) 60 inches
This is a requirement of the International Residential Code Chapter 3. It is a safety precaution against cut injuries caused by a fall while using a stairway.

70. (b) 4
This is a requirement of the International Residential Code, Chapter 3. It is a safety precaution against injuries caused by a fall while using a stairway.

71. (d) filler strip
Occupants may not be able to fully open doors and drawers of cabinets that meet at perpendicular corners. This makes all or part of either or both cabinets unusable. This can be a significant inconvenience in kitchens with limited cabinet space.

72. (a) makeup air
High capacity exhaust hoods can depressurize the building and cause backdrafting of combustion appliances. The makeup air requirement applies if there is a fuel-burning appliance, including a fireplace, in the conditioned space.

73. (b) throat
The fireplace throat is the area between the firebox and the smoke chamber. The throat directs combustion gasses into the smoke chamber and then into the flue.

74. (c) 6 inches
This is a requirement of the International Residential Code Chapter 10. It is intended to provide structural support for a heavy masonry chimney.

75. (c) pellet stove
Pellet stoves are designed to burn wood-byproducts that have been compressed into pellets. The pellets are fed into a hopper which dispenses the pellets into the stove at a rate determined by the user.

76. (d) concrete
This is a requirement of the International Residential Code Chapter 10 that is frequently ignored. Mortar, the most commonly used material, deteriorates more rapidly than concrete, thus requiring more frequent maintenance, which is seldom done.

77. (a) spalling
Spalling occurs when parts of a material break off. Spalling is a common masonry chimney defect, especially near the top where the chimney is more exposed to water.

78. (c) 2 inches

This is a requirement of the International Residential Code Chapter 10 that is frequently ignored. A chimney is considered within a building if any part of the chimney abuts the building walls up to where the chimney passes through the roof or the eaves.

79. (b) inadequate combustion air

Gas burned without adequate oxygen produces carbon, carbon monoxide, and water vapor.

80. (c) 16 inches

Hearth extension dimensions for a prefabricated wood-burning fireplace are the same as for a masonry fireplace.

81. (a) 0

This is a requirement of the International Residential Code Chapter 3. Doors, except for screen and storm doors, should not swing over steps because the user might fall when stepping backwards to operate the door.

82. (d) ¾ -inch thick plywood

This is a requirement of the International Residential Code Chapter 3, which lists materials that will slow flame spread.

83. (c) bedroom

This is a requirement of the International Residential Code Chapter 3. A garage fire could spread into a bedroom undetected while the occupant slept.

84. (a) ⅝ -inch thick Type X gypsum board on the roof sheathing

This is a requirement of the International Residential Code Chapter 3. A parapet wall is the traditional method of limiting fire in the attic from spreading between townhouse units. Gypsum board is an alternative fire separation method that eliminates the need for a parapet wall.

85. (c) in a house with a fireplace

This is a requirement of the International Residential Code Chapter 3. A carbon monoxide alarm is required in houses with an attached garage, or where there is a fuel-burning appliance, including a fireplace. The alarm should be located near the bedrooms. An alarm is required in a bedroom only if a fuel-burning appliance is located in the bedroom.

86. (c) a lock with a knob on the inside

This is a requirement of the International Residential Code Chapter 3. The egress door, usually the front door, must be operable from the interior without a key or special knowledge, such as a combination.

87. (d) the reasons why the crawl space was not entered

Most standards of practice require reporting if a system or component that is required to be inspected was not inspected, and include the reason(s) why. It is wise to also state that there may be undiscovered defects, and to recommend inspection of the uninspected systems or components, but these are not required.

88. (b) the type of wall covering

Recalls, litigation, and similar conditions are out of scope of a home inspection, and are specifically excluded in some standards of practice. Standards of practice require describing the types of wall coverings, and any defects that may exist.

89. (c) Report both a and b

An inspector should report how attics and crawl spaces were inspected, including any limitations on the inspection. While it may seem obvious that there is no accessible attic above a vaulted ceiling, inspectors are still required to state all inspection limitations.

90. (a) high voltage electric power wires in the back yard

High voltage power wires, and any associated magnetic fields, are specifically excluded from a home inspection. Vegetation and retaining walls are in scope if their condition might affect the house. There is no size limitation on an exterior door, so there is no defect and no exclusion.

91. (b) The inspector is not responsible because the damage was not visible during the inspection.

A home inspection is a visual inspection. Defects that are not visible are out of scope, and the inspector is not responsible for reporting out of scope defects.

92. (a) The electrical panel interior was not inspected because it is unsafe to do so.

Most standards of practice require reporting if a system or component that is required to be inspected was not inspected, and include the reason(s) why Response c does not include the reason why. Responses b and d may be true, and may be reportable as defects, but they do not inform the client about not inspecting a required component.

93. (d) state the implication of the defect

An important part of a home inspection defect statement is educating the clients about why they should care about the defect. This helps the client understand and prioritize defects.

94. (c) is near the end of its service life.

Home inspectors should report only what they see and what they can support with visible evidence. Significant granule loss is a common indication of aged shingles. Inspectors should not speculate about the cause of the defect (d) or recommend specific actions (a and b).

95. (a) The handrail is not graspable and may result in a fall injury.

A home inspection report defect statement should describe the defect and state an implication of not addressing the defect. Inspectors should not state that there is a building code violation, or recommend specific actions.

96. (b) recommend evaluation by a qualified contractor

A low temperature drop is not definitive evidence of an air conditioner system defect. There are situations when a low temperature drop is normal. Evaluation is the best way to determine if a defect exists, and if so, the next steps that the client should take.

97. (c) condensation on the wall at the studs

Wood has a lower R-value than insulation. In the winter the areas along the studs may be cooler than the insulated parts of the wall. If the cooler areas along the studs fall below the dewpoint, condensation may occur. The moisture may trap dust in the air which remains on the wall when the moisture evaporates.

98. (b) arbitration

Arbitration occurs when private, independent arbitrator(s), who are agreed upon by all parties to the dispute, consider evidence and render a decision. This decision can, in most cases, be presented to a court for enforcement. Arbitration differs from mediation in that mediation is a facilitated negotiation. Arbitration or litigation may be the next step if the parties cannot reach an agreement in mediation.

99. (d) an agreement between the parties

A contract is an agreement between the parties. The written document, if any, is evidence of the agreement terms, but it is not the agreement itself. Written contracts are not usually required, unless required by law.

100. (a) inspector

The inspection agreement documents the agreement between the inspector and the client(s). This protects the interests of all parties to the agreement by reducing the potential for misunderstandings about the scope and limitations of the services provided by the inspector.

101. (b) when agreed to by the client and the inspector

A home inspection report is prepared by the inspector for the client. Both the inspector and the client have an interest in the report, so both should agree about distribution to third parties, including any real estate agents.

102. (c) provides an opportunity for the client to negotiate the agreement

A contract is an agreement between the parties. Agreement cannot be achieved without an opportunity to negotiate agreement terms. Even if the client signs the inspection agreement, a court may find that there was no agreement about the terms, thus no contract exists.

103. (d) errors and omissions

Errors and omissions insurance covers inspectors against complaints from clients about an inspection. The insurance company will represent the inspector to dismiss, settle, or litigate the claim.

104. (c) parties involved in the transaction

As a general rule, an inspector may not inspect a property if the inspector has an interest in the property. The spouse's commission on the sale of the property is the inspector's interest. This general rule may be relaxed if the relationship is disclosed to all parties.

Appendix: Performance Programs Company's Test-Taking Tips

Introduction

Effective test-taking is more of an art and a practiced skill than a guarantee of success. Students preparing for the state license exam should take exam preparation very seriously. Since there are no guarantees to passing, it behooves students to optimize their chances of a successful outcome. Simply put, this is accomplished by purposeful, intensive study and question-taking practice. The harder you study and prepare, the better your odds become of passing.

There are a few beneficial pointers that can be made to improve your overall test-preparation effort. These are contained in the following compilation of tips assimilated by professional educators and test-prep experts. Please take the time to peruse these observations as they will serve to better your overall chances of passing. And in any case, we wish you the best of success!!

Make and use flashcards

Understanding tested home inspection terminology is a large part of passing your exam. As you prepare for the license examination, study. Don't just memorize specific definitions and measurements. Memorize contexts of content as well. The more you know about "the environment" of each word, in addition to the term's specific definition, the more likely you will be able to use that information to lead you to the correct exam response.

Take notes

As you read and study, take notes. Often, just the act of writing information down helps cement it in your mind. Visualizing how your notes about a particular topic appeared on the page is helpful for students who appreciate visual cues.

Immerse yourself

Form or join a study group, review topics with friends and colleagues, chat with home inspection experts, and read home inspection blogs. In other words, immerse yourself in the world of home inspection. To obtain a deeper understanding of a term or concept, Google it (using whatever search engine you employ with your computer or phone). This will shed light on varying perspectives or iterations of a term's meaning. Be careful about answering exam questions using information found on the internet. Such information may be inaccurate, or may apply only to a specific region.

Prepare a "date and key quantity" sheet

As a memory device, students are well-advised to create a "date and key quantity sheet" to be able to efficiently refer to in future study sessions. This particular summary sheet includes facts and data that are very commonly tested, including measurements, construction materials and quantities.

Plan study time

Set a goal for yourself. Avoid the trap of just "studying until you're ready." Instead, determine the date you want to apply to take your exam and set aside enough time to finish your test preparations by that date. Try to limit how long each of your study / cram sessions will be. Study periods should not be too much in excess of one hour – after which time students begin to lose concentration and attention span.

Finally, select your study environment so as to avoid distractions and interruptions!

Reading is not studying

It may seem odd, but *reading* is not *studying*. Studying is an active process. Creating and reviewing your flashcards is studying. Develop study guides. Teach someone about difficult or complex topics. Relate what you are learning to your own experiences or the real estate topics you hear about in conversations or on the news. Create your own memory devices such as mnemonics, rhyming, acronyms, or images. These can be invaluable ways to remember cut and dry facts and figures.

Dissect exam questions

Take and review as many practice exams as you can find. Take and re-take quizzes in your textbook and any exam prep resource that you can find. Write down the topics you tend to miss questions on, then re-study those topics. When reviewing a missed question, be sure to understand the correct response and why the incorrect answers were not right.

Review the exam provider's handbook

A wealth of knowledge exists in the Examination Board of Professional Home Inspectors (EBPHI)'s test preparation resources. Review these materials thoroughly! You will learn the general topic areas covered and the relative weighting of a given subject. You can review the NHIE® exam overview document here - https://nationalhomeinspectorexam.org/wp-content/uploads/dlm_uploads/2024/10/EBPHI-Exam-Overview-Packet-2023_Updated-9.13.24.pdf

Exam prep materials generally present the key content of a topic and how many questions will appear on your exam. The NHIE testing service candidate handbook will further describe how your exam is scored. This knowledge will help you to understand how to answer questions you may not be sure about. In other words, you should know whether or not you are penalized for wrong answers.

It's almost time! Your exam is tomorrow. What do you do?

Candidate handbooks will provide full instructions about the exam day itself—what you can and can't take with you, how long you have to complete the exam, and how long you have to wait before you get your results, and so forth.

Immediately prior to the exam, you should limit how much to cram. At some point, nothing new should be introduced into your mind. In short, you either know it or you don't. Make a quick final pass-through, then leave it alone.

Okay, it's exam time. How do I avoid being a nervous wreck?

To alleviate stress, you can do a couple of things:

- Drive by the testing center so you know where it is and how long it will take to get there. On test day, allow extra time for traffic snarls, etc.
- Be sure you have an acceptable calculator (information will appear in the exam provider's handbook). Note that some providers don't allow you to bring a calculator in. Instead, you'll use one they provide or one embedded on the computer you'll use to take the exam.
- Assemble everything you need to take with you. Include test registration documents, required identification, a calculator, and a sweater or light jacket. Put everything in a bag or your car.
- Eat a well-rounded meal the evening before your exam and get a good night's sleep.
- Most exam providers give you a few minutes before you begin the exam to acquaint yourself with how the system works. You can answer a few practice questions, use the calculator, etc. Use this time not only to familiarize yourself with the environment but also to take a few deep breaths and get comfortable. You can do this!
- Budget your time. Know how many questions you must answer (more information from the provider's handbook).
- <u>Read every question carefully</u>. Be sure you understand what it's asking, in particular if the question is in the negative ("which of the following is NOT....," or "which of the following is NOT TRUE....". Then read EVERY possible response before you respond. Exam providers generally want you to select the BEST answer, not the only possible answer.

Answering questions

In most circumstances, you should answer every question. You will certainly receive a score deduction if you don't answer a question, but if you guess, you could guess right. So you come out ahead by answering every question.

This issue raises the question: "how much time should I spend on a question?" This becomes easy math. Know how much time you have for a given section and how many questions you must answer in that section. Then divide the number of questions into your time allocation to get your per-question time allowance. Do not stray too much from that estimate as you complete the section!

If you aren't sure of the answer to a question, keep these tips in mind:

- Are there responses that you know are incorrect? Eliminate them. If you eliminate two responses, you've increased your odds of correctly answering the question to 50/50!
- Dissect the remaining possible responses. Are there key words that indicate a correct or incorrect answer?
  - o Terms like "always," "never," and "only" MAY indicate an incorrect response because seldom are things as definitive as these terms suggest.
  - o Terms such as "usually," "generally," "typically," "most," and "some" are more likely to appear in the correct response.
- If you see a response that includes something you've never heard of, don't choose it! If you didn't see that information in your preparations, it's unlikely to be the correct response.

- Be particularly cautious about organization names. "The Department of Housing and Urban Development" sounds suspiciously like "The Division of Housing and Development."

After the exam

Depending on the exam provider and state, you may know right away if you passed. You may also receive a report from the testing center that details topic area scores.

If you're not successful on your first attempt, don't panic…and understand that you're not alone. Home inspection exams can be notoriously difficult. As soon as you leave the testing center, write some notes to yourself about questions you recall struggling with or topics that you may need to review.

Then, dig in again. Use the textbook, your notes, and the information you remember from the exam and keep studying. Your career is far more important than not passing the test!

Appendix: Useful Websites

The National Home Inspector Examination® Candidate Handbook

This contains crucial information regarding the National Home Inspector Examination®. Make sure to download and read this participant booklet to fully understand the entire test taking process.
https://nationalhomeinspectorexam.org/wp-content/uploads/dlm_uploads/2024/10/EBPHI-Exam-Overview-Packet-2023_Updated-9.13.24.pdf

National Home Inspector Examination®
325 John Knox Rd., Ste. L103,
Tallahassee, FL 32303
847-298-7750
info@homeinspectionexam.org
https://nationalhomeinspectorexam.org/

PSI Testing Service
(Psychological Services, Inc.)
3210 East Tropicana
Las Vegas, NV 89121
800-733-9267
https://candidate.psiexams.com/#

Pearson Vue Testing Service
5601 Green Valley Drive
Bloomington, MN 55437
952-681-3000
https://home.pearsonvue.com/Home.aspx

American Society of Home Inspectors
Regency Towers 1415 West 22nd St.
Tower Floor
Oak Brook, IL 60523
847-759-2820
https://www.homeinspector.org/

InterNACHI
1750 30th St.
Ste. 301
Boulder, CO 80301
303-223-0861
https://www.nachi.org/

If you liked Home Inspector License Exam Prep, check out the other real estate licensing titles of Performance Programs Company!

Cramming for your real estate licensing exam? You need Real Estate License Exam Prep!

Where can you buy Real Estate License Exam Prep?
Real Estate License Exam Prep (RELEP) is available as a printed book or e-book through nearly all online retailers. For 30+ states, there is a state-specific version of Real Estate License Exam Prep.

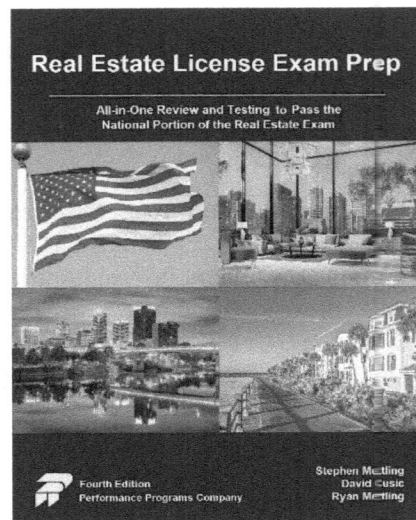

Looking for a real estate principles textbook? Get what all the students love -- Principles of Real Estate Practice!

Principles of Real Estate Practice is invaluable reference material for real estate professionals. Its 495-pages contain the essentials of real estate law, principles, and practices taught in real estate schools and colleges across the country. For many states, there are now state-specific versions of Principles of Real Estate Practice.

Where can you buy Principles of Real Estate Practice?
Principles Real Estate Practice is available as a printed book or e-book through nearly all online retailers.

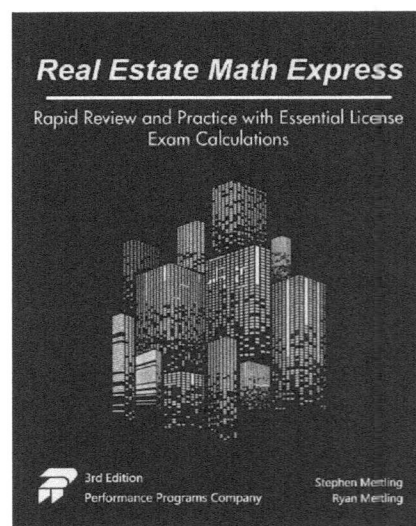

Struggling with real estate math? The solution to that equation is Real Estate Math Express!

Real Estate Math Express is a concise, easy-to-study test preparation guide to help real estate students improve their real estate math scores to pass the state licensing test. The primary feature of Real Estate Math Express is that it contains all necessary formulas and practice questions in 100+ pages.

Where can you buy Real Estate Math Express?
Real Estate Math Express is available as a printed book or e-book through nearly all online retailers.

Publisher Contact
Ryan Mettling
Performance Programs Company
6810 190th St E, Bradenton, FL 34211
ryan@performanceprogramscompany.com
www.performanceprogramscompany.com